Working in the
Twenty-First Century

WORKING IN THE TWENTY-FIRST CENTURY

Edited by

C. STEWART SHEPPARD, Ph.D.
Dean, The Colgate Darden Graduate School
of Business Administration
University of Virginia

and

DONALD C. CARROLL, Ph.D.
Dean, The Wharton School
University of Pennsylvania

This book is based on a symposium co-sponsored by The Colgate Darden Graduate School of Business Administration (University of Virginia) and The Wharton School (University of Pennsylvania) and funded by Philip Morris Incorporated.

A WILEY-INTERSCIENCE PUBLICATION

JOHN WILEY & SONS New York • Chichester • Brisbane • Toronto

Copyright © 1980 by Philip Morris Incorporated
Published by John Wiley & Sons, Inc.

Library of Congress Cataloging in Publication Data:

Main entry under title:
Working in the twenty-first century.

"A Wiley-Interscience publication."
Based on a symposium co-sponsored by the Colgate Darden Graduate School of
Business Administration and the Wharton School, which was held at the Philip
Morris Operations Center, Richmond, in 1979.
Bibliography: p.
Includes index.
1. Employment forecasting—United States—Congresses. 2. Industrial relations—United
States—Congresses. 3. Economic forecasting—United States—Congresses.
I. Sheppard, Charles Stewart, 1915–   II. Carroll, Donald C. III. Colgate-Darden
Graduate School of Business Administration. IV. Pennsylvania. University. Wharton
School of Finance and Commerce.

HD5724.W642   331'.09'05   79-24775
ISBN 0-471-07755-0

Printed in the United States of America

10 9 8 7 6 5 4 3 2 1

Foreword

Not everything a corporation does can be summed up on a balance sheet, nor would we want it to be. In our view, to grow and survive as a company we must do our share to advance the broader interests of the society in which we live and operate.

As the employer of some 60,000 men and women, Philip Morris Incorporated has an obvious direct interest in the changing world of work. Seeking a way to encourage study, understanding, and especially the future direction of this important and complex subject is a responsibility we feel keenly.

Happily, our interest is shared by two distinguished institutions: The Colgate Darden Graduate School of Business Administration of the University of Virginia and The Wharton School of the University of Pennsylvania. In the spring of 1979, under their sponsorship, a group of distinguished spokesmen from business and labor, and from government, science, and higher education assembled at the Philip Morris Operations Center in Richmond, Virginia, to take part in a two-day symposium on "Working in the Twenty-First Century."

It is our hope that the ideas and perceptions of the authors will stimulate the thinking and planning of all of us and will lead to a better life for generations to come.

GEORGE WEISSMAN
Chairman of the Board
Philip Morris Incorporated

Preface

Man has always tried to make out the dim shape of the future. The capacity to imagine the abstraction of time beyond the present is the gift that makes Homo sapiens unique on this planet. But there is something freshly exciting—and appalling—about forecasting what sort of working world we will have in the twenty-first century. The new ingredient in futurism is the dawning certainty that the future is not an accident that happens to us, that we are no longer at the mercy of dimly understood forces. Today, we read our future in the consequences of our own aspirations and behavior.

It was this perception of our responsibility for our own future that Ross R. Millhiser, Vice Chairman of the Board of Philip Morris Incorporated, had in mind when he said, "The knowledge explosion and the revolution in science and technology are continuing to grow exponentially. They promise a quality of life that could go beyond the most fantastic dreams of a generation ago. They also have opened a Pandora's box of problems and threats. However, you will recall that the Pandora legend ended with one thing left in the box—hope."

This book grew out of a symposium, "Working in the Twenty-First Century," co-sponsored in early 1979 by The Colgate Darden Graduate School of Business Administration, University of Virginia and The Wharton School, University of Pennsylvania. The two-day conference was funded by Philip Morris Incorporated, and held at the Philip Morris Operations Center in Richmond, Virginia. There, 350 leaders from academia, government, business, and labor ranged over a wide spectrum of thought and opinion about the working lives of Americans in the century that is only two decades away.

The twentieth century snapped the chain between work and travail. Interrupted only occasionally by economic dislocation and war, the American economy produced a standard of living unimaginable since history first began to be written. Increasingly, most Americans found that work, or at least the kind of work they would do, was a matter of choice.

The end of the gritty struggle for food, clothing, and shelter allows most Americans to ask, "What *else* is there?" In the earlier years of this century, the answer was an outburst of materialism, the pleasurable piling up of goods and conveniences. This tendency toward accumulation is still a strong theme in our mass behavior, but other interests are increasingly compelling. Abraham Maslow's conceptualization of a hierarchy of human needs powerfully explains the shifting attitudes toward work and personal identity. Put simply, we want *more*. Work must provide more than a living. It must yield increasing amounts of leisure, it must be easier, it must be enjoyable, and it must be fulfilling. Attitudes toward authority have shifted commensurately, from a timorous and unquestioning subservience to the boss to a wish—and increasingly, a demand—to control more extensively the rules and content of working life. The drive to take more responsibility for one's work is one more sign of our national urgency about the rich expression of human potential.

These aspirations, and the others outlined in these chapters, are the natural consequences of plenty. The outcry against the erosion of old values and attitudes toward work is understandable, but merely to mourn them is to ignore the new human possibilities emerging in the workplace.

It is the outlook for the future of the human condition that Isaac Asimov, the awesomely prolific science-fiction writer and futurist, sets forth in the prologue of this book. Barring unforeseen disaster, he predicts, our technological genius will free us for the highest of human callings, the act of human creativity.

It was the fruitful deployment of capital and technology that brought us to the point of economic well-being where we can lift up our heads from brutal toil to dream of loftier ends. It is natural enough, then, to devote Section One of the book to an assessment of where emerging technologies and available capital are taking us. With an energy crisis all too evident as this book goes to press, we may for the first time be confronting the possibility that a shortage of natural resources can limit our economic growth. Against that grim scenario, however, we must weigh the effect of the explosion in electronics and communications technology. Its impact on the working lives of Americans will be so profound as to redefine the meaning of work.

Although troubled, the American labor movement remains a vital institution, and the changing expectations and needs of workers, together with an examination of labor-management relations in the future, form the book's second section. In a political climate not noticeably favorable to unions, how do they extend their influence and membership, and what new kinds of demands will they pass across the bargaining table in the twenty-first century?

Section Three presents a fundamental change in what Americans say they want from their working lives. Here we confront a shifting away from materialism, the striving for personal self-fulfillment, a new set of attitudes toward marriage and the family, and the whole range of values that center on the desires of the individual.

In Section Four we scrutinize America's chances for maintaining economic growth in a world of nations so interdependent that one author believes "it is now possible to plan the international economy." Here also is a discussion of the vital role of the American entrepreneur in tilling the soil of capitalism in creative ways.

This book is, in sum, optimistic about America's outlook. Although there are danger signals in plenty, including the decline in productivity in this country, inflation, the emergence of new international competitors, the failure of trust in American institutions, and a host of other economic or existential concerns, the common thread, discernible in most of these chapters, is how much the future is within our conscious control. We can, if we are wise enough and believe enough in ourselves, make the economic marvel of the twentieth century seem but a stepping-stone. As commentator and reporter James Lehrer observes in his epilogue, "We human beings do have the ability to make the right decisions for the future."

The greatest danger to this scenario, we think, is our difficulty in reaching a political consensus about what we want to do and where we ought to go. In addition, there is a dark side to the insistent striving for individual fulfillment, and that is that it could dissolve into unproductive egocentrism. But to the extent that Americans truly want what Maslow called "self-actualization," we have at work a motivating force so powerful as to make our possibilities almost limitless.

C. STEWART SHEPPARD, PH.D.
DONALD C. CARROLL, PH.D.

Charlottesville, Virginia
Philadelphia, Pennsylvania
October 1979

Acknowledgments

We gratefully acknowledge the distinguished speakers who participated in the "Working in the Twenty-First Century" symposium and whose papers form the substance of this book.

We also wish to thank our academic colleagues who served on the Conference Committee. James C. Dunstan, D.B.A., Professor of Business Administration, and William E. Zierden, Ph.D., Associate Professor of Business Administration, represented The Colgate Darden Graduate School of Business Administration. Representing The Wharton School were Edward B. Shils, Ph.D., Director and Professor of Management, Wharton Entrepreneurial Center, and William Zucker, Ph.D., Associate Director and Adjunct Professor of Management, Wharton Entrepreneurial Center.

The conference would not have been possible without the funding provided by Philip Morris Incorporated, and the counsel and support of the Philip Morris executives on the Conference Committee. Our gratitude to: Ross R. Millhiser, Vice Chairman of the Board; Clifford H. Goldsmith, President; Hugh Cullman, Group Executive Vice President and Chairman and Chief Executive Officer, Philip Morris U.S.A.; James C. Bowling, Senior Vice President, Assistant to the Chairman of the Board, and Director of Corporate Affairs; W. Wallace McDowell, Vice President and Executive Vice President, Operations, Philip Morris U.S.A.; Benjamin A. Soyars, Vice President and Senior Vice President, Manufacturing, Philip Morris U.S.A.; Frank A. Saunders, Staff Vice President, Corporate Relations and Communications; and James M. Frye, Director, Community Relations, Philip Morris U.S.A.

David Maxey, former editor of *Psychology Today*, worked with our contributing authors in the preparation of the manuscript, and is responsible for the continuity and cohesion of the papers. Joan Mebane, Conference Coordinator and Manager, Communications Research, Philip Morris Incorporated, provided editorial assistance.

C.S.S.
D.C.C.

Contents

PROLOGUE   The Permanent Dark Age: Can We Avoid It?   1

Isaac Asimov, Ph.D.
Author, Scientist, Futurist

SECTION ONE   Work in the Next Century: The Effect of Natural
Resources, Capital, and Technology,   13

Chapter 1   A New Economic Agenda,   17

W. W. Rostow, Ph.D.
Professor of Economics and History
The University of Texas at Austin

Chapter 2   Two Promising Technologies: The Biosciences and
Information Sciences,   24

William E. Bonnet, Ph.D.
Vice President—Environmental Assessment
The Sun Company, Inc.

Chapter 3   The Post-Industrial Boom in Compunications,   30

Walter A. Hahn
Senior Specialist, Science, Technology, and
Futures Research
Congressional Research Service

Chapter 4   Technology and Society in the Next Thirty Years:
             We Have Manageable Choices,   39

             Irving Leveson, Ph.D.
             Director of Economic Studies
             Hudson Institute

Chapter 5   The Twenty-First Century: Will There Be
             Collective Bargaining?   49

             Theodore W. Kheel, Esq.
             Administrative Director
             Institute of Collective Bargaining and Group
             Relations, Inc.

SECTION TWO Work in the Next Century: New Trends and
             Perspectives for Labor,   59

Chapter 6   Pyramids of Wealth: A Threat to
             Labor Relations,   63

             William W. Winpisinger
             President
             International Association of Machinists
             and Aerospace Workers

Chapter 7   Trends in the Work Force: Individualism,
             Inflation, and Productivity,   69

             James H. Jordan, Ph.D.
             Vice President—Employee Relations
             ICI Americas Inc.

Chapter 8   Can We Find Good Jobs in a
             Service Economy?   80

             William Lucy
             International Secretary-Treasurer
             American Federation of State, County
             and Municipal Employees, AFL—CIO

Chapter 9   Toward a More Participative Work Force,   90

A. H. Raskin
Associate Director, National News Council
former Labor Editor, *The New York Times*

Chapter 10   Women: The Emerging Labor Force,   98

Pat L. Burr, Ph.D.
Associate Professor of Business
The University of Texas at San Antonio

Chapter 11   Personnel Policies for the 1980s,   106

Jerome M. Rosow
President
Work in America Institute, Inc.

**SECTION THREE   Individual Lifestyles and the Work
Environment,   119**

Chapter 12   Our Changing Structure of Values,   123

Louis Harris
President
Louis Harris and Associates, Inc.

Chapter 13   Texture in Living and Working,   131

Stewart Brand
Editor and Publisher
CoEvolution Quarterly

Chapter 14   The Mosaic Society,   134

Ian H. Wilson
Consultant, Public Policy Research
General Electric Company

Chapter 15   Shifting Values: New Choices and
              Old Dilemmas, 145

              Suzanne Keller, Ph.D.
              Professor of Sociology and Architecture
              Princeton University

Chapter 16   The Irresponsible Society, 155

              James O'Toole, Ph.D.
              Center for Futures Research
              Graduate School of Business
              University of Southern California

Chapter 17   Beyond Conventional Wisdom: Lifestyle
              Long Shots, 169

              Theodore J. Gordon
              President
              The Futures Group, Inc.

SECTION FOUR America's Quest to Maintain Economic Growth in
              a Global Society, 179

Chapter 18   Entrepreneurship: Engine of Growth, 183

              George J. Vojta
              Executive Vice President
              Citibank, N.A.

Chapter 19   The United States and the Third World in the
              Twenty-First Century, 191

              Cecilio J. Morales
              Manager, Economic and Social
              Development Department
              Inter-American Development Bank

**Chapter 20 Global Challenges in the Twenty-
First Century, 204**

Jack N. Behrman, Ph.D.
Luther Hodges Distinguished
Professor
University of North Carolina
Graduate School
of Business Administration

EPILOGUE Ours Is the Power to Choose, 213

James C. Lehrer
Associate Editor and Washington
Anchor
The MacNeil/Lehrer Report

BIOGRAPHICAL NOTES 215

SELECTED BIBLIOGRAPHY 223

INDEX 227

Charts and Tables

CHARTS

1   U.S. Population and Projections (By Age Groups)
    1950–2000,   4

2   Growth of Civilian Labor Force and Projections
    1950–2000,   72

3   Employment: By Type of Industry 1950–2000 (est.),   84

4   Employment: By Type of Occupation 1950–2000 (est.),   86

5   Profile of Significant Value System Changes 1970–1985,   141

TABLES

1   Flexitime Usage Rate,   101

2   Key Effects of Flexitime,   102

3   Population by Age Group and Annual Rates Change,   137

4   Population and GNP: Industrial Countries and the
    Third World (Years 1970 and 2000),   195

5   Selected Regional Indicators, 1970 and 2000,   199

PROLOGUE

The Permanent Dark Age: Can We Avoid It?

Isaac Asimov, Ph.D.

Forty years ago, science fiction was strictly for youngsters and idiots, of which, at that time, I was both. Since then youth has vanished, but I have clung to my idiocy. What has changed has not been the science fiction. What has changed has been the conception of what science fiction really is. It may not always be a blueprint of the future, but it always carries the message that the future will be different from the present.

It always has been so, but for most of history the tides of change have progressed at a slow rate so that in one man's lifetime one could not see any change of importance. There were, indeed, all kinds of trivial changes. Kings have died, other kings have come to power, armies have passed and killed half the population, plagues have struck and killed the other half, but all of this—except for the individuals immediately suffering—is trivial. When the pestilence passes, things go back to what they have been before, and it is usually assumed that things will continue as before. Or as Ecclesiastes says, "There is nothing new under the sun."

This is a rather pessimistic view because it makes impossible the notion of progress. Indeed, the notion of progress is a modern phenomenon that arose only when the rate of technology became great enough to make it possible to see in one lifetime the changes that occur. What makes it necessary for technology to increase is rate of application. Why might not technology decrease its rate? The answer is that technology feeds upon itself. The more new advances, the larger the base

1

on which further advance can be made. Through all history the rate of technological advance has progressed faster and faster. If it ever really slows it will be because civilization breaks down, because the human race will finally recede into a perhaps permanent dark age. This, naturally, nobody would want to see; but can it be avoided?

Let us make the assumption that it can be avoided. It is much more pleasant to make that assumption, and if we don't, then much of the discussion of working in the twenty-first century will have to go out the window. So, what is required for civilization to survive?

It seems to me the first thing that is required for survival of our technological civilization is a solution to the population problem. If population continues to increase without limit, no solution is possible for any of the problems that face us today. Nor can we suppose that we can bleed off the superfluous population of the earth by expansion into space. Heaven knows that I, more than anyone, am an advocate of the exploration and exploitation of space. I, more than anyone, I think, appreciate the potentialities—and have no fears that the effort will fall short. Nevertheless, let us be practical.

In the next century we can put into space, let us say, a hundred million people. There will be many people who argue that we can't do it, but let's say that in the next century we can safely place a hundred million people in space. Yet if here on earth we continue to increase population at our present rate, then in a hundred years we will have a population about seven times what it is now. We will have added something like 25 billion people to the population of the earth. If from 25 billion people you subtract 100 million, you are still left with almost 25 billion people.

It follows that while we can get a great deal out of space in the way of providing room for some people, and making available for ourselves energy and material resources, nevertheless, we must solve the population problem here on earth. Space will not be developed fast enough to catch up with the fertility of human beings.

There are only two ways in which the earth's increase in population can be reversed. That is fortunate. If there were 50 ways, we could never choose among them. One way is to increase the death rate until it at least matches the birth rate; the other is to decrease the birth rate until it at least matches the death rate. I suppose you could say that a third method is a combination of the two.

If we restrict ourselves to the first two, we will see that both have their advantages. Increasing the death rate is nothing about which we have to make a strong decision, or take hard measures. All we have to do is to continue as we're going now and we will find that nature will do the job for us. Nature will raise the death rate on our behalf by means of starvation, disease, war, and, of course, death, which happen to be the Four Horsemen of the Apocalypse. Eighteen centuries after Revelation was written, they are *still* the Four Horsemen.

The only trouble with that system is that raising the death rate is synonymous with the destruction of our civilization.

The alternative is to lower the birth rate, but the difficulty is that it has never really been tried. At no time in history has there been a massive reduction of the birth rate worldwide. There have been local reductions in the birth rate, particularly amongst the upper classes almost routinely. What we need is a reduction that is worldwide. Fortunately, there are signs that this may come about.

In Europe and in North America the birth rate has dropped sufficiently to place us within reach of zero population growth. In fact, in four countries, West Germany, East Germany, Austria, and Luxembourg, all German-speaking for some reason, there is actually negative population growth. The population is going slightly downward from year to year. This phenomenon is likely to spread.

Even in countries which are not "developed," and in which high birth rates are traditional, the birth rate is dropping. We are told that is true in China. How they do it in China I don't know, but apparently social pressure does the trick. The local party functionary probably speaks so long to the young couple that they have no time to contribute to population increase.

Let us suppose, then, that we will survive by developing a low worldwide birth rate. How will a society with a low birth rate differ from what we have now? Just consider. A low birth rate means a relatively small percentage of young people. If civilization continues, medical technology will advance, which means that life expectancy will be increased even further. As the young people decrease in percentage, the old people will increase in percentage, and we will have an aging society.

This process of societal aging has been going on in the United States for a century. As the birth rate has dropped, as the death rate has dropped even more, as life expectancy has increased, we have already become here in the United States an aging society.

More and more, from decade to decade, we have become a society which revolves economically around pension plans, Social Security, Medicare, and all the other facets of taking care of old people. Furthermore, there is nothing much we can do about it because although we

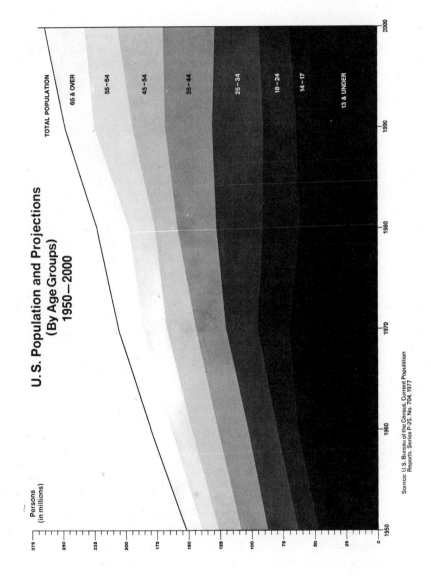

U.S. Population and Projections
(By Age Groups)
1950–2000

Persons
(in millions)

TOTAL POPULATION

65 & OVER

55 – 64

45 – 54

35 – 44

25 – 34

18 – 24

14 – 17

13 & UNDER

275 250 225 200 175 150 125 100 75 50 25 0

1950 1960 1970 1980 1990 2000

Source: U.S. Bureau of the Census, Current Population
Reports. Series P-25, No. 704, 1977

cut off the voting limit so that no one under 18 can vote, we didn't cut
it off at the upper end. Consequently, the aged have become an ever
more powerful voting force. And their vote is to their own interest, as
all such voting blocs are.

There is little that those of us who are young and vigorous can do
about this bloc of the aged because all of us expect, if we are fortunate,
to join the bloc. Those who are willing to take strenuous measures
against these old people are held back by the thought that there is no
way—except an unacceptable one—to avoid joining the club. Consequently, we must look forward to a low-birth-rate society, that is, an
aging society, and one in which it may be that a disproportionately
small number of young people will serve as the economic and social
support of the world. They will be weighed down and finally broken
by the ever increasing percentage of old people who do not contribute
to the social and economic welfare of the world, but who instead are
drains upon it. Instead of dying in the explosion of endless population
growth, we will expire in the whimper of old age.

But is this so? Why do we expect the aged population to be useless
dead weight? On what basis do we suppose that people, if they grow
older, become burdens? Eventually, of course, if you get old enough,
deterioration of the physical body advances to the point where you
cannot pull your weight. But when will this happen?

Right now, 65 is the age of eligibility for Social Security. We know
that after 40 we rarely have the vigor of youth, at least mentally. In
fact, we all have the feeling (except those of us who are advancing, like
myself, and approaching late youth) that you can't teach an old dog
new tricks.

There is something glorious in youth. That is the time for vigor and
ambition and daring and imagination and the ability to seize new initiatives. These wither with advancing years, and we soon become
stodgy and conservative. Even before people become physically inca-
pacitated, we are sure that they are already mentally stodgy. But is this
true?

We have had very little experience with old people because for most
of human history the old have been relatively few in number. In addition, we have been a youth-centered society, psychologically as well as
physiologically. Not only have the young people literally comprised
most of society, but we have concentrated our attention on them, and
we still do.

I would suggest that the most youth-centered aspect of society is education. It is assumed that education is for the young. You send children to school, you teach them just enough to enable them to read a newspaper headline and traffic signs and perhaps No Smoking signs. In fact, I'm no longer sure of traffic signs. Have you noticed they are being replaced by pictures?

As long as education is confined to the young, our civilization cannot progress, and for a very simple reason. Every child who goes to school, no matter how young, naive, or stupid he or she may be, cannot fail to notice that everyone in school is as young as he is. He cannot fail to notice adults do not go to school. If there is anything in school which is irritating, which makes children feel in prison, which arouses resentment, that's it. And let's face it, there is always something that will occasionally arouse the resentment of the inmates.

The child feels he is young and weak. As soon as he grows up, he knows he will get out of there and show them, and that is what he aims for. Virtually every child in school looks forward to the time when he doesn't have to be in school. Not being in school is a sign of being grown up. It is the end toward which he is striving.

Once he gets out of school he no longer wishes to do any of those things that are characteristic of school. Why should he? Those activities were for the days when he was a child. Any time the child gets out of school as a young man or woman, the tendency is no longer ever to want to read another book, think another thought, or have another idea. He's finished with that. That was his rite of passage, that was his passage into adulthood. Anything that would drag him back into childhood is shameful.

You might think that somebody who has gone through school and has forgotten virtually everything he or she has ever learned would be embarrassed if you were to say to him or her, "What is the capital of Paraguay?" And get "I don't know" as an answer. But, no. He no longer wears diapers either, and he is not ashamed of that.

If we continue in this fashion then, we cannot survive. There will be fewer and fewer people who will be fresh out of school and who presumably know something, and there will be more and more people who are old and out-of-date, who will remember only vaguely what they learned as teenagers and will, therefore, be stodgy and conservative.

In short, we create the very old people we think of as a drain on society, and we must stop creating them. How are we going to do that?

It seems to me that we must completely reorganize our educational system. We must make sure that education is for all ages, that people must learn as long as they live, just as they must breathe as long as they live.

This sounds queer, since we all know that it is a matter of certainty that everyone is supposed to hate school. However, it is the kind of schools we have that they hate. I cannot believe that this means they hate learning. Learning is fun. Everybody loves to learn if he learns what he wants to learn.

If we are to persuade people to learn all their lives, then we must let them do it in a pleasant way. After all, in any form of life which is sufficiently advanced so that we can interpret the emotions with which creatures do whatever they do, it would seem that there is pleasure in doing what there is physical adaptation for doing. A bird enjoys flying, a fish enjoys swimming. A seal *certainly* enjoys swimming; he shows off for us if we give him half a chance.

What is it, then, that a human being particularly enjoys doing? He's got three pounds of extremely complex brain wrapped around with the protective bone of the skull, and it's got to be used. It's just got to be. If it isn't, we suffer the agonies of boredom, and there's nothing that is worse than that. Frankly, I think a great deal of the mischief that people get into is simply because mischief is better than doing nothing.

To make full use of the brain we cannot expect to get very far if we do things en masse, if we have large numbers of people who are all taught the same thing at the same time without regard to their personal interests, their personal preferences, the rate at which they feel like going, and the direction in which they care to go. The first task of a true education would be to attempt to find out what it is that a particular human being would like to know and teach it. For that, you must have a one-to-one relationship. One teacher for one student.

But how can that be done when there aren't enough teachers in the world?

Once, a rich family could hire a tutor for its children, but only a few could be educated in that way. Since we have adopted the philosophy of mass education, it's had to be one teacher for many students, and a curriculum whereby everybody must learn at the same time and at the same speed.

Even today we have small teaching machines. We see pictures of a child with earphones on and a machine telling him that he is wrong, to try again. There you have one teacher for one person.

Of course, it's a simple machine at the moment. It can only work for simple teachings, such as spelling, addition, and other straight factual things. We are not going to remain at this level.

If there is one thing that has been developing before our eyes with remarkable and even frightening speed, it is the computer. The computer has changed from a relatively simple machine that took up an entire wall and used up enough electricity to support an entire huge building into a little thing you can hold in your hand and that will run on a few small batteries. It can do more, considerably more, considerably faster, considerably more reliably than that huge machine could 30 years ago.

What's more, the computer is continuing to develop in this fashion. I am absolutely certain that if society survives, technology will continue to advance, and that computers will become far more elaborate, far more convenient, than they are now. Furthermore, if we continue to build communication satellites that are more elaborate and versatile, it will mean that there will be millions, even hundreds of millions, of different television channels available. Every person conceivably could have his own television channel. All human knowledge could be computerized and kept in a central library or several central libraries. Every single computerized machine could be hooked up to the gathered knowledge of the human race. It could then teach any subject by presenting the known information on it. It could respond to each student's personal needs.

I foresee a future in which every human being can learn, study in his own house or place of residence at any time he wants to, at any age. All knowledge will be available to him, and he can study what he wants.

This doesn't mean that he will simply be tied to a machine with no human contacts at all. The machine is an added option. There will always be some things that can be taught best by human beings rather than by a computer, but there are other things that can be taught best by machine.

If computer education takes place on that scale and people are learning all their lives long, age will not matter. People will remain as vigorous and as mentally alert into advanced age.

If we have a situation such as this, what more does it mean? If everyone can study anything that he wishes to study, learn anything that he wishes to learn, what guarantee will he have that he will learn things that are needed to run the earth? Won't everybody simply learn stamp collecting or girls' telephone numbers (or boys', as the case may be)?

It seems to me that there will always be many people who will want to know those things that keep the world going. They will want to understand about scientific research, about the maintenance of the machines, about the designing of computers, about all kinds of complex things. In fact, it seems to me that such knowledge will be the most desirable, for there is a keen desire to be useful and to be applauded. There is no danger that there will be too few of such people because the routine work of the world is going to be increasingly done by computers.

We are facing an increasingly automated society. We are facing a society which is going to change fundamentally in the nature of the work expected of human beings. This has happened once before in history. At the time of the Industrial Revolution, steam engines and other devices began to do the muscular work of human beings.

Even as late as 1800, 95% of all human beings lived by digging in the soil and growing food. When the United States first became a nation, 95% of the Americans labored in agriculture. They supported themselves, as well as the other 5% who were parasites on them—the doctors, lawyers, preachers, merchants, artists, and so on.

In the United States today, less than 5% of the population is involved in growing food and working in the soil. What of the other 95%? Why, they do other things. If this were two hundred years ago, they wouldn't have the opportunity to do other things. They wouldn't work in factories, they wouldn't work in show business, they wouldn't work as clerks, they wouldn't work as engineers, they wouldn't be all the myriad of things they are. They would have no option except to be working in the soil.

We can't help believing that what we have now is a better system, that people have a greater variety of work open to them, that there are more interesting things to do than to have everyone grubbing in the soil.

Computers will take over the unnecessary mental labor we now do routinely and repetitively, and we will spare the human brain unnecessary work that is beneath its dignity, just as in the past we have spared human muscles the indignity of working day by day by day with no opportunity ever to look up at the sky.

You might wonder whether, if the computers do all the work, it might not mean that eventually the human mind will decay for lack of anything to do. We might have thought the same when the Industrial Revolution came—might not the human body decay for lack of any muscular work to do? To be sure, there are a great many flabby human beings now who have sedentary jobs, but they don't *have* to stay flabby.

We are now in a kind of self-help revolution in which everyone is laboring to keep fit. From where I sit in my apartment overlooking Central Park I can, at any time, look out and watch people jogging away, puff, puff, puff, all up and down the park. I find that watching them is enough exercise for me.

Anyone who wants to can keep his body reasonably fit doing something he enjoys doing, rather than keeping it fit by doing things he hates doing. In the same way, the fact that computerization is going to remove a great deal of the kind of work we do now does not mean that human beings will have their minds decaying at all. It simply means that their minds will be doing other things. They will be engaged in more creative endeavors.

It may be that the twenty-first century will be the great age of creativity in which finally machines will do the humdrum work of humanity. The computers will keep the world going, and human beings will be free at last to do things that only human beings can do—to create.

The work of the future will be creation, done by each in his own fashion. People will judge you not by how long you work or how many routine units you turn out, but rather by how much you increase the joy of the world. They will want to know how much of what you do gives pleasure not only to yourself but to others. How much is useful. That is what will count.

It is difficult to work out the details of such a world because we continue, even against our will, to think in the terms of the world as it now exists. If this were 1800 and I tried to describe the world of 1979, and if I said that people would be moving around at unprecedented rates and constantly in communication with each other over huge distances, the question might be, "How does one develop horses that run that fast?" Or "What kind of megaphone do you use to enable you to shout loud enough for someone to hear you miles away?"

If you tried to explain that machinery does this, then they would want to know just exactly how the machinery would affect life as they know it. They would ask, for instance, how the lower classes could afford the machinery. You would say that the concept of upper and lower classes has greatly changed. And they wouldn't comprehend that.

When I describe what I see in the future, I fail to be specific for a very good reason. I don't know the specifics.

The best imagination in the world would fall short, and perhaps I'm not the best. Therefore, it would be better if instead of one person working on the problem, we have groups in which one will advance one clever facet and another will advance another clever facet and out of all of them put together we then may begin to get a glimpse of a twenty-first century. This much I know: it will be as far advanced beyond ourselves as we are beyond the Middle Ages.

Remember, though, that all of this presents a deliberate and voluntary choice on the part of humanity. We don't necessarily have to choose a twenty-first century of computerization and total education. We don't even have to choose a twenty-first century that will involve the survival of civilization. We can choose to go on as we are doing today, placing most of our concerns in national strife, in competition of armaments, in increasing population, in ripping off the environment, in allowing the energy supply to decrease through waste as much as through use and, in so doing, deliberately choose suicide.

I hope we don't do that and I hope we all just remember that whenever we look forward into the future, we are looking forward to something about which we have a choice. That is for our benefit and our good—if we choose wisely.

SECTION ONE

Work in the Next Century: The Effect of Natural Resources, Capital, and Technology

Wbegin by taking inventory of our national assets, those we
have in hand and those we can expect to develop.

The activities that we call "working," after all, cannot take place
merely because individuals in a society declare themselves willing. We
need the base provided by natural resources and by capital, plus innovative technology to further reduce brutish work and free humans to
work at their highest potential.

W. W. Rostow leads off this section by saying that we are trying to
solve today's economic problems with yesterday's economic thinking.
We have, he says, a generation of economists so steeped in Keynesian
thinking that they ignore the supply side of the economy: "Their theoretical structures, their textbooks, their arguments with one another
are set up in such a way that one might assume that energy, food, raw
materials, and technology arrived by Immaculate Conception, or that
the stork brought them."

Insisting that our future will be the accumulation of all the economic
moves we make in the short run, Rostow asks, "How do we get from
here to there?" How do we overcome our very real energy problems? Is
our national emphasis on the good things of life, on consumption, now
so overwhelming that we perilously ignore saving, and hence the accumulation of capital for investment? Rostow lucidly lays out his
agenda for answering those questions in a positive way.

That we are entering a technological revolution in electronics and
communications seems beyond question, and the changes this revolution will bring in the way we work will be pervasive. William E. Bonnet forecasts a revolution in our understanding of human biological
and biochemical processes that could lead to a life expectancy of 100
years. That, he thinks, might mean a vivid revolution in the definition
of a career, with multiple careers and alternation between periods of
schooling and work. Taken together with a quantum leap in our ability
to move information, not people, and the intense use of robotics and
automation, we can look forward to a substantial increase in the level
of training for virtually all workers.

The amalgam of computer science and communications, reports
Walter A. Hahn, will ease our transition to a post-industrial society,
but the change will be much more rapid than our earlier shift from agriculture to industry. We are headed, he says, for a paperless office
filled with electronic hardware. Just beyond is the checkless, cashless
society, with banks shuttling funds back and forth by electronic
means.

15

These changes, says Hahn, must produce turbulence as well as opportunity. There is the risk of alienation as social patterns change because of a reduced need to communicate face to face. A rising anti-technology sentiment is also a possibility. But there is a redeeming fact if we are wise enough to perceive it. Although technologies provide their own imperative, we still have explicit choices about the kind of technological future we want.

Irving Leveson echoes the theme of manageable choices, and one that worries him is that we may make the political choice to reduce economic incentives for innovation and development. Especially troublesome is the falling United States spending for research and development in proportion to total world spending. "The world of the twenty-first century can either be an aging society and economy or a mature economy and society," says Leveson. He hopes for the latter, but is moved to conclude: "The most likely outcome is a bittersweet mixture of the two."

Theodore Kheel, from the vantage point of 40 years in industrial relations, begins the discussion of human expectations that will continue throughout this book. The trade union movement, young even for an American institution, will have much to say about working in the next century, so Kheel sketches its history as prologue.

A common theme in this section, as elsewhere in the book, is that we, as a society, stand in the presence and peril of choice. As a maturing society, we have the power to choose the economic blueprint by which will be built the world of work in the twenty-first century. It is sobering, then, to perceive that our working future could be less than excellent because we lack the social technologies, as Walter Hahn calls them, to agree about what our future should be.

C.S.S.
D.C.C.

CHAPTER 1

A New Economic Agenda
W. W. Rostow, Ph.D.

There are, if one strains, two ways to look at "The Effect of Natural Resources, Capital, and Technology on the Nature of Work in the Next Century." One requires a straightforward analysis of what life would be like in the twenty-first century in the light of the natural resources available and the capital and technology that we might generate. Another way is to ask this question: What will be the effects of our present and foreseeable problems of natural resources, capital formation, and technology generation on what the twenty-first century will be like? I have chosen the latter concept because as an economist and historian, and as someone who has from time to time served in public policy, I am inclined to take seriously the problem of getting from here to there rather than focusing on comfortable long-term projections.

I recently completed a private intellectual adventure. It began when I was 17 and finished when I was 61. It consisted of writing a history of the world economy over the past two centuries. At the close of that book, when I looked ahead, I concluded along the following lines:

- If we—the human race—are to be wise and lucky in the next quarter century, we will have brought the crude birth rate in the developing continents down under 20 per thousand from its present level of 35–40 per thousand.
- We will have avoided Malthusian disasters over that quarter century and generated enough food so that the children born will be able to fulfill their innate talents and possibilities.
- We will have generated a new round of agricultural technologies,

as the devices and tricks that we used in the last generation ran into diminishing returns.

- With respect to energy, we will have somehow scrambled through and kept the growth process going with presently known energy resources and technologies while we generated new, hopefully infinite, hopefully nonpolluting forms of energy for the next century.
- We will have solved a whole set of probable raw material problems with new materials, substitution, and recycling.
- We will have learned how to bring inflation under control. We will have learned that the Keynesian revolution—with its assumption that unemployment is an act of man and not of God—has brought about a much more difficult problem which we are all handling very badly. That is, the control of inflation, with its enormous, potentially corrosive results on our societies.
- We will have found the terms for an authentic North-South partnership in the world; and, with another quarter century or so of growth, the presently developing countries will have come to stages of development where they will be more resilient, more capable of making adjustments and facing the future successfully on their own.

That, roughly, is what I take to be the agenda. I have systematically disagreed, as an historian and an economist, with the notion that one can effectively separate the long run from the short run. I believe the long run is the accumulation of what you do in the short run.

Now, when I look at this array of problems, I ask three questions. One, are the resources and technologies, known or probable, sufficient to produce a favorable result? Is this a manageable agenda from the point of view of resources and technology? On that point, I am almost sure the answer is positive. I then ask: what are the economic problems involved in dealing with this agenda, including some rather difficult problems with respect to energy and the costs of containing pollution? My conclusion is that I have seen a lot more difficult economic problems solved. I believe that the most difficult problem in getting successfully through the next quarter century lies in the world of ideas and political action. And that is the central theme I shall now try to illustrate. I shall talk mainly about the United States. The relevance of these ideas to other parts of the world we can explore later.

With respect to ideas, I think we are trying to cope with the agenda that is upon us with a set of ideas that are profoundly inappropriate.

They are ideas which have their origins in the 1930s; they were generated in the Depression. They gained strength and currency in the 1950s and 1960s, a period in which we were all spoiled rotten by the falling or low price for energy, food, and raw materials. We were spoiled because we took those prices for granted and, in both concept and policy, focused on how to manipulate effective demand.

That is what we roughly call the Keynesian revolution. The great minds in the world of economics concerned themselves almost exclusively with this problem. They argued, of course, to a degree. You have so-called conservatives, like Milton Friedman, who have said you can do it all with monetary policy: just set the right rate of growth for the money supply and forget about the rest. Others say, let us do it with fiscal policy. And there are arguments about the so-called Phillips Curve trade-off: it is better to have, a conservative would say, a bit more unemployment and damp the rate of inflation. Others say no, let us take the risk of a bit more inflation to get a slightly lower percentage of unemployment. Somewhat oversimplified, those two arguments—about the proper mix of fiscal and monetary policy and the Phillips Curve trade-off—have taken up about 90% of the great debate among economists.

Meanwhile, the world enjoyed a boom in the 1950s and 1960s unexampled in the history of the past two centuries. That boom was, in part, based on the new virtuosity of governments in the control of effective demand. But it was also based on something else which most economists did not understand. From 1951 to 1972, the terms of trade for the advanced industrial countries improved by about 24%. In the United States, the relative price of electricity fell 43% in this period. One can hardly find a reference in the reports of the Council of Economic Advisers to this shift in the terms of trade. With this enormously powerful lift to real income, we went into an era in which the automobile, durable consumer goods, and the life of suburbia spread not only across the face of this continent but also to Western Europe and Japan. Some other rather creditable things were done with this great lift in real income. There was, for example, the allocation of increased resources to higher education and to health services. And, with real incomes rising, the voters were willing to allocate a quite substantial increase in the proportion going to the poor and disadvantaged, within their societies and overseas.

Then came a reversal in terms of trade. It started in the United States about 1969, but the big reversal came with the rise in wheat prices in 1972, and the rise in energy prices in 1973. These price increases were foreseeable, if one had looked deep beneath the surface of affairs in the 1960s and examined grain stocks in relation to global consumption, or U.S. oil and gas reserves in relation to consumption. A turn was bound to come. And it came for the fifth time in the last 200 years.

In the face of this switch in the terms of trade, and the consequent damping or reduction in the real income of people in the advanced industrial world, the mainstream economists have been virtually helpless. We have shifted to an era, like the other four eras in which the terms of trade turned unfavorable for advanced industrial countries, where the critical problems lie on the supply side. They lie in technology, in productivity, in generating new energy resources, and in ways to save energy. They lie in getting our transport system in some sort of rational shape. They lie in the supply of water and the supply of viable acreage. We take our food surplus as some sort of permanent act of the Lord, but we shall have to struggle to maintain it. The generation of economists that are now the prime leaders in our country have no way of dealing systematically with the supply side. Their theoretical structures, their textbooks, their arguments with one another are set up in such a way that one might assume that energy, food, raw materials, and technology arrived by Immaculate Conception, or that the stork brought them. From this point of view, we look rather pathetic. We are led by men whose minds were set in another period to solve other kinds of problems. We economists seem incapable of guiding the political leaders of the world onto the agenda that I have outlined.

President Carter, for example, came to office with the hope of carrying forward the great social achievements of the 1960s: a national health program, a national welfare program, and enlarged programs for the cities. In fact, he and his colleagues have been faced by a nation in which social services are degenerating, and in which there is a Proposition 13 tax revolt because real incomes are falling and people want to save that marginal dollar for themselves. Concept and reality are out of phase.

I am concerned about the gap between concept and reality because I am conscious that we economists are implicated in one great failure, and I do not wish us to fail again. Between the two world wars, economists were so fixated on what had worked before 1914 that they were incapable of dealing with the interwar reality. By the time they did get around to it, Hitler was in power, and the Japanese military was moving. Right now I believe this kind of time lag in concept has a profound meaning not only for our economic policy but also for our strategic position in the world. In this kind of world, where there are no agreed working concepts that grip our agenda, in the minds of economists or politicians, political life becomes fragmented. It is impossible to generate a lucid picture of what the nation's priorities are. It is impossible to unite business, labor, and our citizens to make the mutual sacrifices or adjustments to move forward on these matters. The democratic political process, in a quiet way, is thus endangered.

It is possible, of course, to look beyond difficulties. My friend Herman Kahn, in his book *The Next 200 Years*, notes that if trends are projected from before 1914 down to the 1960s there is a great deal of continuity. We were practically on the trend curve in the 1960s. He also noted that we had two world wars in that time, a depression, and a good part of the world taken over by totalitarians. Perhaps, once again, long-run hopeful trends will assert themselves, and there will be some sort of recognizable continuity between trends now and trends through the twenty-first century and beyond. My comfort in that possibility is limited. I would rather not see us go through the traumas of war, the destruction of democratic societies, and all the rest, which I think are thoroughly possible unless we get on to the agenda—and very soon.

There's an irony here. Right now, economists and governments are worried about slow growth and high unemployment. I believe that if we got on to the right agenda, those problems would largely disappear. But in the time ahead, expansion will not be based on investment flowing from what the economists call the accelerator; that is to say, investment will not flow initially from the expansion of consumers' real income. The critical dynamism will come from investments on the supply side which will expand income. To use economists' jargon, the multiplier would be the initiating force.

In a paper recently published by the American Association for the Advancement of Science, I measured the amount of investment required to reduce our oil imports to six million barrels a day. That import level was President Carter's 1985 target in his 1977 plan. I found that the increase in investment related to energy would be about 2 or 3% of the gross national product (GNP). At that time the investment gap keeping us from sustained full employment was about 1.7% of GNP. I could demonstrate quite well, I think, that if we took energy seriously, our problem would cease to be a problem of underemployment and slow growth in the United States. It would be one either of priorities or, as I would prefer, raising our investment rate. We have a low investment rate in this country, say, 16% of GNP. But as I've looked at energy and its requirements; at the requirements for contain-

ing air and water pollution which require another 1% of GNP investment by 1985; at the fragmentary data on what we require to get a
rational transport system, one where the trains don't fall off the tracks
and the bridges don't threaten to cave in; at problems of water conservation and, perhaps, water transfer; at soil conservation; at productivity and the requirements for increased research and development—it
seems palpable that we're a society where, if we face up to these supply problems, we ought to have an investment rate of, say, 20 to 22% of
GNP. This is no astonishing figure. It is what most European countries
achieve. The Japanese have run as high as 35%. I drive this point home
because it is one practical, operational meaning of the approach I com-
mend from the supply side.

Once we get the hang of the period we're in and break loose from the
fixations, ideas, and policies of the past, we're going to be looking at
the people in the slums of the Northern and Midwestern cities not as a
sad, intractable social problem but as real live human beings that we
need for the working force. It is a quite different image from the conventional image of the next 25 years. But we haven't got the hang of it
yet, by any means.

Now, a few words about energy. I once gave a talk entitled "The
Years the Locust Hath Eaten." I returned to the biblical phrase used by
Churchill in his first volume on World War II where he describes the
wasted years of 1931–1935 when the British and French failed to face
up to the security challenge.

We have now had at least five and a half Locust Years in energy.
We're heading into a period when the 1977 predictions of the CIA will
come true; that is, the demand for OPEC oil will exceed OPEC production capacity by 1983. The CIA projection may even turn out to be
over-optimistic. The Iranian crisis and the secondary effects of that crisis have brought that time closer—perhaps a couple of years closer.

What we are now experiencing is a kind of premonition of a more
serious crisis to come. The situation may or may not ease up in 1980;
but we are on a collision course with stagnant American energy production. We have done rather well in conservation by bringing our energy—GNP ratio down to .6; but even with a low 2.5% growth rate, we
need a 2% increase in energy consumption, and we are producing no
increment in energy production for the year 1979. And so we are relying on increased imports, even with a slow rate of growth and a good
conservation performance. We are consequently heading into a dangerous global economic crisis with serious security consequences.

Is there any hope? Well, yes. I've never believed that my ideas, arrived at even after the best quiet study I was capable of, came down from a mountain carved in marble like the Ten Commandments. My test of whether a set of my ideas and perceptions is correct is whether others, out of their own experiences, came to similar views. There are a few cases where I see that happening. One is among the Coalition of Northeast Governors. They have decided that they want an energy corporation for the Northeast, not merely to help with the energy problem, but also to generate an extra $100 or $120 billion of energy-related investment that would help galvanize the somewhat sluggish Northeast. By my calculations, a slightly larger amount is needed in the industrial Middle West. My point is that the Northeast Governors are beginning to perceive the linkage between the resource side and growth and full employment. Then again, quite on its own, the Joint Economic Committee of the United States Congress made what might turn out to be an historic statement on March 19, 1979. It said that the 1950s and 1960s were a time of orientation toward demand, but that we have now entered a supply-oriented era and that the energy problem is the symbol of that era. The acceptance of this idea is a big change, and I believe it is the first time in a long while that the report is bipartisan.

I agree with the temperate optimists that the next century could be less difficult, economically, than the twentieth century, and hopefully less bloody than this rather murderous century. All sorts of technologies are emerging that could play a constructive part: automation, lasers, all manner of communications possibilities, fusion power, derivations from the remarkable work on the human brain. Although the link between science and invention is oblique, one cannot look at the state of contemporary science and not feel that there are great potentialities for human welfare. But if we don't get on to the supply side agenda that I outlined at the beginning and generate the intellectual framework to cope with it—if we remain fixated, on the one hand, with what worked in the 1950s and 1960s, and, on the other hand, with the glamorous potentialities of science and technology—if we don't face up to this urgent agenda, we may, perhaps, get back on some kind of curve in the twenty-first century, but it may be in a world that has suffered a great deal; and it may be a much less attractive world for human beings with our values than we'd like to see. Therefore, I do think we should focus some thought on getting from here to there.

CHAPTER 2

Two Promising Technologies: The Biosciences and Information Sciences

William E. Bonnet, Ph.D.

O ver a decade ago we began an era of quantum jumps in our basic knowledge of the biosciences. The expansion of that basic knowledge is still proceeding at an extremely rapid pace. It will have innumerable practical consequences, some of which are now appearing and many of which will emerge during the next century.

One of the principal developments will be the ability to do things biologically in a controlled manner. For example, we will be able to build organisms to accomplish specific tasks. A recent instance was the production of insulin by organisms created through genetic manipulation. We will be able to produce all sorts of biologically active substances, many of which can now be made only in the human body. Organisms will be developed that have important industrial uses, including the processing of organic waste into fuels or sugars. We will develop techniques for the microbial processing of dilute ores or seawater to recover metals.

A second area of development will be the modification of plants and animals through genetic engineering. It is highly likely that plants will soon be developed that are able to fix their own nitrogen and therefore not need fertilizer. We will develop nutritionally improved foods, such as high-protein grains. In the animal family, we will probably be able to produce nutritionally controlled meats and dairy products low in fat and cholesterol.

A third area of development will be the understanding of human biological and biochemical processes. The two major impacts of this will be good health and long life. The probable result is that everyone will be able to have a life expectancy equal to the apparent maximum human life span of about 100 years. Eventually, the life span itself may be lengthened. The important part of this development is that the 100-year life span will be a healthy one. Major physical disease should be controlled or eliminated, and there probably will be some control of mental disease by drugs.

It is this last aspect—advancement in the biological sciences—that will most affect the workplace. The whole concept of a working life will be different. People will retain their full mental and physical capabilities into their 60s, 70s, and 80s. The traditional working life—leaving school or college at 18 to 25, working for 30 or 40 years, and retiring for 5 to 10 years—will disappear. Instead, people will take a flexible approach to multiple careers. The individual who can identify an interest might start work fairly early in life. If he is uncertain, he can work for awhile and then go back to school; there will be no hurry to begin a career. People will probably work at two, three, or four careers during their lifetime, returning to school several times for training in a totally new field at ages as late as 60 or 70. Combined with changes in social values, good health for 100 years will revolutionize our view of a working life.

Another branch of technology that will have an even more profound effect on the way in which we do our everyday work is that category known as the information sciences. This category includes developments in electronic hardware, computer hardware and software, and communications techniques. It also includes the area commonly called automation or "robotics."

Among the important technical developments in information sciences will be very low-cost, very large-scale information storage techniques. We have already seen the beginning in the electronic circuit chip that goes into a digital watch or a very small calculator. This trend toward smaller, more capacious storage units will be carried much further, so that one can visualize and reasonably expect an information storage chip the size of an aspirin tablet that will hold the contents of 20,000 large books. There will be improved communication techniques utilizing satellites, compact two-way personal radios, and fiber optics. There will be improved communication between people and computers, so that this function will cease to be limiting, as it frequently is now. We will see the development and widespread use of very simple computer terminals. By the middle of the next century, voice communication with computers will be fairly well developed. One can even speculate about the very far-out possibility of direct connection of the human nervous system to a computer.

The development of these techniques will have three general effects. One will be to move information, not people. This trend will be enhanced by the reduction of mobility resulting from high energy costs. A second effect will be to upgrade people in the sense that they will be doing more intellectual, higher-level work, with machines taking over many of the more menial and unpleasant tasks. The third effect will be to expand the work force. Since it will no longer be necessary to move everyone to a central workplace, those for whom such moving is inconvenient could then enter the work force.

One of the possible economic advantages of the electronic age will be an improvement in the productivity of the service sector. This has been a concern to economists, because currently low productivity of this kind of work has tended to retard economic growth rates.

Robotics and automation, for instance, will be substantially advanced. It will be possible to build much more complicated programmed and controllable machines. For example, coal mining will probably be done from the surface rather than underground, utilizing machines, control devices, and televised visual communication. Generally speaking, unpleasant and dangerous tasks will be automated. Assembly lines should be much more highly automated. The reliability of electronic devices will be substantially increased by redundancy of circuits, which can be achieved very cheaply with the low-cost hardware that will be developed.

A major effect of all of these new techniques will be the requirement to substantially increase training for everyone. Given the need for a much higher level of technical sophistication and a long life with multiple careers, an important function of industry will be in-house training of employees to undertake new careers.

One of the easiest and most obvious examples is the retraining of a traditional clerk or stenographer to be a computer programmer, able to be part of the computer revolution. At a different academic level, a lot of polymer chemistry has pretty much matured. When interest shifted to the biological sciences, we encouraged polymer chemists to obtain training in that area. A third case occurred when we decided to go into the coal mining business. We retrained rough-necks from the oil fields to be coal miners.

All in all, I have a fairly optimistic view of the effect of technology on working life. I see the development of long, multiple-career working lives with higher productivity and the elimination of unpleasant and dangerous jobs. While there may be many social, political, and economic difficulties in transition to this kind of a workplace, it seems to me that its eventual emergence is inevitable and highly desirable.

I am not as optimistic about the condition of our natural resource supply. The problems in this area, which have begun only recently, will be with us for a long time and will delay our reaching the desirable state of the workplace that technological development will make possible.

From the late nineteenth century until World War II real economic growth in the United States averaged slightly below 3% annually. After World War II a unique set of circumstances—abundant cheap energy and other resources, pent-up consumer demand, high financial liquidity, technological advances—led to a long economic boom and a higher-than-average level of economic growth rate, almost 4% annually. These forces have spent themselves, and we will now tend to fall back to the longer-term growth rates. In addition, a set of forces bearing on the long-term trend is likely to push it down somewhat. The most important of these is the rising cost of energy.

In the 1970s this nation entered a basically new era when the supply of cheap energy ran out. We are now in a period of transition where oil and gas will become increasingly expensive and eventually in short supply. We will be steadily replacing oil and gas with more costly alternate sources of energy.

There will be no cheap technical solution to this problem. Most alternate energy technologies are mature and expensive: for example, the liquefaction of coal or the production of gas from coal. They also frequently have environmental problems, as in the use of oil from shale. In some cases, they are just plain expensive—solar energy will be used, but it won't be cheap. The public is doomed to disappointment in the expectation that the style of living and working will not have to change because of the energy problem.

In the workplace, many of the changes may not be too apparent. There will be a series of modifications in equipment and systems design, as well as in operating practices and ways of building equipment. In the past we have substituted capital equipment for labor as its cost increased; in the future we will substitute capital equipment for energy as its cost increases. It does, however, seem doubtful that energy will ever cost so much that we will substitute people for energy.

A more noticeable effect of high energy costs on our working lives will be a reduction in the mobility of people. Transportation will become much more expensive and subject to fuel supply interruptions. Most forecasts call for an increase in mass transit into the center city. However, I do not think this route will be followed, even though it would increase energy efficiency. It seems to me more likely, given our present trends, our lifestyle preferences, and a still substantial but reduced mobility, that we will see the development of both smaller cities and satellite complexes around larger cities, which will contain all the elements of living—commercial, industrial, and residential—in close proximity. The trend, I think, will be to eliminate commuting, rather than increase its efficiency through mass transit. People will tend to live much closer to their work.

The most noticeable effect of high energy cost on the workplace will be the retardation of new job creation because of increased inflation and lower economic growth rates. This effect will be increased by other resource problems. While there is little chance of a worldwide physical shortage of any important mineral resource, in general costs will slowly rise as ores get leaner and require more and higher-cost energy for recovery of the metal. Although not a widespread problem in the Western world, localized water shortages could inhibit economic growth. This is especially true of alternate energy source development in the western United States. It seems clear that for health, aesthetic, and economic reasons the developed world must, and will, reduce the level of pollution of the physical environment. This will increase the real cost of producing goods.

Some analysts have forecast catastrophe resulting from these and other resource problems—the "limits to growth" concept. While it is unlikely that such widespread collapse will occur because people will react and adapt, there seems little doubt that rising energy, resource, and environmental costs will inhibit new job creation.

In summary, I am pessimistic in the short term about the effects of resource limitations on the workplace, but optimistic in the long run about the kind of working life that technological change will make possible. This kind of forecast has many serious implications outside the realm of the physically possible. A long period in which the nature of work is constantly changing, in which groups of workers frequently become technically obsolete, and in which economic growth is not too vigorous, is likely to be a time of intensified conflict between labor and management. The definition of "labor" will change substantially, with the white-collar component coming to dominate the traditional blue-collar group. Pressure for an increase in the role of the government as a manager or regulator of the economy will rise. There must be greater recognition by both labor and management of the need to deal responsibly with normal resistance to change and to adapt to the workplace of the future.

CHAPTER 3

The Post-Industrial Boom in Compunications
Walter A. Hahn

My grandchildren will have just entered the work force at the start of the twenty-first century. I assume that they will perform some mixture of three kinds of work: activity to earn a living, activity for self-fulfillment, plus those activities for necessary maintenance of body, habitat, and possessions. We can hope that the first two activities will be one and the same, but history is replete with examples of their separation. It is likely that even in the future, some will work only to live, while others will gain satisfaction and recognition from it as well. Presumably, at least through the twenty-first century, we will still perform functions that are today called house-work, yard-work, hobby-work, and the like. Since I am not speaking in economic or social structure terms, I will lump the above types of work into a single category and suggest the impact of technology on all three activities that my grandchildren—and yours—may experience.

It is tempting to spread out a futuristic smorgasbord of gee-whiz, technology-based gadgets and to discuss which ones we want to encourage and which ones should be suppressed. It is more responsible, though perhaps less entertaining, to explore a few highly likely trends in two key technologies that most of us in the futures field "know" will influence work (and many other things) in the twenty-first century. Futurist Robert Theobald warns us:

> We should recognize that we must move away from an industrial/mobile society toward a communication/community society. The shift will

require modifications in our societal patterns which will be at least as great as those which occurred between the agricultural era and the industrial era but they will take place far more rapidly. One of the most worrying aspects of the present period is the failure to understand the speed and scope of the microelectronic revolution which will change so much of our lives in the next decade.*

Using Harvard professor Anthony Oettinger's word for it, I will explore "compunications"—computers and communications. While for some technical purposes it might be meaningful to examine these subjects separately, it is in their combination that the major social, economic, environmental, political, and other technological impacts will be seen.

It was only in the nineteenth century that we saw devices that today we would call computers. First, there was Charles Babbage's Analytical Engine (1834). This was followed by statistician Herman Hollirith's punched cards, which appeared in 1885 in time for use in the 1890 census. MARK I, developed by Howard Aiken of Harvard in association with IBM, was the first program-controlled computer, but it was still electro-mechanical. It quickly yielded in 1946 to the first electronic digital computer, the ENIAC (electronic numerical integration and calculator), which used close to 20,000 vacuum tubes. Today, a single, fingernail-sized semiconductor chip can perform similar functions while consuming negligible power and needing no massive air-conditioning equipment. In simpler and cheap form our children carry calculators to school in their pockets, and their affluent fathers wear them on their wrists, complete with timers, as status symbols.

We are all aware of the giant step in human communications that came with Gutenberg's printing press. But point-to-point communication for literally thousands of years was limited to the range of the eye and the ear, for example, signal fires or lights and drums. Distances were extended by fast horses and slow ships, but Ben Franklin was little better off than Julius Caesar. Samuel Morse's electric telegraph is less than 150 years old. Its wires and cables rapidly spread across continents and under oceans, even though they only operated at the now astoundingly slow rate of two words per minute. Alexander Graham Bell added voice communications to wired transmission in 1876, and Marconi, just before the turn of the century, demonstrated communica-

* Robert Theobald, *Special Study on Economic Change,* Testimony Before the Joint Economic Committee, U.S. Congress, May 31, 1978.

tions without wires. Since then, through satellites, we have seen the horrors of war on our home televisions, listened in on working conversations between two men on the moon, and permitted sports fans all over the globe to watch their Olympic athletes compete.

Computers never were very separate from communication devices. No modern communication system operates without its own internal or attached version of a computer. Similarly, advanced computers are often so large they require specialized communication links among their parts. Also, as we see with increasing frequency, an instrument the size of a portable typewriter, or even a touch-tone telephone, will let any of us communicate with distant computers from our nearest phone booth. Compunications, or whatever you wish to call it, is here.

Compunications and its integral microelectronics are both the driving and dependent technologies behind the so-called information explosion. Today, approximately 47% of the total labor force in the United States is engaged in information-related occupations. Gross 1977 revenues of some of our major information industries give us some perspective: telephone, $40 billion; postal service, $13 billion; computer systems and software, $29 billion; newspapers and wire services, $13 billion; and schooling, $130 billion. One could go on citing additional large numbers for radio, TV, movies, magazines and books, advertising, brokerage and banking, and 80,000 units of federal, state, and local government. Changes in these industries and occupations in turn affect less information-dominated occupations such as agriculture, some manufacturing, and the arts. And all of this will affect our personal lives.

Historically, it was a very long transition from a hunting to an agricultural society, albeit one with cities. Then came the industrial society, still with cities, but now with suburbs and the retention of some farms and agribusiness. Except in the oceans, most hunting is now for sport. One popular phrase describing the next stage we are entering is "the post-industrial society." As one might expect, the post-industrial society has the vestigial aspects of all that has gone before, but the emphasis will change. According to Daniel Bell, the economic sector will shift from producing goods to producing services. Professional and technical classes will dominate. Theoretical knowledge is to be the source of innovation and policy formulation. Technology will be controlled through information—information about the technology per se, and about its impacts on society, the economy, and the environment. Authors Peter Drucker, the late Carl Madden, and a host of others also have described the beginning of the next century as an era or age of information. Let us look at some selected technological trends, or possibilities, that will influence this coming information society and, in particular, have an impact on work.

Today's managers, secretaries, clerks, accountants, and others work in a paper-bound office, but in the future they will work in an electronic one. Some form of word processor will likely be the most visible aspect of the paperless office. Visualize a typewriter-like keyboard below a television-like screen. An unobtrusive but significant difference from today's scene is the presence of a telephone coupler leading to and from electronic storage devices. Possibly it also connects with a large computer, and maybe to printing equipment, or to lines to similar devices in other offices. Almost any unit of the system can furnish a duplicate of the screen's display on paper, but the "carbons" will only exist in quickly accessible electronic files. Small text revisions (e.g. different addresses) or even major ones can be made with the need only to proofread the changes.

One can visit an office much like the above today since all these functional capabilities currently exist. But at present they are usually in parallel with all the familiar paper paraphernalia—files, cutters and punches, envelopes, the ubiquitous in-out and hold boxes, wastepaper baskets, and possibly a shredder. Sometimes the new machinery has replaced the typewriter or accounting devices at the clerical employee's work station, but in most current setups they usually stand ready nearby. In the electronic office of the future, more than likely, all people, regardless of rank or task, will have displays and keyboards.

In the electronic office, most of the paper-handling routines that consume so much time and space will be gone. Mail sorting, opening, stamping, physical transportation, or searching will decrease significantly but not disappear. During the transition to a relatively paperless office, some of this work will be done at a central location, where printed information will be converted to electronic form and transmitted throughout the enterprise. This is actually being done today in the Equitable General Insurance Company's home office in Fort Worth. Future optical character readers will further automate the translation of the information received from nonelectronic offices or individuals who still use paper and handwriting.

Social patterns will change in the office of the future. There will be fewer reasons to move around the immediate office and building. Will we see in office workers the boredom and adverse reactions in health and attendance that we now see in highly automated factories? What novel excuses will be invented to meet that new person on the fifth floor?

Two fears immediately face workers: the elimination of their jobs, or of their own abilities to convert to the new technologies. These fears will apply to managers as well as to the mail clerk—and they are real. Many other jobs as we know them today will disappear or undergo major change. Bank tellers and their accounting, auditing, and financial colleagues will be seriously affected by EFT—electronic funds transfer. In the coming checkless, cashless society, the honest citizen will lose the currently legal benefits of float, and the robber will find little cash to extract from his victim. Government monitoring for policy purposes, control, and tax collection will be eased by the centralized and more standardized electronic financial systems. But the Mafia will have to find a substitute for cash to transfer unrecorded wealth.

Electronic mail will convert the materials-handling task of the post office to an information-handling one. Sea-mail between continents is all but gone now, and more mail-sorting rail cars are reported to be in museums than on the tracks. What will happen to the U.S. government's largest automotive fleet, the mail vehicles? The fuel savings and reduction in traffic of the transformation are appealing generally, but not to the vehicle operators and materials handlers.

With over 97% of U.S. homes already housing a television, will the daily newspaper eventually be "delivered" electronically on a wall screen? If so, there goes one of the last allowable jobs for young people, along with those of the printers.

Printers and binders are further threatened by the electronic library, sometimes called the multimedia library. Microsystems consultant Jon Roland forecasts that if performance increase and cost reduction trends continue at their present rate, by the end of this century it may be possible to store the entire contents of the Library of Congress "in a volume no larger than a single book costing no more than a single book does today."

Roland may be very optimistic as to that early date, but few would doubt that we will have that capability in the first half of the twenty-first century. The Library of Congress already is scheduled to close the card catalog in 1980—25 million cards cannot be maintained, or even effectively used, by mere humans. Both the master card catalog and the books it represents are in Washington, D.C., and partial duplicates of each exist in both domestic and foreign locations. If the memory and access capabilities Roland predicts are combined with compunications, the information on any of these cards and in the books can be instantly made available anywhere else on the globe, and, yes, in space. It is staggering to note that all the great and small libraries in the world could be simultaneously linked and, technically at least, made accessible to any individual on earth. The economic, procedural, and social processes to convert technical feasibility into daily global operations are formidable. So is the making of an *explicit choice* to implement that capability or to prevent it.

And we do have explicit choices. The experience from preceding decades would lead many to believe in the technological imperative: if something *can* be built, it *will* be built. More recently, we have been disillusioned by the way many technologies generated unforeseen and dire social or environmental consequences.

Among the various responses to technological side effects have been demands for the social management of technology, a rising anti-technology mood, and technology assessment (TA)—the review of possible and probable impacts, prior to introduction of the new technology. Being against technology, or viewing TA as technology arrestment (as some did when it was introduced a decade ago), is as unproductive as the unquestioning, uncritical approach. Technologies do have something of an imperative which, when allied with parallel economic, social, and political imperatives, can move selected technologies into practice with great speed. This appears to be the case for compunications and microelectronics. To control and direct genies already out of the bottle will require similar sophisticated technologies—both physical and social. We must choose those paths that will, at a minimum, assure our ecological and social survival. In theory we can do more. We can also select those social, technological, economic, environmental, and political paths that we want.

Regrettably, choosing our future may be the biggest rub of all. Developing concepts, procedures, and institutional forms to set goals, to plan strategies, and to develop institutions to achieve them are social technologies. It is by the use of social technologies that we get agreement on the proper course for our society. Yet, social technologies lag hard technology by many generations. My point on "explicit choice" is this: the lack of adequate social technologies may have even more impact on the nature of work in the twenty-first century than the consequences of the rapid and ubiquitous information technologies discussed previously. We know much about developing sophisticated hard technologies and too little about how to reach a consensus on doing so.

Meanwhile, the march of hard technology proceeds. If one can install the advanced word processing and compunications systems in an office, they also can be installed in a home. This is already being done in scattered and elementary form, and predictions are that home offices will increase very rapidly. The time and cost advantages of noncommuting are direct benefits to the employee. Offsetting the capital or rental cost of equipment and communication lines are reduced costs in physical working space and a variety of overhead at a central office. For employees with families it is not at all clear that the interruptions at home will be any less than those at the office. Computerand teleconferencing are already demonstrating some advantages over face-to-face meetings but with some obvious losses in interpersonal discourse and group dynamics. Time may be as big a variable as distance. The employee can adjust electronic work hours to almost any reasonable schedule agreed to with the employer and other workers. Electronic storage devices, after all, are infinitely patient, and computer-controlled transmitters can time and route messages in almost endless variation. Many questions of management control, secretive dual employment, and the various effects on the home environment will need to be resolved.

One could explore in equal depth the notion opposite to the home office—the centralization of work at one or a few geographic centers. Insurance and banking institutions are taking the lead in this direction. Time-sharing on computers is offered as a commercial service, and huge networks such as those of IBM and General Electric are already in operation on an international basis. World time zones aid in load balancing among computer centers located thousands of miles apart. Domestic airlines already handle almost all reservations centrally, and some foreign airlines even use U.S.-based computers. How the relative balancing of these centralizing and decentralizing forces will come out is not at all clear. Many of the technical and social changes will present us with new problems for which the knowledge and means of solution do not yet exist.

Other problems of unprecedented scale and intensity will also face us. Security and privacy are key examples. If those who want access to each other via communications can do it so easily, so can third parties. Computer crimes, once the stuff of science fiction and comic strips, are routinely tried in the courts of today. There is a larger fear that much of such crime may go undetected. To a limited degree in current practice, and optimistically in theory for the future, information scientists and engineers tell us that transmissions and stored information can be physically protected and coded to prevent unauthorized access. While this is reassuring, how can the layman be sure? The situation is more difficult than just translating complex science and engineering sophistication into understandable form for the public. It involves rebuilding trust in institutions and their leaders which many people feel has broken down today. History tells us of the early distrust of paper money. Will citizens of the twenty-first century have any reason to trust the technology of compunications or the veracity of the huge public and private institutions that produce and operate the systems and equipment? Many do not even believe that today's energy shortages exist, and the data that prove it does are more extensive and verifiable than they will be for electronic money.

The talk about these new instruments and processes is enough to give any of us a feeling of obsolescence. As the complexity and pace of change continue, we will face even more severe problems of retraining. Multiple careers, retreading, lifelong learning are but a few of the everyday topics now emerging. Fortunately, many of the same machines and techniques that will cause the obsolescence of some tasks are extremely useful for teaching new ones. Computer-aided instruction, educational television, audio and video cassettes, microform reproduction, and remote access are only a few of the approaches available. But we will face the usual problems of acceptance of these new gadgets and approaches, and must resolve many questions, such as who pays for the materials, equipment, and time required? What are the personal and societal criteria for selecting the next career? What is to be done for those incapable of change?

Below the euphoria of the new technologies and global vistas are some grubby leftovers that must be dealt with. Who will do the dirty work? Compunications cannot clean streets, attend the ill in hospitals, or slaughter cattle. Who will engage in the high-risk occupations that require great human judgment: rescue squads, fire fighting, and crowd control?

Reportedly, up to 20% of the U.S. population is functionally illiterate. These people cannot make change, do their income tax, or fill out many of the governmental and private forms needed for current living. Will the even higher educational and intellectual demands of emerging technologies create a still larger functionally illiterate class? And since this new class may be of even higher native intelligence than the present one, can we predict how or if they will accept the role? It would be too much at this point to do more than acknowledge the vast problems of the ever more rapid transitions from the present to a compunications society.

It boggles the mind to note the huge number of technologies that exist or may come into being to aid or to threaten us. Compunications and microelectronics will have many more impacts and wider areas of impact than are even hinted at here. These are not notes of despair but rather of hope. Nature has taught us the survivability and delights of diversity. The possibility that we could be overwhelmed by it all exists. But the possibilities seem greater that we can use these advances to make wise choices for a better world for all of us and for our grandchildren.

CHAPTER 4

Technology and Society in the Next Thirty Years: We Have Manageable Choices[1]

Irving Leveson, Ph.D.

The advantage of talking about the twenty-first century used to be that it was so far off that one could consider developments which might take a long time to occur and imagination could run free. As in many other ways, life is no longer so simple. We have become acutely aware of the more gradual changes which can have very profound impacts on society, such as the aging of the population and the gestation periods for development of new energy sources. We have become cautious about accepting pictures of the future unless accompanied by a reasonable explanation of how we get from here to there. And the twenty-first century feels like it is almost upon us.

The advanced capitalist nations today are going through a difficult period of rapid change, structural shift, and adjustment. That process has a number of causes, but central to them is the notion of the transition to a post-industrial economy, one in which growing attention is devoted to service industries, leisure, and personal pursuits.[2] In the next three decades, we face the challenge of managing that transition, and our success in doing so will have a great impact on life and work for a long time.

Perhaps the most important observation that can be made about the effect of natural resources, capital, and technology on the nature of work is that the disasters which we hear about so often are extremes in a range of possibilities which are as unlikely as the most blindly optimistic projections. This does not mean that we can relax, since it is only through vigilance that some disasters will be avoided. And it does not mean that none will occur over an extended period of time. But it does mean we do not have to hold back development in fear that every potential advance will raise the likelihood of future disaster.

The rate of growth of world population will fall dramatically as birth rates in more and more countries decline with rising incomes. But the absolute numbers of people added will be far greater than ever before—about a billion a decade over the next three decades. The rate of growth of output per capita will be slower in industrial countries in the next 30 years than in the last 30, but development will spread to more nations, and the rate of growth of gross world product per capita will not decline.

With unprecedented additions to output resulting from productivity changes as well as population growth, possible pressures on resources and the environment cannot be ignored. But neither can the capacity of modern societies to solve these problems. Problems will be contained by shifting away from production methods and products which are harmful or rely on resources which become scarce. Rising prices of basic materials and energy will encourage exploration and creation of substitute materials. New technologies will increase resource recovery, conserve scarce commodities, and reduce environmental impacts. In fact, our existing environmental rules were implemented with the knowledge that the costs they impose would be far too high unless major technological changes did occur.

The need to substitute for scarce goods or pay higher prices, and the costs of reducing environmental impacts, will make commodity prices rise faster than the general price level, and keep economic growth slower than it otherwise would be. But in the most likely scenario, the world of work will not be dominated by draconian measures or sudden large-scale shifts in production methods and products, except in isolated instances.

Neither is the most likely projection for capital one of sustained shortage. Fears of capital shortages have been generated by several factors that do not portend long-run problems when put in proper perspective. Credit crunches, the most often cited form of shortage, have been the result of attempts to slow the growth of the money supply to curb inflation. They have been a phenomenon of the current form of the business cycle rather than of long-run growth. While personal savings have been reduced by the growth of pension benefits, history has shown that when large supplies of capital were needed to support strong economic growth, the largest swing factor has been corporate profits. Corporate profits have not fully returned to a satisfactory level when put on a historically comparable basis,[3] but in the current recovery they have sharply responded to increases in demand as in the past. The rapid growth in the use of debt is a rational response to low interest rates in relation to inflation and to the tax treatment of interest payments. It is not a signal that markets are not working. The mechanisms of the economy, in short, are in far better working order than some have suggested. A disturbing exception, however, is the state of our incentive structures.

Today, incentives are distorted by a climate of high risk, inflation, costs of energy, heavy taxation, and intense regulation. A reaction to the distortion of incentives has set in and may last for several years. But in the long run, there is likely to be a return to the growth of regulation and an increased role for government. These will result from intensification of forces such as localism, risk aversion, and preoccupation with health and safety. Such movements to place social limits on growth have shown a strong tendency to increase with rising affluence. This does not mean that a decade from now we will see a big burst of government spending and regulatory activity, such as in the 1960s and early 1970s. Fluctuations in economic and social behavior will probably be less intense in the United States in the next three decades than in the last. But there is good reason to expect that forces which have reduced incentives for innovation and development will grow in importance once again.

There is special need to be concerned about pressures that have arisen that shift the burden of proof from the government to the innovator. The innovator increasingly needs to prove that every possible harm will not occur. Formerly, society asked that problems of importance be addressed once a product or technique was in use. With the burden of proof on the entrepreneur, development can be slowed enormously.

There will be some slowing of economic growth in the United States because certain traditional sources of growth, such as rising education, have diminished in importance because of rising costs of resources and because of legitimate responses to environmental problems. But the greatest concern is that increased bureaucracy and actions taken in the name of achieving increasingly discretionary personal preferences will continue to retard incentives and reduce the ability of growth to occur. Less growth will mean less productive capacity to deal with problems of environment and resource scarcity, to reduce poverty, to increase leisure, and to seek self-fulfillment. Incomes will continue to rise, but not as much as they could.

At the same time that incentives have been distorted, the economy has undergone an extraordinary amount of structural change, including the shift to flexible change rates, widespread declines in city populations, rapid increases of women in the labor force, and a dozen other major developments. While there is no indication that the economy has become permanently more unstable as a result of these changes, many years of difficult adjustment lie ahead, and the amount and the length of the adjustment period will vary greatly among sectors. Financial institutions may largely adapt to high inflation rates within a decade, while shifts to lower density lifestyles and adjustment of physical structures to energy costs will take far longer.

In order to depict correctly the role of technology in the future, it is necessary to consider some of the reasons for the slowdown in technology today. A large part of the decline in research and development spending as a percent of GNP in the last decade is the result of reduced federal funding for defense and space research. Both sectors are highly volatile and are at low points, as the mounting pressure for increased defense spending indicates. Inventive activity has been especially hurt by the adverse economic climate of the 1970s. This includes the impact of high risk, the effect of inflation requiring high interest costs in the early years of a project, pressures on government spending, and slower growth of demand in a period of reduced income and population growth.

As problems subside and the economy adjusts to new conditions, the incentives for higher R&D spending will increase. Responses to problems of energy and environment have begun to stimulate more R&D activity, and substantial further increases are likely in these areas. On the whole, we would expect the gains from R&D in the United States over the coming decades to return to levels close to the peak rates of the 1960s.

When we look at this country's share of technology development activities in the world, rather than in relation to its production, we get a very different picture. The U.S. proportion of world R&D spending, manpower, and invention has fallen dramatically. The number of countries with incomes at levels near those of the United States has grown, and as technology development spreads the U.S. share of gross world product continues to fall. It is natural that as other countries progress they will also invest heavily in R&D, drawing on their own strengths and the availability of world markets. Part of the uneasiness about this shift in relative importance results from the fact that the United States is no longer alone at the top. Part stems from the fact that individual companies may be losers in spite of improvements in the general good.

Fears of loss of international competitiveness and its impacts have been exaggerated. The world has become more competitive, and that takes some getting used to. Foreign technological advances may require adjustments in exchange rates which will result in slower growth in the real standard of living. But the United States increasingly will be able to benefit from productivity improvements and from new products made possible by the importation of technology developed elsewhere. Competitive challenges will encourage innovation in the United States. The Hudson Institute recently held a conference for government agencies to examine structural changes and adjustment problems in OECD countries.[4] The latest evidence indicates that:

1 Problems of employment adjustment due to import competition have been exaggerated.
2 Competition from imports is often used as a handy excuse for adjustments to many of the other changes which are taking place.
3 The greater danger is that increasingly detailed regulation of international transactions and subsidies and restrictions to prevent adjustments from occurring will impede the processes from which we can derive large gains.

There have been an increasing number of statements to the effect that a slowing of technological change has occurred because of a Schumpeterian cycle—that technological opportunities developed earlier have been fairly well exhausted and new R&D efforts will have to continue for a while until a new wave of innovation occurs. These arguments are not only largely incorrect, but also provide too easy an excuse for those who do not see a need to improve the incentives for innovation and technological change.

The impressive economic growth after World War II was in part made possible by technologies developed during the war years and the Depression. And while those opportunities may have been exhausted in the long period of strong economic growth over the last 30 years, the United States has returned to a period in which technological change continues at a more normal historical rate. Technological change continues to be strong, but we bemoan the passing of an unusual era. Moreover, we have so taken for granted the institutionalization of technological change and the regularity of major developments that we no longer see them as having the importance that they do.

We tend to misread the technological examples before us. Those who focus primarily on new product development to draw conclusions about the pace of technological change miss the degree to which technology has responded to problems on the supply side, through automated factories, resource recovery techniques, lower-cost medical diagnostics, new materials, and information handling. New product development itself reflects the problems of the current economic climate rather than technological insufficiencies. Certainly the development of mid-sized, wide-bodied jets is not exciting after the jumbo jet has arrived. But SST was held up for environmental reasons, not because the propulsion technology was unavailable. Yet a major new wave *is* beginning in computer and related technology, and one is likely to occur at some time in the next century in space.

The United States is currently entering what might be termed "the second computer revolution." The impacts of very low-cost computers, distributed computing, and microprocessors are likely to be enormous. Major applications are apparent in telecommunications, office automation, financial services, medicine, entertainment, personal business, and learning in the home. Computer-type devices link with other recent technologies in videotaping, text editing, telephone dialing, and a number of other uses. The effects of the computer on society will parallel those of advances in transportation, communications, and energy in earlier generations.

At the same time we are entering a new era in which the service industries can no longer be viewed as backward and incapable of advances in productivity. The service economy is experiencing major improvements in the organization of human activities, and increasingly, it is taking full advantage of more technology to provide new services or provide old ones at lower cost. While the gains from the new era of service industry productivity growth are often unmeasured, they are clearly large.[5] Many potentially dramatic changes are possible in this climate, ranging from automated fast-foods to the extensive use of videotapes or discs in higher education and continuing learning.

THE FUTURE FOR LABOR

Since the mid-1960s, the U.S. labor force has grown at about 2% per year, double the rate in earlier years. The impetus was the entry of the postwar generation into the labor force, the rapid growth of women in the labor force, and shifts away from capital intensive production.

During this period many factors also discouraged capital investment. The passing of the youth bulge will lead to smaller growth in the labor force, the rise in female labor supply will slow, and the incentives for capital investment will improve. At the same time, the high ratio of labor to capital raises the rate of return to further investment. As a result we can expect a substantial rise in capital spending in the first half of the 1980s and a reversal of some of the movement toward a more labor-intensive economy which has occurred thus far. The wave of capital spending will improve productivity, but it will have some profound effects on the labor force.

While there has been some occupational advancement among females, the most rapid growth in employment during the decade of high female employment growth has still been very much in traditional occupations—secretaries, salesworkers, and so on. As we look at the prospects for rapid automation during the coming years, there emerges a picture of particularly far-reaching changes in just those occupations. Teller machines should substantially reduce demand for not only tellers but other employees in bank branches. Tens of thousands of telephone operator jobs will be eliminated in the next decade by automated systems. As we go further out in time, we may see a significant impact on demand for salesworkers in department stores and other retail units. The rapid growth of catalog shopping keyed to opportunities for mail and telephone ordering may become attractive once video discs and cassettes allow products to be viewed inexpensively and conveniently in the home. The demand for secretaries may be decreased by the use of text editing machines and automatic telephone dialing systems, and we would not be surprised to see rapid introduction of devices that permit dictation and other voice recordings to be directly translated into typescript by machine.

The result of these technological changes will be weak demand for labor in the occupations in which females still tend to be most highly concentrated. This should slow the rate of growth of female employment and create pressures for women to move into traditionally male areas or to be upgraded within their current work environments. There could be considerable frustration about opportunities for advancement and increasing sexual politics. One manifestation may be the extensive use of trade unions to pursue feminist goals.

The picture is not one of technological unemployment on a national scale. Rather, the growth of demand for workers has been extraordinary, just as the supply has grown rapidly, and the future slowing of demand will come at the same time as supply growth falls off. The importance of technological changes will be in their incidence and in the adjustments which are required.

The competitive environment, along with continued strength in service employment, will mean no gains and probably further losses in the proportion of U.S. employees in unions for at least another decade. In a decade or two the declines should stabilize, however, and some increases may occur as new jobs become more standardized.

In the long run, the increased experience of the female labor force and improvements in the utilization of female labor in job assignments can be looked to as an important source of productivity gains. By the first decade of the next century, there will have been sufficient time for women to adapt their skills to new demands, and for enough adjustment to have occurred so that women have occupational positions and pay equal to those of men with similar work histories.

Horatio Alger is not dead; she is very much alive. The age of the anti-hero has passed. The last few years have seen an extraordinary increase in new business formation and an explosion in female self-employment. The rise transcends not only the traditional dress shoppe and beauty salon but also the proliferation of needlepoint, pottery, art, and music establishments. We now see women in large numbers as travel, employment, and real estate agents; tennis club operators; and restaurateurs. And there is every indication that self-employment and management responsibilities for women will continue to increase and break new ground.

In a study I did on self-employment a decade ago, I used the concept of "dynamic career ladders" to describe the creation of opportunities by changes in technology, economies of scale, and growth of markets over a long period of time. The rise from pushcart to grocery to supermarket symbolizes not only the gains that were made from one generation to the next, but even at times by the same individual as opportunities grew. Something very much like that is happening today. The woman who began as a real estate salesperson with a local community firm, because she could work closer to home in familiar surroundings, now may become an executive in a major national organization such as Century 21.

Opportunities of this nature are by no means limited to women. There will be many such examples in this new era for the service industries. Advances in consumer electronics will create numerous jobs in sales and service, in specialty stores, in distribution outlets, and there will even be an electronic analog of the interior decorator.

In thinking about the years ahead, it is useful to have a picture of the way things will look as the forces that are expected to predominate become important. In my illustrative view, the world of the twenty-first century can either be an aging society and economy or a mature economy and society.

The aging paradigm* is characterized by a loss of technological leadership and failure to meet challenges from international competition. Institutions and processes are increasingly rigidified. The aging of the population leads to loss of vigor and innovation, and emphasis on status and position. Social forces that tend to limit growth strengthen to produce an increase in territoriality, overreaction to risk and change, and an unwillingness to work toward compromise for the greater good. Detailed forms of regulation permeate all levels of government. Vast resources are devoted to working through cumbersome processes rather than finding ways to accomplish desired goals. Decisions are often ad hoc and unpredictable, and successes are not easily copied. Periodic crises result from the inability to respond quickly and strongly to challenges to environment, resources, and public dissatisfaction. A bureaucratized climate impedes human happiness and creativity to a degree that would make even Ibsen cringe.

There is another world, not of aging but of maturing, which is hopeful and free. The maturing model of the post-industrial society holds forth promise that increases in affluence and leisure will provide a basis for greater self-expression and self-fulfillment. Flexibility in the amount, nature, and timing of work and in travel and study will create new opportunities for those who seek them. Role differences will be less rigidly defined, and changes in roles will not be difficult to make. Learning will be even more of a continuing process, and the thinking of the best minds will be available to all in forms that can be widely understood. Technology will free us from burdens of mounting paperwork. More and more activities will be pursued for their own sake. The time, resources, and experience of the many older Americans will help guide the process with wisdom and appreciation of the society which has developed.

* Paradigm: a model; a frame of reference for looking at the world.

These paradigms of an aging and maturing society are both too simple. Both aging and maturing societies will have their problems. Dropouts may occur more easily through reaction to rigidities than through a general rise in leisure and flexibility of work hours. Boredom, alcoholism, and drug use may be more prevalent in an affluent, carefree society than in one in which life is a continuous struggle. We need not resign ourselves, however, for we can influence the outcomes by the choices we make and the values for which we stand. The most likely outcome is for a bittersweet mixture of the two.

What is most amazing is the extent to which our society takes progress for granted. We have always known that the ability of a civilization to progress has depended on the existence of frontiers such as the opening of the West. It is a tribute to our civilization that, increasingly, the future is the frontier.

REFERENCES

1. The ideas of this paper are drawn from a book in preparation on *The Economic Future of the United States,* to be published by Westview Press, Boulder, Colo.
2. See Herman Kahn, William Brown, and Leon Martel, *The Next 200 Years* (New York: William Morrow, 1976) and Herman Kahn, *World Economic Development* (Boulder, Colo.: Westview Press, 1979).
3. Irving Leveson, *Quarterly Economic Update,* Hudson Institute, January 1979.
4. The papers and proceedings will appear as Irving Leveson and Jimmy W. Wheeler (eds.), *Western Economies in Transition: Structural Change and Adjustment Policies in Industrial Countries* (Boulder, Colo.: Westview Press, 1979).
5. Irving Leveson, *The Modern Service Sector,* Joint Economic Committee, U.S. Congress, forthcoming (late 1979).

CHAPTER 5

The Twenty-First Century: Will There Be Collective Bargaining?

Theodore W. Kheel, Esq.

It is certainly wise to lift our eyes from the day-to-day world of work to form a vision of the future. It is our best chance of making sure that the new facts of our working lives do not appear as accidents, or unwelcome surprises. As others in this book point out, our society has social choices to make. And an uninformed choice, one that lacks a coherent vision of the future, is no choice at all.

But in looking to the future, we cannot escape our current institutions and beliefs. Whether we like it or not, they inform what we are likely to think about the future. More importantly, the institutions that govern the world of work are the mechanisms that govern how we will get from the present to the future.

Manifestly, one such institution is the modern trade union. Unions are now so much a part of our working lives that we forget they have been part of society for a relatively brief time. They came into existence to protect workers, to give them the added strength they achieved by joining together. This led workers to seek to bargain collectively, and collective bargaining has become the main business of unions. So as we attempt to get a clear picture of the future, it is well to keep in mind how unions became legally strong, flourished, and developed with employers the practice and procedure of collective bargaining.

I began to accumulate my information on unions on the day 40 years ago when I reported for work at the National Labor Relations Board

(NLRB) as a lawyer. I had been hard pressed to find a job and was de-lighted to be employed and pleased with the annual stipend of $2000 I had accepted. I was no sooner at my desk in an unadorned government office when an officious functionary of the union of lawyers at the NLRB entered my office and demanded to know how much I was mak-ing. When I told him, he immediately said that it was a violation of the union's contract with the Board, that I was entitled to $2600, and that I should file a grievance. When he saw me blanch, he promptly added, "Or we will." I put in the grievance, got the $2600, and have believed in unions ever since.

I came to learn about collective bargaining, the main business of unions, the very next day. As a novice I was assigned to answer letters referred to the NLRB by the White House. The first one came from a worker imbued with the enthusiasm the New Deal had inspired among workers to join unions and bargain collectively with their employers. This worker wrote President Roosevelt to say that he wanted to bar-gain and collect from his boss but that his boss wouldn't let him.

To this day, many workers and their employers think collective bar-gaining means bargaining and collecting from the boss. In the early days of the New Deal, it certainly looked that way. Wages were de-pressed, workers flocked to unions, and unions won money and bene-fits for them.

This was not surprising. The National Labor Relations Act of 1935, held constitutional in 1937 in a momentous 5 to 4 decision, was pure civil rights legislation for workers. Called the Wagner Act, in honor of its principal sponsor, Senator Robert F. Wagner of New York, it con-demned employers for having denied workers the right to organize and bargain collectively and declared it to be the policy of the United States to encourage "the practice and procedure of collective bargain-ing" and to protect "the exercise by workers of full freedom of associa-tion, self-organization, and designation of representatives of their own choosing."

Twelve years later, in 1947, Congress decided that the pendulum had swung too far in labor's favor. It passed the law named Taft–Hartley after its principal sponsors, Senator Robert A. Taft and Representative Fred Hartley. To this day, this law is the foundation of labor relations in this country, even though it has been amended on several occasions, notably in 1959 by the Landrum–Griffin Act. Taft–Hartley is pure reg-ulatory legislation. It did not simply guarantee workers the right to join unions, but also the right not to join. It not only required employers to bargain collectively with unions, but ordered unions to bargain collectively with employers as well.

Taft–Hartley also contained the first and, as far as I know, the only definition of collective bargaining in any law of any country. Even though the term is in general use, few people know what it actually means. To many, it still means the same thing that the worker who wrote Roosevelt thought it meant.

Actually, the definition of the NLRA is exceedingly simple. It says that collective bargaining is "the performance of the mutual obligation of the employer and the representatives of the employees to meet at reasonable times and confer in good faith with respect to wages, hours, and other terms and conditions of employment." There is more, but that is the heart of it. What is so complicated about that? The only question is, what if the company and union meet and confer in good faith and can't agree? The law covers that contingency. It says the obligation to bargain collectively "does not compel either party to agree to a proposal or to require the making of a concession." What then? Another section covers what the union can do. It says that nothing in the law "shall be construed so as either to interfere with or impede or diminish in any way the right to strike." What about the employer? What are his rights? Answering these questions calls for a little more analysis of what collective bargaining is all about as a practical matter.

We start with a simple definition. Collective bargaining is bargaining collectively. And bargaining is negotiating, and negotiating is what we mostly do in our dealings with other people. When two or more people get together, they inevitably negotiate with each other whether they realize it or not. Decisions on the most routine matters are products of negotiations. Where shall we go to dinner? Shall we see a movie? Let's go shopping. The aim is agreement, a joint decision. That is what negotiation is all about. But it can be exceedingly simple or terribly complex. For our purposes, negotiation should be divided into two classes: negotiations between individuals and between groups. In the latter case, the negotiating or bargaining is through representatives, and that brings into play a host of complications not present when people bargain on their own behalf. Communication, and the media through which it is transmitted, is among the most important complications. So are face and the loss of it, and many other factors growing out of the group relationship, as well as the subject matter of the negotiations.

Negotiation is always about changing or not changing the status quo. In collective bargaining, it is the union that most frequently wants to change the status quo. The cost of living has gone up, for instance, so the workers want an increase. In most instances, the employer is content to let things go along as they have been. When pressed by the union to make a change, he must decide whether or not to agree. The law says he does not have to agree, but if he doesn't, the union can strike. The employer weighs the consequences and then decides what he wants to do.

In some cases, the employer is dissatisfied with the status quo and wants to change it. In the summer of 1978, the management of *The New York Times, Daily News,* and *New York Post* decided that the labor force in the pressrooms was too numerous. They wanted to reduce it. By law, they were obligated to meet and confer with the union at reasonable times in good faith. They were entitled to insist on a reduction. But the union was not obligated to make a concession, and it did not want to. As a result, the publishers and the union reached an impasse after "good faith" bargaining. (Neither side complained to the NLRB about the other side's good faith, though they said a lot about the lack of it in public statements.) At the point of impasse, the employers became legally empowered to change the status quo despite the union's objection. The New York newspapers did precisely that by posting new tables with reduced labor forces, and the union responded with its legal right to strike. That is how that strike got started. It was the union's response to the employer's right to change the status quo unilaterally. This shows that the right to act unilaterally is the employer's usual equivalent to the union's right to strike.

This may sound complex, but it's pure and simple Adam Smith marketplace economics. The union or employer bids, the other side asks. They negotiate. In most instances, they reach agreement. If they don't, the party seeking to change the status quo makes the next move. If the union is dissatisfied, it seeks to force a change through a strike. If the employer is displeased, he proceeds with a unilateral change of employment conditions within his control.

I have spent time on this analysis of collective bargaining because I do not believe that the negotiation of changes in the status quo of the conditions of employment is going to be very different in the twenty-first century, at least if we are successful in preserving as much of our system of free enterprise as we now possess. Collective bargaining is one of our current freedoms. But it is not a totally free institution. In a completely unregulated market, an employer could refuse to bargain collectively with the majority representative of his employees. But he could also agree voluntarily to bargain collectively. A union could refuse to bargain in good faith, as difficult as that may be to determine. But it could also bargain in good faith. Under the law, these freedoms are curtailed, but the freedom to say yes or no is usually retained. But not always.

In disputes that threaten national health and safety, the President may enjoin for a period of 80 days a strike or a unilateral change by an employer that precipitates a strike. Similar provisions apply to the railroad and airline industries. Strikes during the term of contracts with procedures for arbitration can be enjoined, notwithstanding the anti-injunction provisions of the precursor of the Wagner Act, the Norris–LaGuardia Act of 1932, also a major piece of civil rights legislation for workers. Damages can be recovered in suits for breach of contract. Jurisdictional disputes can be enjoined and forced into arbitration. Certain types of picketing can also be enjoined. And Congress has on several occasions imposed compulsory arbitration to prevent strikes that might imperil the economy of the country. These are all part of the system of collective bargaining that has developed during the last forty years. I do not see vast changes in the next century in the system.

So far, I have been speaking of employees in the private sector. The employment relationships of those who work for federal, state, and municipal governments present an entirely different picture. For the most part, their right to strike is limited. That means that they cannot bargain collectively as do their counterparts in the private sector, since there can be no free choice in the event of an impasse. This also limits the public employer's right to act unilaterally. Nor are public employers oriented to the marketplace. Their incentive is not to make a profit, and their concern is not over the price they can charge. It is the taxpayer who has become their principal disciplinarian. Besides, since the decisions of government are the product of many deliberative bodies and officials, public employers are incapable of arriving at bargaining decisions with the flexibility of private employers. These are a few of the principal reasons that the development of collective bargaining in the public sector has been so troublesome. Undoubtedly, these factors also explain why collective bargaining in the public sector has lagged behind the model provided by the private sector.

Employees in the public sector came to enjoy the benefits of legislative protection long before the Wagner Act was passed in 1935. In the latter part of the nineteenth century, federal employees were granted the eight-hour day. All levels of government adopted civil service, a form of job security, in varying degrees. Pensions were also awarded at an early date, and public employment tended to be regular and not subject to layoffs as in many private industries. But wages tended to lag behind the private sector. The great success of unions in the private sector in the years following the Wagner Act stimulated employees in the public sector to seek improvements through negotiation. Besides, employment in the public sector was growing by leaps and bounds. The combination of these ambitions produced the clashes of the 1960s, and the dust still has not settled. But we better understand the problems today than we did during those tumultuous years. And we can draw some conclusions that might be useful in assessing the future.

Collective action by public employees is bound to continue. They will meet and confer with their employers at reasonable times through organizations called unions. The negotiations will be conducted in good faith, and agreements will be made. There will also be disagreements, and undoubtedly some strikes. It is not likely, however, that strikes by public workers will be legalized. There is no sentiment for it at the present time, and I don't believe that popular support is likely to develop. The possibility of illegal strikes will nonetheless infuse the negotiations with some of the urgency now present in collective bargaining in the private sector. Third-party decision makers will continue to be used to cope with impasses, but with increasing uneasiness on the part of governments because of the dilution of their authority that these outsiders produce. Unions will be inhibited because of the negative publicity of strike action, as well as the resistance of public employers in the face of taxpayer protests. But the dynamics of the relationship will require accommodation. Unions will come better to understand how to function in the governmental arena. They are already fairly skilled in how to do it. Public employers will accept the unions for what they are: a force that must be taken into account in the decision-making of government. I foresee many problems ahead as unionism in government expands, but I am not alarmed. I think that by the beginning of the twenty-first century, we will have an expert understanding of how unions of government employees should function, and it will be substantially different from the way we act in the private sector.

While unions in the public sector have been growing rapidly, the same is not true in the private sector, and there will be little major forward thrust of organization in the foreseeable future. My crystal ball is too cloudy to indicate what labor relations will be like at the turn of the century, but I don't see any significant retreat from the current levels of unionization. There are major concentrations of unionization in autos, steel, aerospace, transportation, communications, construction, entertainment, mining, and manufacturing. The concentration is heavy in seven states: New York, New Jersey, Pennsylvania, Ohio, Illinois, Michigan, and California. There will probably be some increase of unionization in the Sun-Belt states as industry continues to move there and grow. Blacks, Hispanics, and other minorities will play an increasingly larger role in union affairs. So will women. Integration in the workplace will continue to move ahead, despite the obstacles of fitting latecomers into the employment structure. But as the minorities break through, they will also come to enjoy the protection of seniority, a must for trade unions.

Unions will continue to merge. This is essential to keep their expenses down. They have the same problems in this respect as companies. They will face challenges within their own ranks, but they always have. Unions are political organizations. As soon as one faction is elected, another comes into existence to oppose it. It is the same in all organizations of people. The Landrum–Griffin Act has made opposition within union ranks easier. But the incumbents always have an advantage. It is true of our political system as well. But the incumbents are the constant target of politicians and the media. Unions make good copy, and that is partly why they are the frequent subject of investigations of one sort or another. The pressure of scrutiny is not likely to diminish.

There was a time when workers and their unions enjoyed the sympathetic support of most of the public. That time has passed, because unions have succeeded too well in improving the lot of their members. The lumpen proletariat now organized is middle class. They worry about taxes and the decline of their neighborhoods. They are, in turn, part of the problem, like any other group in our society. They are given no special sympathy because they are workers who belong to unions.

The urge to converge is very strong in our society. We get together for all purposes—buying, selling, renting, praying, learning, traveling. We are a society of special-interest groups, most of them legal. The 13 states of the original United States got together in 1776 to form a more perfect union. Groups have been forming ever since, and they will continue to do so. The term "union" is not as popular today as it once was. But even in the early days, employee groups that did not wish to be tarnished with the predominantly blue-collar color of early unions, formed organizations of precisely the same character. They often used the word "association," instead of union, to describe themselves. The

National Education Association (NEA), the major organization of teachers and others in education, originally sought to distinguish itself from the American Federation of Teachers, which openly called itself a union. Now the NEA recognizes itself as a direct competitor. The associations of professional athletes likewise chose that term instead of "union" but now unashamedly admit their identity as labor organizations. The same is true of organized policemen and firemen. Now lawyers, doctors, architects, and even churchmen are ready to accept the union label to describe their joint activities.

The union of unions—the American Federation of Labor/Congress of Industrial Organizations—may go through changes in the future. Its venerable leader, George Meany, is necessarily at the end of his long term, although it might not have been as soon as some might have liked. But the basic structure is unlikely to change, no matter who succeeds Meany. Most people do not realize that the AFL-CIO, a merger of two unions, is not itself a trade union. Workers do not belong to it. They belong to unions that belong to it. It does not bargain collectively. It is mainly a lobbying spokesman for labor on Capitol Hill. The AFL-CIO has not been doing too well in that respect lately, although it does many things for unions that are not as publicized as its failure to get legislation on situs picketing or labor law reform through Congress. The unions will always need a spokesman in Washington, even though several major unions—the Teamsters, the auto workers, and the coal miners—remain outside the main body. They will likely be back in the fold by the next century, if not a lot sooner. It is more a matter of personalities than ideological differences.

I see collective bargaining continuing through the remainder of this century, and on into the next. The subject matter of bargaining—wages, hours, and working conditions—is not likely to change very much. New problems will inevitably arise, involving health, pensions, and job security in the face of environmental and energy considerations, as well as the rapid change in the location and technology of industry. But a strong professionalism has developed on both sides of the bargaining table that enhances the capability of industry and labor to cope with these problems.

The emotionalism that is inherent in any human relationship will inevitably continue to surface from time to time. But it is likely to be the exception rather than the rule, involving, in most instances, the security of jobs. That is the issue that arouses the most feeling. This is merely a reflection of the importance of jobs in our society. The workplace is where most people spend most of their waking hours. It is a part of their social and business existence. It will continue to attract more attention, with greater focus on the so-called quality of work life.

Some form of association of employees on the job will always exist, whether called a union or by some other name. In one form or another, collective bargaining is here to stay. But it does not exist in isolation. Collective bargaining is affected by changes in our society, whether they be economic, social, or cultural. We have stable industrial relations when our society is stable. Inflation exacerbates conflicts in collective bargaining. It is not the only disturbing force, but one of the main ones. So is unemployment.

The problems that face collective bargaining are the problems that face everyone. The system of collective bargaining we have built during the last 40 years works pretty well. It is not perfect, obviously, but no method of resolving the problems in human relationships is, or ever will be. Collective bargaining is subject to "the thousand natural shocks that flesh is heir to." Without being able to predict what these may be, I am pleased to predict that collective bargaining and trade unions will be with us in the twenty-first century.

SECTION TWO

Work in the Next Century: New Trends and Perspectives for Labor

Organized labor in America has come upon difficult times, and the decades ahead promise little in the way of peace or relief. What began less than a century ago as a growth industry in the redress of social and economic imbalances has become an American institution with diminished prospects for extending its membership and influence.

The authors in this section, expert in labor relations and personnel management, might well agree with such a gloomy generality, but they diverge in sharp and interesting ways about why unions are troubled and what should be done about it.

In his passionate call for a new brand of democratic socialism, William Winpisinger sees economic power now so concentrated in giant multinational corporations that labor, under present national labor relations policy, can no longer act as a counterbalance. The remedy, in his view, lies in legislation that extends the scope of collective bargaining into what have been the exclusive provinces of management, and in policies and procedures for settling labor-management disputes on an international scale.

But turning to government for legislative help, writes James Jordan, would be a tragic lowering of labor's private and independent voice and a precursor of an economic system unattractively like Great Britain's. Labor unions are so powerfully part of our society, Jordan says, that the danger is not their disappearance. Indeed, larger unions are on the way. But will they be imaginatively led and able to grapple with the decline in productivity, the ambitions of minority groups and women, the shifting age distribution in the work force, and the rise of individualism within it?

America is moving rapidly from being a goods-producing economy toward an economy in which service workers predominate; today, fewer than one worker in four is employed in manufacturing. It is not progress, says William Lucy, to see high-paying blue-collar jobs traded in for routinized, lower-paying clerical work. As service and clerical work become a matter of poking buttons on a sophisticated machine, he asks, what premium will young people place on education? His fear: when getting an education no longer means getting ahead, we may not avoid a downward spiral of indifference and alienation.

An answer to worker alienation, writes A. H. Raskin, may well be found in a "vibrant form of industrial democracy." The rise of individualism within the work force, and the consequent demand by workers to take part in decisions that affect their working lives, are forces

61

unions and management have been slow to respond to. But respond they must, "to make the worker a full citizen inside the office or factory."

By about 1985, the traditional white, male breadwinner will be in the minority in the American labor force. One reason for the shift, points out Pat Burr, is the powerful need of American women to work. It is a need based on economic necessity and not on misty dreams of self-realization. And yet, the traditional demands of child care collide with our standard ways of organizing work. The effect of the collision is to deny women access to jobs in the first place and continuity as they try to climb the organizational hierarchy. Private sector employers, Burr suggests, should lead the economy in organizing and partially subsidizing child care centers, and in scheduling work with greater flexibility.

Jerome Rosow closes this section with an intense look at the demographic shifts that are changing the make-up of the labor force. We face a shortage of young workers in the 1980s, but intense competition in the 25 to 44 age group for promotion. This struggle will be exacerbated by large numbers of qualified women and minorities, the newest players in the game of recognition. And older workers will increasingly elect to stay on the job, backed up by legislation that has moved the mandatory retirement age from 65 to 70.

Moving beyond the question of who will be doing the work in the next two decades, Rosow assesses the attitudes workers will pack with them to factory and office. Foreshadowing the ideas presented in Section Three, Rosow examines the broad-gauge decline in worker satisfaction, the emerging demands for more control over one's hours of work and leisure, the decline in tolerance for authoritarian bosses, the unwillingness to defer gratification, and a clutch of other issues that are part of what has been called "The Age of Me."

C.S.S.

D.C.C.

CHAPTER 6

Pyramids of Wealth:
A Threat to Labor Relations
William W. Winpisinger

Our government tells us that by the year 2050, if the current inflationary trends persist, we will be living in a country in which a loaf of bread is going to cost $37.50, a medium-sized car $281,000, and a modest home in an average neighborhood nearly $3.5 million. Since per capita consumer debt in our country already amounts to 20% of annual income, then the real question, in terms of the twenty-first century, will be how to break the bonds of economic and human bondage.

That grim scenario, in my judgment, becomes all the more plausible when I view the extreme concentration of wealth and income in our country today and the enormous concentration of control and power that is exercised in the marketplace by relatively few giant corporations.

Consider first, the pyramid of wealth. One-fifth of 1% of adult Americans own an impressive laundry list of things. They own 20% of all corporate stocks and all the private bonds and notes in a literal sense. The wealthiest 1% of Americans own 14% of the real estate; more than half of all of the corporate stocks, and 14% of the cash in every checking account, savings account, pocket, and purse in the country. If those figures fail to daunt one's consciousness, then consider the other end of the pyramid, down at the base. Seventy percent of Americans had a net worth of $10,000 or less in 1972, and 24% had a net worth of less than $1000. Since then, of course, inflation has increased the value of their assets, but only relatively, because inflation applies the same percentage to rich and poor.

Similarly, we should examine the personal income pyramid. The top

5% of Americans get more, in total cash, than the bottom 40%. The top 20% get 40 cents out of every dollar of personal income. The bottom 20% get one nickel of every dollar of income. If you took blocks representing those figures and stacked them against the 853-foot-high Transamerica pyramid out in San Francisco, 98% would lie at the base, less than one foot off ground level. The remaining 2% would stack right up to the tip of the pyramid, and if the blocks represented wealth rather than people, we would perceive the mirror image of an inverted pyramid, with the tip at the bottom and the broad base at the spire.

So, harsh and unfair economic realities exist all around us. Unless some genuinely major changes are made in our socioeconomic policy, these shameful disparities will continue to exist well into the twenty-first century. I foresee poverty, a loophole tax system that favors the few truly wealthy, subsidies for giant corporations, and wage controls for nearly everyone else, except a few chief executive officers and independent professionals. The basic prices for the necessities of life will be soaring 12 to 14% annually, and that is not a prescription for hope or optimism.

The dogma of free enterprise has it that competition forces profit-making companies to serve the public and restrains unbridled corporate behavior. But the concentration of corporate control over markets and prices has, I think, effectively eliminated competition and eradicated that basic premise of the system. At the end of World War II, for instance, the 200 biggest manufacturing firms held 45% of the United States' industrial assets. Today, that figure is 60%. In 1960, 450 firms controlled one-half of the nation's total manufacturing assets. Now, they have 70%. Today, fewer than 1% of American manufacturers control 88% of all industrial assets and receive more than 90% of the net profits of all industrial firms in the country.

At the broad base of the business world, we find 11 million business establishments, but half of them are firms having annual gross receipts of $10,000 or less. The assets and sales of Fortune 500 companies are ten times greater than the assets and sales of the second 500 on the list. The pyramiding of America, then, provides the broad backdrop—the single and overwhelming economic fact of life—against which labor relations in the twenty-first century must be contemplated.

The reality today is that economic power means political power. They are virtually synonymous. In my particular institution, the union, we have come to call the phenomenon of economic pyramiding "The Rise of the Corporate State." As the statistics I have provided demonstrate, the corporate state is already a reality. Beyond mere quantification, we see the corporate state dominating our political economy—and hence our lives and livelihoods—in myriad ways. We see it in Proposition 13 activities; in the drive for a balanced budget; in the dismantling of federal regulatory agencies; in the price deregulation goals of the energy industry; in the Business Roundtable's secret agenda for controlling government; in the Carter Administration's distorted and grossly unfair anti-inflation program; in the union-free environment, about which we hear much, and the drives by corporate employers to take back hard-won gains and benefits; in the outlaw conduct of firms like J. P. Stevens and hundreds of others; in budgetary favoritism toward the military-industrial complex; in the fierce resistance of the medical industry to comprehensive national health insurance; in the multi-million dollar expenditures by corporate and trade association political action committees on behalf of presidential and congressional candidates; in the flight of capital and technology to foreign shores; in the rape of human rights and trade union rights in developing nations; in the Trilateral Commission's prescriptions for a global economic order and its recruitment of President Carter and Vice President Mondale to its ranks; in the OECD's domination of international economic think tanks, international economic analyses, and the dissemination of information.

All are symptomatic of what I think of as a disease. In each of those instances, the corporate state is bringing about a disequilibrium in the balance of power of a magnitude never before experienced in American history. When that power is amplified by corporate control of technology, then I think one can begin to perceive, abstractly at least, the problematical dimensions of labor relations in the twenty-first century.

I can only suggest that the most effective counterbalance to the corporate state's pyramiding of America will be a dynamic and progressive democratic socialist movement, indifferent to previous ideologies or theories. It will be a socialism, born of economic, political, and social necessity, with a very pragmatic approach. It will champion the common good, as opposed to narrow parochial self-interests—and that includes those of my own institution as well. This counterbalance will be a people-oriented socialism, clashing with the socialism of the corporate state.

There must be class struggle toward an equalization in society, toward an equalitarian society, but not necessarily a violent struggle. Events, and the intensity of corporate America's intransigence, will determine the nature and the parameters of the struggle.

A major element will be the national labor relations policy that exists in the twenty-first century. There has been no major change in that policy since enactment of the National Labor Relations Act in 1935. The typical collective bargaining agreement that is born of that statute still provides four basically fundamental features: (1) the recognition of the union, (2) grievance procedures, (3) wages and working conditions, (4) seniority rights. Innovations that have extended the scope of bargaining have been essentially limited to pension, health and welfare benefits, and supplemental unemployment benefits, and all of these have been incorporated in one way or another under the wages and working conditions clause.

As we view the behavior of the corporate state today, it is apparent that the existing labor law and the limitations in the scope of bargaining are no longer adequate to ensure the domestic tranquility and the maintenance of industrial democracy and peace. If the disequilibrium of power in labor-management relations is to be redistributed toward equilibrium, then national labor relations policy will have to be redefined so as to encroach on management prerogatives and proprietary information rights. If trade unions are to survive, and if labor is to escape maltreatment and social discard, then the scope of bargaining must be extended to include a measure of worker control over corporate decisions affecting manpower, investment, and the organization of production processes. It is possible that this control can be shared with the public at large through the kind of socialization of industry about which I have spoken. In the meantime, it may take the form of the more familiar codetermination agreements, labor representation on boards of directors, or outright employee ownership, such as we see in some of the European countries today. Labor is already beginning to exert leverage on corporate decision-making powers through the use of pension fund placements. I expect that practice to accelerate. But I think the existing ERISA law prevents full utilization of that particular device, and much needs to be done.

Federal legislation as an expression of public policy could also expand the scope of bargaining beyond the four fundamentals, and that would be a rational, sensible, and democratic path. If we fail to extend the scope of bargaining, I predict that the twenty-first century—and maybe even the time before that—will be marked by intense effort on the part of labor and trade unions to puncture the management prerogative and proprietary information shields, and those efforts will be backed by strike action if it is necessary. And as job displacement due to technology accelerates, the problem will become more acute, and the courts will not long stand in the way of remedial action by workers.

We must come to grips with the reality of international economics and international labor relations policy in the twenty-first century. Global aggression by the corporate state is not strictly American, or a phenomenon of East versus West or North versus South. For all practical purposes, the corporate state of the West, the North, and Japan functions in the same manner as corporate stateism in the Eastern nations and in the totalitarian and military regimes of the Southern Hemisphere—which is to say in an anti-democratic manner and method. Thus the Business Roundtable in America is the rough equivalent of the Politburo in Russia. The Trilateral Commission and the OECD play similar roles on grander global and regional scales, though perhaps with less official authority.

There can't be any mistake about the impact of the behavior of multinational corporations on labor relations. Multinationals are unchecked, respect no boundaries or flags, and answer only to a few individual boards of directors and a few government officials. Multinational corporations are entities unto themselves, transcending the power of national governments in many instances. The runaway shop is certainly a multinational phenomenon, and so is the flight of capital and technology. Violations of human rights and worker rights, through indifference or contempt toward democratic and social values, are a corollary of their proliferation. Trade unions can neither checkrein the power and mobility of multinationals nor effectively bargain with them, even in the four traditional areas of collective bargaining. Existing labor relations policy, in short, is bankrupt with respect to the behavior of multinationals, and, as the twenty-first century approaches, it is absolutely essential that the workers from diverse and different countries, whose livelihoods depend on the same employers, design ways and means to collaborate in collective bargaining.

In the twenty-first century, international strikes and boycotts may become the rule, rather than the few faltering exceptions we have experienced thus far. International tribunals and agencies may be forced to develop codes of conduct governing corporate behavior and to piece together an international labor relations policy.

The twenty-first century, I believe, will see the first attempts to establish procedures for settling labor-management disputes on a global scale. Voluntarism is already feebly forcing these issues into the international dialogue, but voluntarism, I predict, will fail, as it inevitably does. Strong sanctions will have to be written into an international labor code and into national codes. Trade union representation and participation in international agencies, heretofore the exclusive domain of academics and business and management personnel, will become absolutely essential.

The alternative to these developments is continued aggression by the corporate state around the globe and eventual indentured servitude and subjugation for billions of no-longer-so-ordinary working people. Such subjugation cannot and will not be lasting, for people have the innate desire to be free. Without economic freedom, there cannot be genuine political freedom. That is the irrefutable lesson of our history.

CHAPTER 7

Trends in the Work Force: Individualism, Inflation, and Productivity
James H. Jordan, Ph.D.

The state of the union movement today is murky at best, as viewed by the unions themselves and by their political and economic adversaries.

As Irving Kristol, professor of urban values at New York University, has noted: "One cannot—at least I cannot—envision a decent society without free trade unions, but it is getting increasingly difficult in an age when one or two unions can bring the entire economy to a grinding halt to understand how to go about living with them. So it's time, I suggest, that we start thinking seriously and coherently about their place in the modern world."

A major question is, can they continue to grow? Union membership reached a peak of 18,477,000 in 1956, some six times its size in 1933. One of every three employees in nonagricultural establishments and one in four of the overall labor force were organized. By 1976, however, union membership had grown to only 19.4 million, and the portion of the private sector labor force that was organized slipped to 20%. Recent union organizing efforts have not been very successful. Beyond the numbers, this speaks to an overall decline in unionism.

The traditional base of organized labor's strength—the manufacturing sector—is being overshadowed by the number of blue- and white-collar employees in the service industries. Nor is labor monolithic. Many of the political demands of various segments of the labor movement increasingly conflict with one another. For example, municipal

69

workers want more money, while municipal taxpayers who also belong to private sector unions do not want to foot the expense. And labor's advantage as a primary source of political contributions in
election campaigns is beginning to be matched by business political
action committees.

The conservative swing of the American voter, disillusioned with
big government and its frequent ally, big labor, resulted in the unions'
failure to obtain enactment of the core of their legislative agenda in the
last two Congresses. This is all the more significant because the Demo-
crats have enjoyed virtually a two-to-one majority in Congress since
1975 and were joined in 1977 by a Democratic President in the White
House. Instead of a string of victories, the unions suffered decisive
defeats on such key issues as labor law reform, national health insurance, construction site picketing, and requiring foreign oil to be
shipped in American-flag tankers. Labor also experienced significant
setbacks in such issues as indexing the minimum wage, worker compensation, and various tax reform proposals.

The current conventional wisdom is that labor is in decline. But labor has entrenched itself as a permanent and important part of our political and economic process. Too great a denial of labor's needs still
can result in harm to the whole system. The unions are strong enough
to cause serious trouble—to the majority party at the polls (witness
McGovern's debacle in 1972), to the hope of containing inflation (wage-
price guidelines), and to the growth of international trade (multinational trade negotiations).

Labor is not being eliminated or even reduced to a minor role. It is,
however, currently unable to enlarge its power. And to a degree, that
implies diminution.

The basic philosophical difficulty for organized labor is that Americans, more than ever, conceive of themselves and their society in highly individualistic terms. Unions, on the other hand, are built on a
foundation of group control, and their behavior is predicated on a notion of group action that contradicts the central tenets of individualism. Unions must be viewed as "job-control" mechanisms, in which
the individual subordinates himself to the group.

Management, on the other hand, has a philosophy predicated on individual merit and the progress of the individual. The work of a manager is to preside over change. Innovation and flexibility are his prime
requirements. Thus, management's institutional framework coincides
with the new attitudes toward individualism that are emerging in the

work force. This activist approach to change derives from the nature of management's task and does not reflect a desire to be anti-union.

Labor-management relations in the 1980s must be approached in this context, not as a continual refighting of the battles of the 1930s. Those issues have long since been resolved, but it would seem that the leadership of the labor movement is still taken with reliving the glories of days past. The major difficulty between labor and management now is whether the union can adapt and embrace institutional changes that will be required in the future.

There are three broad categories that largely determine the course of labor-management relations—social, economic, and political.

In the category of social forces, I place the individual first. We have moved into an age where emphasis has shifted from collective action to the person, a time in which institutions are distrusted. This individualism has been coupled with a shift in personal priorities and a relative decline in the importance of financial incentives. Money and jobs are still valued, but there has developed as well an emphasis on self-satisfaction.

The individual's ability to manage and control his or her time and its use is becoming more important. By way of illustration, we have seen develop an entire range of time-saving innovations—the 7-day, 24-hour shopping center, microwave ovens, frozen meals, fast-food restaurants, and day care centers.

People in the workplace are also moving away from a fixed schedule. There has been a substantial increase in the number of part-time workers, and the prospects are that more jobs will be shared by part-timers. Similarly, flexitime, which allows a worker to vary arrival and departure times, is taking hold in many industries.

The second social force is the changing character of the work force. Nonwhite minorities in the work force will grow from about 12% to 20% by 2000, as pressures mount to remedy minority unemployment. Working females will constitute at least half of workers by the turn of the century. There will be more two-worker families and single head-of-household workers. As early as 1985, we will have reached a major turning point: the white, male, family breadwinner, known in the past as the "typical" worker, will be in the minority.

At the same time, the working population will age as the postwar babies mature and the decline in the birthrate makes itself noticed. By 2000, the 35 to 55-year-old group of the work force will be 50% of the total force.

Most significant of all, there will be a temporary decline in the size

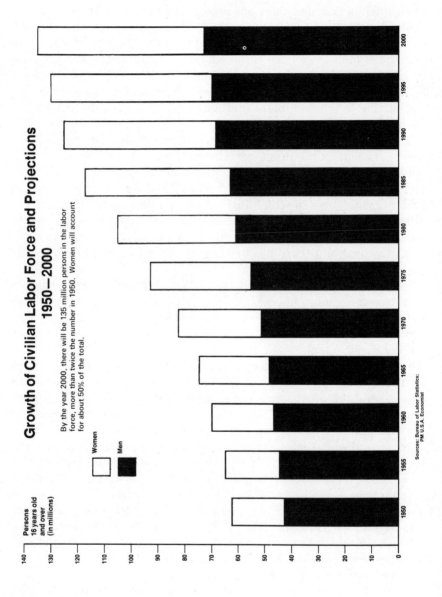

Growth of Civilian Labor Force and Projections 1950—2000

By the year 2000, there will be 135 million persons in the labor force, more than twice the number in 1950. Women will account for about 50% of the total.

Women

Men

Persons
16 years old
and over
(in millions)

140
130
120
110
100
90
80
70
60
50
40
30
20
10
0

1950 1955 1960 1965 1970 1975 1980 1985 1990 1995 2000

Sources: Bureau of Labor Statistics;
PM U.S.A. Economist

of the work force. In the 1970s, we have been used to an average annual increase of about 2%. This figure will slip to about 1% between 1985 and 1990, until the children of the baby boom go to work and reverse the pattern. In the meantime, we are faced with an immediate future characterized by labor shortage, not by labor surplus and unemployment. A surge of entry-level job applicants will follow in the last decade of this century and into the next.

The dominant economic force is rampant escalation of the cost of living and devaluation of our currency in defiance of all efforts to control it. The prospect of continuing inflation has created a defensive philosophy throughout industry. It has taken its toll in capital formation, which, in turn, adversely affects the ability of business to update existing plants and to create new plant capacity. The rising costs of manufacturing—both raw materials and labor—should be bringing increased reliance on technology, and yet, the rate of innovation is lagging.

Running in tandem with inflation are the effects of our abrupt switch from the abundance of cheap, plentiful raw materials and natural resources to an economy of shortage. What has happened with petroleum is no longer unthinkable across a wide range of commodities, so the impact of a truly international economy for the first time must be taken into account in labor-management relations.

A decline in the growth of productivity is a key to the parties' future relationship. We are not keeping pace with the rest of the world. In the 20 years between 1947 and 1967, productivity in the U.S. private sector rose at an average rate of 3.2%. By 1977, however, the rate of increase had fallen to 1.6%, far behind the rates of our major trading partners throughout the world. From 1962 to 1977, the average annual increase for the United States was 2.7%, against 5.5% in Germany; 5.6% in France; 6.9% in The Netherlands; and 8.4% in Japan. Consequently, America is finding it increasingly more difficult to compete in world markets.

To bring the economic factors into sharper focus, consider the behavior of unit labor costs. Between 1967 and 1977, average hourly wages rose 120% while average hourly output advanced only 20%. Under accelerating inflation during this period, hourly pay rose more than twice as fast as it had in 1957–1967, while the annual rate of gain in productivity was one-third less than before.

Foremost among the political factors that will shape changing labor-management relations is the growth, both in size and in involvement, of government. The ever-increasing pervasiveness of government has produced increasingly voluminous, highly complex, and very costly regulations.

Government intervention, for example, has become much more detailed and complex through the intrusion of the National Labor Relations Board into the substantive terms and conditions of bargaining, with both sides seeking to gain a tactical advantage through its use. Similarly, the other agencies of government—EEOC, OSHA, for instance—limit the scope of what were the traditional domains of labor and management.

However exciting it might be to do so, we cannot forecast radically different and brave new worlds suddenly coming into being. History teaches that social change comes gradually, and I do not foresee any great social changes that will call for a shift in public policy to greatly enhance the power of either unions or management.

There is, however, a real danger that unions, frustrated at the bargaining table and unable to make gains in membership, will turn to the government to solve their problems. Considering the importance that labor has placed on its legislative programs, I cannot help remembering the old warning, "the weaker part always will turn to the legislature for solution to its problems."

One of the strengths of the American labor system has been decentralized private decision making, in which the needs of both workers and industry can be accommodated. If American unions try to turn toward a political solution, as did the British, it will inevitably lead to wage and price controls or an incomes policy, and the same disastrous results as in the United Kingdom. There is simply no way to set wages and prices and, equally important, the terms and conditions of employment in such a diverse and decentralized economy as ours without permanent damage to our economic system.

Labor will see its primary target for unionism, the manufacturing sector, continue to shrink. The prospect is that by 2000, blue-collar workers may well constitute the same proportion of the labor force as farm workers in 1979. Casting for membership elsewhere, labor will seek by legislation to give it advantage in the bargaining unit election process. It will put forth increased efforts to organize the professional, technical service, and government workers who will be, by far, the largest segment of the labor force.

Thus, the political arena will become a more important battlefield for labor and management. The unions, understanding that there is, at present, no broad public support for a policy that would materially strengthen unions, will seek to change their image as a special-interest group. Therefore, I can foresee labor seeking to endorse the aims of groups such as Ralph Nader's and other corporate critics. It will be looking to direct coalitions composed of its old friends, such as the minorities and the intellectuals, as a means to influence the legislative process.

Legislative goals in the future will concentrate on improved labor laws, protection of jobs, protection against runaway plants, national health insurance, and antitrust enforcement. I expect to see concerted drives by unions to shift their business and funds away from banks, suppliers, and manufacturers that are nonunion or support nonunion enterprises.

The labor movement will not, of course, be different from any other institution in its need to respond to the new forces that will shape coming decades. Moreover, the mere passage of time will bring about a change in the composition of union leadership.

About this new leadership we can be certain that it must differ from the old guard which still holds sway. A product of the present age, the leadership of the future will be better educated, will have matured in an affluent society, and, unlike its predecessors, will be removed from personal contact with a time in which the economic survival of the working class was a viable concern.

The AFL-CIO Executive Council, which purports to represent 40 million American women but has not allowed women one seat on the council, will reluctantly come to add women, blacks, and other minorities to its ranks in its effort to become more representative and responsive in the next century.

Another factor that will bear on the future of the labor movement will be its duplicating the trend of corporate mergers. Larger unions are on the way. The United Steel Workers, for example, will become the sole survivor in the chemical industry, where at present at least five international unions compete for membership.

Union structure will further adapt in at least two ways:

1 There will be more concentration of authority and control at the top. The AFL-CIO will become much more important in setting national policies and objectives and will give new direction to organization and legislation. It will also provide systems to expedite union mergers and to settle jurisdictional disputes.

2 The international unions will establish new relationships for the individual with his local and the local's relationship with the in-

ternational. The new role of the ombudsman is one we will see enlarged as unions struggle with the age-old problem of achieving a balance between the needs of the individual and those of the organization.

Unions will be forced to undertake a new examination of their leadership in the next century. Representation is the crux of the union movement, and no matter on what side of the table one sits, there is obviously a problem in effective union representation. Not only is the present top leadership two generations older than the bulk of the workers it represents, but the vast majority of its international representatives have been outclassed by the highly educated, articulate work force whom they seek to organize and represent. The worker enjoys wages and benefits better than those of the international union representatives, who have had great difficulty gaining representation of their own with their union employers.

Planning for a trade union leader's development and ascension to power is difficult, given the political nature of unions, but the need and opportunity will be there. There will be a cadre of college graduates, underemployed in industry, who could effectively blend into the ranks of union leadership. If they do not, they will certainly be a dissident force in the future. The question will be whether the unions can find a way for this potential new source of leaders to emerge.

And what will be the result of all this turbulence on the outlook for unionization? Although there will be changes in labor legislation, primarily in the area of expediting timetables for elections, the percentage of the civilian labor force that is unionized, currently around 24%, will remain fairly stable. However, the growth of unionization in state and local government and teaching—where the issues of representation, due process, and governance have not yet been solved—will continue its dramatic rise.

The economic climate in which bargaining will take place will be rocky. The shortage of capital, the rate of inflation, the drop in productivity and real profits, the international competitive picture, and the scarcity and cost of natural resources will force hard bargaining. Labor and management will have to divide up an economic pie that, for the first time, may not be capable of supporting a rise in real wages.

The accelerating speed at which global, political, military, and financial events will take place should be a reminder that governments in the United States and elsewhere will have very little control or influence over the major developments crucial to corporations, investors, and, therefore, unions. There is a basic trend in the world of growing volatility, instability, vulnerability, risk, and uncertainty which will carry into the twenty-first century. The pressure will be for flexibility and change, and management will look to build work forces with those characteristics—be they union or nonunion. Anything that inhibits these needs will be firmly resisted.

Despite the hope of many for industrial peace, we should expect collective bargaining to continue to be an adversary proceeding as long as wages are to management a cost of production and to the worker his standard of living.

I do not look for any great changes in the structure of bargaining. If anything, our decision making must become more decentralized. The pressures for adaptation and change will keep the focus of bargaining at the local level, and the scope and content of bargaining will not be radically different.

Man-days lost due to strikes do not constitute a major problem now, nor will they in the next century. For the few disputes that do create national problems, we will find that the public interest will be asserted in much the same way as it has been during the twentieth century. I do not look for compulsory arbitration or any panacea to emerge, but rather for the government to use an arsenal of weapons ranging from "jawboning" to specific legislation and threats of deregulation.

One of the most significant problems will be the training of a new generation of collective bargaining practitioners. They must learn to avoid the problem that arises when new labor and management leaders learn only by mistakes at the bargaining table. I look for the Federal Mediation and Conciliation Service to undertake the training of new leaders in the bargaining process. The aim should be to assure complete understanding of each others' roles and needs before "crisis bargaining" begins.

Forecasting the topics for the bargaining agenda is difficult, but one direction seems visible and important. We have been steadily moving away from the idea that an employee is a variable cost to be hired or fired at will. The forces of technology are making that concept obsolete, and the twenty-first century will complete the job. In plants where it may take a year to train one employee who controls over $10 million in capital, layoffs are not the way to control costs. Labor-management history also teaches us that workers who are concerned with job security can do nothing but resist change. Ways and means to assure job security will, therefore, become a common goal of management and union, and labor will become increasingly a fixed cost of production.

Trade-offs for job security will come in job flexibility—the old distinction between a production and maintenance worker will disappear, for instance—and in the elimination of work rules and overtime restrictions.

The cost of fringe benefits has been growing at a much faster rate than direct compensation for the past 25 years, and the trend will continue. There will be virtually no limit to the invention of totally new benefit plans. Some, such as legal assistance, adoption assistance, and automobile and homeowner's insurance, are already on the horizon. Since women and part-time employees will make up a much larger portion of the work force, there will be more emphasis on benefits important to these groups— flexitime, four-day workweeks, part-time production, and new ways to schedule work will become commonplace. The "cafeteria" approach, in which the employee selects the benefits package best suited to his age, family circumstances, and other needs, will be even more widespread.

Ultimately, the only limitation on benefit growth and diversity will be the total compensation cost the system can absorb. In large companies, employee benefits costs have increased from 24% of pay in 1957 to 41% in 1977. If these rates continue, employee benefits will outstrip the cash pay employees receive shortly after the turn of the century.

Collective bargaining, however imaginative, will remain a limited-purpose instrument. It simply is not capable of developing solutions to the broad social problems of the entire economy. It is here that I see a constructive role for government. Rather than becoming increasingly involved in specific labor-management issues through regulation and direct intervention, government can work to create the economic framework in which these problems can be solved.

The strength of the U.S. economic system has been our ability to develop new technology and to build a work force fully capable of using it. It is government's task to encourage that process. Unions cannot accept changes that will create high unemployment any more than management can accept a situation in which it does not pay to invest in new technology. But government can help unions, management, and individuals meet the issue of technological innovation by assuring that the burdens of change are fairly distributed.

There will be opportunity for a government–labor–management partnership to train displaced labor for new jobs, to facilitate the movement of workers from one area to another, and to give economic security to displaced workers searching for new jobs. Furthermore, the problem of unemployment of blacks—particularly young blacks—is one that cannot be solved through collective bargaining. And our society cannot bear much longer the prospect of 40% unemployment in this area.

The drive for individualism will be the biggest issue in collective bargaining. Reconciling the individual worker's values with the organizational needs of a centralized bargaining structure will be a major challenge. Within the union structure, we will need a new mechanism for identifying individual needs and placing priorities on them. From this need will emerge the concept of the skeletal contract. It will be written to permit personal options while protecting the rights of the union and the group.

These overall contracts will be much more general than those we now have. They will allow working committees—smaller units—to develop specific provisions. Issues of overtime, work scheduling, job assignments, flexibility, and job training are examples of provisions that might best be left to working committees rather than being solved in traditional collective bargaining negotiations. The conventional contract would continue to protect the interest of the group, while a whole new set of relationships will spring up on the shop floor. They will have to do with the individual choices and issues which are not permitted to emerge now in collective bargaining—issues of pride, respect, independence, which contribute much to the quality of working life and to the higher quality of the product.

Involvement of the individual worker in making decisions on matters that affect him directly will be the solution. No longer will it be desirable simply to assign workers to a prearranged environment. Instead, they will have a voice in improving and designing the physical place in which they work. Such consultation will also apply to issues such as health, safety standards, schedules, hours of work, training, steady employment, product quality, and productivity. These issues can be moved out of the adversary process with the opportunity to develop responsibility and product pride.

Looking ahead to the world of work in the twenty-first century is not just a matter of looking down a road, but around several corners. The most likely scenario must take into account many, often contradictory developments not only in the workplace but throughout society.

CHAPTER 8

Can We Find Good Jobs in a Service Economy?
William Lucy

We have many scholars who can give us a fairly detailed description of our nation's emerging work force. They can tell us everything we need to know about the occupational futures of bellhops and ceramic engineers, urban planners and dining room attendants. They can estimate, with reasonable certainty, the number of openings for motion-picture projectionists in 1985.

All these numbers are useful, but we need to know far more about the emerging labor force. We need to know the human implications behind these statistics. What sort of lives do working people have to look forward to in the work force of the future?

At my union, the American Federation of State, County and Municipal Employees, we have been asking this question, and we have been disturbed by the answer we keep getting back. Our national employment goal is a decent job for everyone who wants one. We see emerging, unfortunately, an economy that will be increasingly unable to supply those decent jobs. We see, if current trends continue, millions of people working far below their potential, contributing precious little to our society: a labor force mired in frustration and measured in injustice.

I would hasten to add, however, that the nation is by no means headed inexorably to an employment calamity. Conscious economic, political, and social decisions have shaped our current employment realities. Conscious decisions can change them for the better.

There are, to be sure, tough choices to be made. The nation must face and make them, armed with a systematic understanding of the dangers and trends we are facing.

The United States economy, once the world's most efficient producer of goods, has become an economy of services. This is the overriding economic fact of life that shapes our nation's work force.

The story is familiar. The Civil War opened the way for the creation of a truly national market. In the next half-century, America's factories and forges made the market a reality. Out across the land went the steel rails that linked the nation. Up went great new cities at the crossroads. With bricks and wires and girders, workers fashioned the infrastructure of a modern industrial nation.

About 60 years ago this era of industrial development began to change, or "mature." The insatiable demand for manufacturing and construction labor ebbed. In 1920, nearly half of the labor force—46.6% —worked in goods-producing sectors. A decade later, the percentage was down to 40.6%. In 1970, only 33% of the nation's working people were producing goods.

As the economy shifted, it thrust forward virtually whole new sectors of employment. In 1870, for instance, only one-sixth of 1% of the nation's workers labored as clericals. One hundred years later, clericals totalled 18% of the work force. Overall, the numbers of workers providing services increased ninefold from the turn of the century. Today, we have a situation in which less than one worker in every four is involved in manufacturing.

Originally, sociologists and other observers uncritically and almost universally hailed the goods-producing to service-providing transformation as a great advance. The shift, often described as a change from blue- to white-collar labor, was accepted as a step up in job status, an upgrading of the general level of skill among workers.

Nowadays, there is an understanding that the situation is not that simple. In fact, it has become increasingly apparent that the blue-collar jobs the nation is losing are good jobs, relatively high-paying, stable openings. The bulk of the new jobs being created are not. As Columbia University's Eli Ginzberg has pointed out, two-thirds of the jobs created since 1950 can be classified as low-paying, high-turnover, part-time. Service sector jobs averaging $146 per week are replacing goods-producing jobs paying in the $200s. Jobs requiring skill and judgment are disappearing. Jobs requiring minimal skills and decision making—and paying correspondingly less—are growing.

Our society's overly rosy image of office work concealed this reality for a long time. Years ago a worker who left the shop floor for the office was automatically assumed to be making a step upward. Office work was deemed to require more "intelligence." Perhaps there was some truth to this assumption back in Dickensian days when companies were small and clerks were trusted and indispensable confidants. But the reality is very different today. The same forces of mechanization that have helped reduce the number of production workers are now changing the nature of clerical and service occupations. More and more modern secretaries, for instance, are confronted with elaborate new office machines that demand less, not more, skill. The machines "remember" form letters, and the secretaries who use them have little need for stenographical, grammatical, or sophisticated typing skills. They merely press a button and watch the machine regurgitate the proper response. The situation of supermarket checkout cashiers provides a similar example. In the traditional setting, supermarket cashiers are models of dexterity and concentration. Their fingers fly over keys with lightning speed. Their minds are walking encyclopedias of prices. In the new computerized checkout systems, the cashier merely passes a magic electronic wand over each item's "Universal Product Code." The only skill required is the ability to find the code and pack the bags.

According to Franz Schurmann, University of California professor of history and sociology, and Sandy Close, managing editor of the Pacific News Service, we are "becoming a nation of traders, information-processors, and providers of services." These jobs, they could add, require less and less training and are more and more interchangeable. Because they provide so little challenge or opportunity for advancement, turnover is high. Because so many people can perform them, there is always a ready supply of new people to fill the openings. High turnover, constant supply: together they ensure low wages which, in turn, ensure still higher turnover and start the cycle all over again.

There is another related and disturbing trend. As low-paying, high-turnover service jobs proliferate, they set the tone more and more for the manufacturing jobs that remain. Many manufacturing establishments today are dependent on part-timers. Less than two years ago, we read a report about a St. Paul, Minnesota plant based exclusively on part-time production help. The owners boasted that their labor costs were half as high as their competitors'.

There are no indications that the trend toward clerical and sales/service jobs is receding. The Bureau of Labor Statistics, as a matter of fact, estimates that more new jobs will be created in the clerical and service sectors between 1976 and 1985 than in any other category. The number of clerical "opportunities" will be up 28.8%. Service work will jump 23.4%. The total job increase will be only 19.2%. By 1985, adds the Congressional Joint Economic Committee, 80% of the work force will be in other than the goods-producing sectors.

Economic change naturally brings social and political spin-offs that, in turn, rebound back and reshape economic trends. If we assume the continuation of present employment trends, what spin-offs can we expect? I would like to offer the following list.

1) An Increase in Inequality

We have, up to now, considered the work force as an undifferentiated whole. But there are, of course, vast and important social differences among working people. The better jobs of our society—the stable, well-paying manufacturing, mining, and construction slots—have traditionally gone to white men. The poorer jobs have been the special—and forced—preserve of minorities and women.

Black, brown, and female workers no longer accept the racist and sexist stereotypes of "their place," and society, on paper, is committed to ending inequality and discrimination. But if the number of good jobs is decreasing, how is justice to be served?

If the nation accepts productive stagnation, it is making a mockery of the commitment to equal justice. In an economy where good jobs are increasingly scarce prizes to be hoarded and jealously guarded, affirmative action programs will become fierce battlegrounds. The winners may vary from battle to battle, but the war's ultimate victors will be hate and intolerance.

2) An Increase in Alienation

"Young people don't work like they used to." That claim is often heard. There should be an equally standard retort: jobs are no longer what they used to be.

I have already mentioned the growing routinization of clerical and sales work. This trend has gone much further than people imagine. In modern fast-food outlets, for instance, the cash register keys that clerks punch are marked only by pictures of hamburgers, french fries, milk shakes, and the like. Clerks punch the order in pictures, not prices, and the register does all the numerical computing.

As jobs demand less, training becomes less necessary—if necessary at all. Schooling becomes increasingly irrelevant to the job market. "Getting an education" no longer translates into "getting ahead." In the decade ending in 1985, there will be 10.4 million college graduates en-

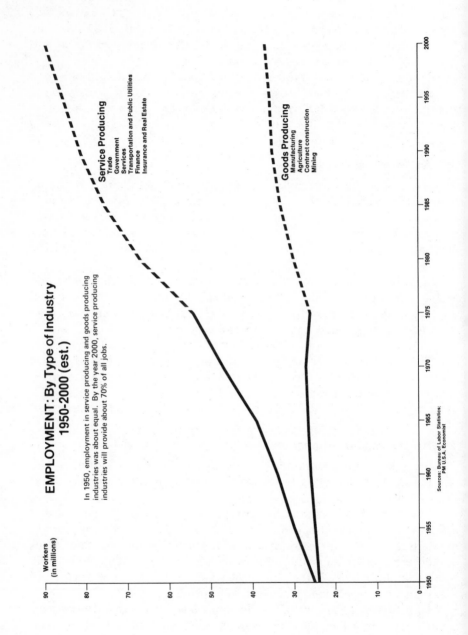

EMPLOYMENT: By Type of Industry 1950-2000 (est.)

In 1950, employment in service producing and goods producing industries was about equal. By the year 2000, service producing industries will provide about 70% of all jobs.

Workers
(in millions)

90

80

70

60

50

40

30

20

10

0

1950 1955 1960 1965 1970 1975 1980 1985 1990 1995 2000

Service Producing
Trade
Government
Services
Transportation and Public Utilities
Finance
Insurance and Real Estate

Goods Producing
Manufacturing
Agriculture
Contract construction
Mining

Sources: Bureau of Labor Statistics;
PM U.S.A. Economist

tering the labor market and only 7.7 million openings for traditional college-level jobs.

Students are not dumb, although the job market may treat them as if they were. In an atmosphere in which it is clear that education has less and less to offer, students' motivation will fall and their performance drop. Poorly motivated students become poorly educated students, unable to take on job responsibility. Absenteeism and shoddy work increase. Employers complain, "Young people don't work like they used to," and demand subminimum wages. Once again, the vicious cycle.

3) An Increase in Anti-unionism

Every reasonable observer of the modern labor relations scene recognizes that trade unions play a crucial role in twentieth century society. They are essential to the health of our social fabric. Through unions workers gain higher wages, better working conditions, and, equally as important, dignity.

Unions encourage and facilitate citizen participation in the political process, and anything that attacks the workers' right to organize in trade unions attacks the heart of American democracy.

In the recent past, many employers have come to understand that unions can help advance the economic interest of business as well as the greater interest of society. By bringing justice to the workplace, unions help create stable work forces. When employees represent a substantial training investment, this stability is a major business plus— and sought after.

However, when businesses have little investment in their workers' skill, stability is less crucial. When employees are interchangeable, excessive turnover is no longer a danger to be avoided at all costs. In such a setting, it matters little whether an employee stays a year or a lifetime. In fact, since worker experience offers no higher productivity to the employer, keeping turnover high pays off in lower wages and pensions.

Is it a coincidence that the nation is now witnessing the biggest upsurge of corporate anti-unionism since the Great Depression? Last year's congressional defeat of a very modest labor law reform bill symbolized this trend. Almost to a corporation, business united behind vulgar labor-haters they would never have countenanced a decade ago. Many of these same corporations are now using high-powered psychological consultants who shuttle from company to company explaining how to wage sophisticated anti-union campaigns.

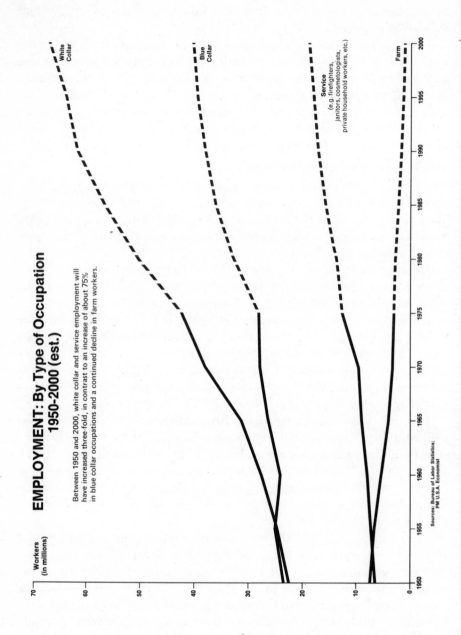

EMPLOYMENT: By Type of Occupation 1950-2000 (est.)

Between 1950 and 2000, white collar and service employment will have increased three-fold, in contrast to an increase of about 75% in blue collar occupations and a continued decline in farm workers.

Workers
(in millions)

70

60

50

40

30

20

10

0

1950   1955   1960   1965   1970   1975   1980   1985   1990   1995   2000

White Collar

Blue Collar

Service
(e.g. firefighters,
janitors, cosmetologists,
private household workers, etc.)

Farm

Sources: Bureau of Labor Statistics;
PM U.S.A. Economist

86

The losers, when unions are attacked, are unorganized workers. A society that squeezes unions inevitably squeezes wages down.

4) An Increase in Economic Instability

An unskilled, unorganized work force is, by definition, also an underpaid work force. The macroeconomic implications of a growing low-wage employment sector are particularly dangerous. The loss of purchasing power to our economy that this entails will make recessions more frequent and longer lasting. Economic insecurity will be the unavoidable result.

5) An Increase in Public Sector "Budget-slashing"

The four factors mentioned previously inevitably lead to a fifth: frustration. Low wages, lousy jobs, dead-end futures, and economic instability create a bitter, unthinking mood ripe for demagogic exploitation. At AFSCME, we know the danger of demagogy well, because public employees have become the scapegoat of the 1970s.

Government is a convenient target, because it often seems the only segment of society that people have the power to alter. People can't cut the price of milk, but they can cut their taxes. Add politicians looking for cheap votes, and the result is Proposition 13 and everything it has come to stand for. Few politicians, as the new federal budget shows, appear immune to Proposition 13 fever.

The government budget cutbacks now multiplying across the nation will have an enormous impact on employment. Public sector jobs have been one of the few bright spots in the overall employment picture. The past generation's expansion of the public sector work force has brought millions of people into the labor force and placed them on the ladder for stable, decent-paying jobs. We are proud of the key role our union has played in this process.

But this process will come to an abrupt halt if Proposition 13-style budget cuts continue. The nation will have closed another employment opportunity door in the face of working people.

Public services, it is important to note, also sharply influence private sector employment patterns. Public monies, for example, fund job-training programs and provide the child care aid that enables women to take decent, full-time positions instead of relying on no-future, part-time work. Slashing programs such as these constitutes a long-term step backward for employment.

The possibility of avoiding a bleak employment future depends first and foremost on our nation's ability to plan and work toward a more balanced mix of jobs that accurately reflects people's needs.

We can start this process by reversing the nation's long-term decline of industrial jobs. Where did those jobs go? The answer is, overseas. The multinational corporate giants based in the United States are transferring their capital and their technology over our borders at an alarmingly rapid rate. Between December, 1973 and December, 1977 the economy lost 500,000 goods-producing jobs. During that time, imports of manufactured products increased 70%. We now import more machinery and transportation equipment than oil.

The technology exports wouldn't be as threatening as they are if the nation had the research capacity to generate new technological advances. But the nation does not have that capacity. Long years of heavy military spending have distorted our research priorities and made the nation less able to match the technological advances of Japan and Western Europe.

The military spending, moreover, has been a bad productive job investment. The dollars we have spent and are spending on ever more elaborate bombs and missiles would produce far more productive jobs if they were earmarked for necessary civilian needs. Chase Econometrics, for instance, estimated during the controversy over the B-1 bomber that the nation could create 30,000 to 70,000 more productive jobs by spending the B-1 money for public works or constructing public housing instead of redundant bombers.

There is no shortage of useful, productive work that needs to be done in this country. The nation's housing stock is dilapidated. Unrepaired railbeds are a barrier to adequate transportation. New energy systems are needed. We can train toward these needs, target our resources toward them, use them to build the momentum for a new productive upsurge. If we combine this reconversion from military to useful civilian production with a new policy that curbs the power of multinational corporations, we can revitalize the manufacturing sector and create the new, good jobs we need.

The same national planning we bring to the goods-producing sector must be brought to the provision of services. We must analyze what the nation needs, look at approaching trends, and try to anticipate changes in the way we live.

To give one example: there will soon be an explosion in the number of elderly in this country. In 1975, there were 18.9 retired workers for every 100 active workers. In the year 2030, there will be 33.6 retired people for every 100 workers. That amounts to almost a doubling of the nation's elderly population.

A demographic shift of that magnitude will have huge social implications. Where will the newly retired live? What new services will they require? If we target those needs today, we can train people to meet them in the future.

There are many other aspects of our social reality that demand perceptive and comprehensive planning for future services. We have only begun, for instance, to comprehend the enormous difficulty of keeping the air, water, and soil of a modern society clean. The recent tragedy in Niagara Falls' Love Canal—where women, in a neighborhood built on chemically contaminated soil, gave birth to malformed children—underscores the deep and pervasive environmental problems we face.

Our past ecological indiscretions will continue to haunt us in the future. Some scientists are predicting an epidemic of asbestosis as the deadly fibers picked up decades ago by millions of workers work themselves into cancer. We must plan the care of these future victims and take the necessary monitoring steps to prevent additional environmental tragedies. Both these objectives will create the potential for huge numbers of new, useful service jobs. But these jobs will only be realized through careful planning and the targeting of resources.

I could make many similar points on education and on the delivery of adequate health care services in general. The useful services exist. The jobs must be created.

These strategic outlines are necessarily brief. Our purpose here is not to map the employment future, but merely to emphasize that the future can still be directed in valuable directions—if the nation has the will. The shape of our emerging labor force will determine the shape of our entire society. There can be few questions more important to the health of the nation than the shape of the labor force to come.

CHAPTER 9

Toward a More Participative Work Force
A. H. Raskin

It is painfully clear that the United States will enter the twenty-first century facing serious global challenges to its industrial preeminence. It is equally clear that one of this country's most formidable obstacles in surmounting those challenges is likely to be a diminishing appetite among Americans for putting up with the traditional rigidities of the workplace or for according work itself its old primacy in their scale of values.

Discontents have always been present in mine, mill, factory, and office. But the last few years have produced compelling evidence that higher levels of education and an inner-directedness, born in part of preoccupation with self and in part of distrust of all authority, are steadily eroding job satisfaction. The quest of workers for self-fulfillment outside their jobs rather than in them shows no sign of abating in the final quarter of this century.

The chances for a reversal of this trend toward disaffection are diminished by a raft of new forces circumscribing the horizons of employee expectation. One is a move into the frozen-food department of the economic pie. Since World War II, Americans have been cutting ever larger slices of pay based on the expansion in real terms of the gross national product. The notion that rising productivity made it possible for everyone to count on a bigger slice of the pie each year without a reduction in the size of the chunk going to anyone else has up to now been the main sustainer of America's high standard of living. It has also been a principal reason why the labor movement in the

United States, alone among those in the industrialized democracies of the West, applauds the enterprise system.

The idea that there automatically will be more abundance to share year after year is already on its way to obsolescence. Slow economic growth, lagging productivity, chronic inflation, and the increasing fierceness of import competition conspire against it. There is a strong possibility that the national output of goods and services will stay relatively static as we turn into a new century. Indeed, even that may prove an excessively hopeful forecast, given the ability of multinational conglomerates to build plants in any part of the world. In addition, there is the announced resolve of the Third World to have at least one-quarter of the global wealth and productive capacity within its borders by the year 2000. Environmental constraints, essential to the preservation of an America worth living in, will put a further brake on economic expansion. So will concern for the protection of employees and the community against the high price of carcinogens, toxic waste, and other breeders of death in the workplace.

Even with the first commercial dividends of our huge investment in space exploration and in tapping the riches under the oceans, it is not inconceivable that far from having a bigger pie to whack up each year, the United States will have to adjust to a smaller one. Such an unpalatable accommodation may be in store for all the developed countries, but it will be more irksome for us than for the others because we have viewed "more" as our birthright to an extent that makes us unique. That philosophy was laid down as organized labor's central prop by Samuel Gompers and other founders of the old American Federation of Labor almost a century ago. The early merchant capitalists and the robber barons always embraced that same philosophy. Madison Avenue has exalted "more" to the status of a religion. If material rewards have lost much of their allure for millions of younger Americans, it is less because they scorn affluence than because they take the comforts it provides as a matter of entitlement.

There is plentiful current evidence to support anxiety that the political impact of a leaner economy will be to accentuate the trend toward a protectionist society in which those with a firm handhold on the opportunity ladder fight against government initiatives aimed at redistributing resources, access, or power. One need only remember the support given to George Wallace's brand of redneck populism in the late 1960s. Large numbers of white- and blue-collar workers showed the shallowness of their adherence to the 1930s-oriented programs of social reform that remain the bedrock of the legislative platforms of organized labor. The heritage of Vietnam and Watergate and a thousand lesser scandals in government, industry, labor, and most other institutions has been a cynicism so widespread that many, if not most, citizens conduct their daily lives in the belief that "rip-offs" are the rule and that they are regularly being betrayed, out of incompetence or avarice, by those who profess to be their protectors.

It is easy to imagine this sense of letdown causing the emergence of a demagogic leader, especially if there are new humiliations on the international scene. And there are other developments that could contribute to hunger for a "strong man." One would be a major recession marked by high inflation and high unemployment. Another would be the removal of labor as an effective countervailing force in economic and political affairs. Danger signals already visible indicate that trade unions could lose much of their standing because of sophisticated employer resistance and because the leaders of the labor movement fail to modernize their tactics and organizing appeals.

My own hope, in the face of all these sources of anxiety, is that our traditions of dedication to individual dignity and social justice and the basic good sense of our people will keep us from riding a totalitarian treadmill into the twenty-first century. I prefer to believe and to expect that the magnitude of the nation's problems will cause us to seek democratic solutions based on reestablishment of a foundation of trust in the adaptability of our institutions and the integrity of our leaders. The erosion of that trust is our single most troublesome roadblock; none of our institutions can be repaired permanently until their performance begins to match their claims of virtue and effectiveness. On the blithe assumption that this seemingly uncrossable gulf will be bridged before this century expires, let me make some diffident predictions about the world of work a couple of decades down the road.

Automation, which has been on a sputtering fuse for a full generation, will begin to make a consequential imprint on the character and volume of work. New machine tools of extreme flexibility will usher in the era of the multipurpose factory, capable of swift conversion from one product line to a quite different one in response to shifts in consumer demand or intensity of overseas competition.

That development will be of utmost importance in maintaining America as an industrial power. But its human implications will require changes in public policy beyond the necessary adjustments at the collective bargaining table. The extent to which existing skills will be rendered valueless, and workers who have spent a lifetime acquiring them relegated to the scrap heap, has already been illustrated dramatically in the mechanization of coal mining, the movement of containerized cargo through the nation's ports, and the automation of newspaper composing rooms. Increasingly, an answer has been found in agreements guaranteeing displaced workers lifetime job security in exchange for the installation of new technology and the establishment of work rules that are free of featherbedding.

Unfortunately, such answers are usually a lingering death sentence for the unions that sign them, dooming them to disappearance when their present members die off or retire. That melancholy fate is already in view for the mechanical unions in the newspaper field. The early years of the next century will almost surely see newspapers home-delivered via television, with printout attachments available to give the reader an instant copy of any article he wants to keep. In the fully automated factory, the need for workers chiefly will be for monitors of the control panels and for repair mechanics to hold breakdown time to a minimum. But the problem of cushioning the displacement shock for the existing factory work force will be an even harder one to handle through labor-management negotiation than have those in longshore, newspapers, or mining. That is because employers will tend to house their robots in completely new plants in new locations, most of them in the Sun Belt where unions have traditionally been weak and seem likely to remain so for at least a generation.

The tilt of population, markets, and industry toward the South and Southwest, plus the choice open to many corporations of moving to other countries for cheap labor or tax advantages, present novel problems. They make it improbable that permanent job guarantees or other forms of attrition and early retirement can handle the twenty-first century industrial transformation unless government steps in as the principal underwriter of such assurances of protection for workers.

Political pressure from the Northeast, Middle Atlantic, and Midwest states, in danger of degenerating into industrial deserts, can be expected to push the national government into a central role in assisting in that monumental process of adjustment. If such a government obligation is accepted as public policy, the vaporous beginnings of national economic planning embodied in the Humphrey–Hawkins Full Employment Act will have to be strengthened and implemented in a way that will reverse the current trend toward "less is better" for government's role in managing the economy.

The prospect that government will expand, not contract, seems to be heightened by the likelihood that an incomes policy regulating both prices and wages will be a permanent fact of life in an increasingly interdependent and competitive world. The rules of trade and a check on the destruction of monetary values by chronic inflation will be twin governmental responsibilities that cannot be met without far-ranging reliance on economic planning. This will have to be conducted at a central level, but it will be best executed in a democracy if it represents a partnership endeavor of public and private interests.

My overall conviction, however, is that the workplace of the twenty-first century will be a more congenial place to work if only because many of the more disagreeable jobs will have been taken over by machines, and these, in general, will be quieter and cleaner. The movement from blue-collar employment to white-collar and professional jobs will continue, and the range of fringe benefits employers provide as an extension of the paycheck will be widened to include many options in mental health, adult education, and leisure.

Flexibility will be the keynote of work arrangements as the ratio of women in the labor force reaches parity with that of men. Not only will millions of workers be allowed to set their own starting and quitting hours, a practice already well launched, but opportunities may be widespread for job-sharing on a systematic basis. One worker might take the morning hours and another those in the afternoon, or one might work six months of the year and a second take care of the other six. A similarly pluralistic approach would extend to fringe benefits, providing workers with a cafeteria range of choices. Included in the range of benefits is likely to be a system of employer-financed sabbaticals—for foreign travel, study in cultural or job-related fields, and mid-career self-inquiry. In this restless era, when personal wants and the needs of society change so dramatically, many workers may well capitalize on such sabbaticals to switch into wholly new lines of endeavor.

The standard workweek, unchanged since passage of the Fair Labor Standards Act under Franklin D. Roosevelt, is likely to move from five days to four, with legislation rather than collective bargaining the principal instrument of change. The cost implications would be staggering in the absence of any parallel shift in other industrialized countries, but the trend toward more paid leisure is universal. Six-week vacations are common in Western Europe. Cutting a day off the workweek might appeal more to American workers than added vacation time, though so many now look forward to going away in mid-winter as well as mid-summer that management policies may be broadened to include personal selection of shorter hours or longer vacations.

We will not have succeeded by the year 2000 in breaking down all the walls of exclusion that have slowed job access and job progress for women and minorities. But it is reasonable to believe that our stickiest problems in the equal opportunity field will be behind us. That forecast, to be sure, can be made with somewhat more confidence in the case of women than it can for blacks and Hispanics, especially those who are young and poor and ill-educated.

One abomination of the workplace is overdue for elimination by the year 2000. That is the double standard that has condemned most blue-collar workers to being paid by the hour while white-collar and professional workers share with all levels of management the comparative dignity of salaries issued weekly or monthly. No more humiliating kind of second-class industrial citizenship is conceivable than this chaining of the blue-collar work force to the clock. The astonishing thing is that unions have not only agreed to this practice, but fostered it. Unquestionably, the absence of this degrading policy at IBM helps explain why unions have found so little receptivity to their organizing drives in that company over the years.

In the women's field, the next two decades will see "keep out" signs vanish from practically all the traditional areas of male employment, from ditch-digging to flying airliners. The continuing problem will be in barriers to advancement. Women will still have an uphill fight to achieve top rank in corporations, unions, and public life. Here the task of absorption, especially in the intermediate levels of skilled and managerial employment, will be aggravated by the fact that through most of the next 20 years, a huge bulge will appear in the number of workers in the prime working age group from 25 to 44. Qualified seekers for promotion, male as well as female, will be far more numerous than the slots available.

The same competition will slow the upward climb of minorities, undoubtedly more seriously. The heritage of racial discrimination in ghettoized existence, low income, and wretched education is still proving an intractable handicap for many. The survival of this heritage helps account for the frozen lump of unemployment among young blacks and Hispanics. Their hopelessness remains an explosive mine field menacing the smoothness of our transition into the new century.

Early in the century, we will need to rethink the country's public and private programs for the elderly. Many Americans are opting for retirement in their mid- or early 50s, while many others are pressing, with the law behind them, for the right to stay on the job until age 70 or longer. Varied as the individual decisions are, the lengthening of life expectancy for workers of both sexes is causing a worrisome rise in the number of fully retired persons and in the burden of sustaining the cost of their pensions, medical care, and other needs.

Congress already has recognized the need for building a cost-of-living escalator provision into Social Security as a means of safeguarding purchasing power. Retired federal employees have the same kind of protection for the purchasing power of their pensions. Very few private pension plans established through collective bargaining have any comparable inflation hedge, but it is inconceivable that this can continue into the next century. Every union is pressing for cost-of-living clauses to guard the value of the wage dollar for all its active members.

Certainly, equity requires that when a worker retires after three or four decades, he should carry with him solid assurance that the living standard his pension is supposed to provide will remain secure. The reality, however, is that in the absence of any turnaround in the ability of national and world leaders to clamp inflation, the economy will be incapable of sustaining the weight of a fully indexed system of public and private benefits now in existence. Linking Social Security, civil service, and industrial retirement systems into a network that combines stability and fairness is a national necessity. Regrettably, we may not get around to addressing the issue until one or more of the giant industry-wide programs collapses and makes intervention inescapable.

Another source of tensions will involve animosities within the work force—between the unionized workers in the public sector and those in the private sector who resent paying the increasingly high bills for civil service support and resent even more the coercive tactics that often deprive them and their families of vital services, forgetting the frequency with which their own unions have used precisely the same tactics in battles with corporate employers. Comparable strains, long muted in the name of labor solidarity, are likely to surface between the "have" unions in auto, steel, oil refining, and other high-wage industries and the "have-nots" in the garment trades, textiles, and the service fields, where most minority workers and women still work.

What gives me hope that all these tensions will be eased and that the country's workers and employers will respond constructively to the challenges ahead is my confidence that we are moving toward an awareness of the desirability—in my judgment, the necessity—of a vibrant form of industrial democracy. I have in mind a system that avoids the paramilitary lines of command now so general in the workplace and taps the creativity and imagination of a new generation of workers.

From the standpoint of their own feeling of self-worth, workers want to feel that their boss and their union respect the ideas they have about how their own work could be done better, how the plant or office can be made more efficient and pleasant, and what is good or bad about certain equipment, lighting, work flow, or methods of compensation. The benefits to the enterprise of involving workers in decisions on such matters go far beyond having a more satisfied work force; their involvement provides a basis for cooperative relationships indispensable to the welfare of employer and employee and to social stability.

Autonomous work teams, the opportunities of rotated leadership, two-way communication on everything important to the worker in his job, plus a widening list of joint policy decisions at the shop level are inevitable. At the moment, there is little stirring within either labor or management to extend such joint activity to the point of employee or union membership on company boards of directors. The nature of tomorrow's problems, however, makes it probable that workers will want to make their views known and respected at that level as well. To the degree that it does bring a genuine sense of involvement to rank-and-file workers, such a development would be healthy.

My observation of German codetermination and other West European experience makes me doubt, however, that board representation actually does give the average worker a feeling of intimate participation in top-level policy on such questions as capital investment, marketing programs, or product lines. Indeed, few workers have either a desire for such participation or a belief that they have much to contribute in this type of managerial decision. This does not necessarily rule out the idea that a collective worker voice can be useful in decisions on other corporate matters, especially those involving plant relocation or layoff policy.

Whatever the developments on that front, the most needed changes— and those I am most confident will come—are those that make the worker a full citizen inside the office or factory, involved in all the decisions that directly affect him.

CHAPTER 10

Women: The Emerging Labor Force

Pat L. Burr, Ph.D.

Between now and the turn of the twenty-first century, private sector employers have the divine opportunity to show their true concern about "what the economy is coming to." Now is the time to redefine what American industry expects of the labor force, particularly women, and what it offers.

That women will play an increasingly powerful role in the American work force is not in question. They already do, both because they are needed and because they must, as a matter of economic necessity. Consider:

- In 1977, nearly two-thirds of all women in the labor force were either single, widowed, divorced, separated, or had husbands whose earnings were less than $10,000.[1] Earned income, therefore, is a matter of economic survival. The conventional view that men are solely responsible for the economic welfare of the family, and women are responsible for all other care, is no longer true or appropriate.[2]

- In 1977, 37% of black families in the United States were headed by women. In the total population in that year, one of every seven families was headed by a woman.[3] Their interest in working has nothing to do with frivolity.

The earnestness of women toward work shows up also in other statistics. In 1974 the average number of sick days taken by women was 5.6, compared to 5.2 for men,[4] a difference of 3 hours and 12 minutes a year. And despite all the social factors that might be thought to dictate otherwise, women perform about as well as men at staying on the job. In 1968, the most recent year for which statistics are available, the quit rate for women was 2.6% and 2.2% for men. Compared to an earlier study, there is hope that this small difference between men and women is narrowing further.[5]

If planning begins now, women workers can have an extremely positive relationship with American industry in the twenty-first century. The employer, obviously, needs an increased supply of labor and increased productivity in the bargain. The real issue of the women in the labor force is how the employer can meet those needs and how the employee can meet a different, but not necessarily incompatible, set of needs.

Examining the need for employers to increase the labor supply and its productivity, we find that the unemployment rate for white adult men 20 years of age and over in 1977 was 4.6% compared to 6.2% for white adult women. The unemployment rate for minority adult men during the same period was 10% compared to 11.7% for minority adult women.[6] If an increasing labor supply is needed, then it is expected to come from the area where unemployment is greatest, assuming an absence of structural unemployment. And even in the case of structural unemployment, employers can redefine employability by addressing work preparation, work hours, and child care.

For women in the work force, there is an initial period of fairly continuous employment lasting three to four years between school and marriage.[7] Following the birth of the first child, there is often a period of nonparticipation in the work force, which may last between five and ten years. A period of intermittent participation begins as the youngest child reaches school age, after which there is a permanent return to the labor force for some women, though for others participation remains intermittent.

Lack of child care, either public or private, is a critical factor affecting the twenty-first century labor force, and the problem is accentuated when the available child care is affordable by only 10% of working mothers.[8]

The cycle described above is a vicious economic cycle for women who drop from the labor force, lose command of their skills, lose the drive toward upward mobility, and lose their places in line for promotion.

Child care, as a labor force issue, affects the executive working mother[9] as well as the mother who is out of the labor force for child care reasons. For example, a six-state study in 1969 suggested that a potential 63% of nonemployed women receiving aid to families with dependent children would like to work in a steady job if adequate child care were available.[10]

And what is the return on investment to employers who are willing to establish child care facilities for men and women who desperately need them? Larger blocks of time are freed for the potential employee, tardy behavior patterns are minimized, and absenteeism related to child care can be reduced.[11] Morale can also increase with the lowering of anxiety among mothers with small children.

What about the cost? One study has suggested that in 1974 the average annual cost of 2500 hours of child care for a 3- to 6-year-old in a nonsubsidized center was approximately $1300.[12]

While relying upon the private sector employer as the change agent thrusting us toward a more humanized workplace in the twenty-first century, the employee must be willing to share the cost. In addition, the parent-employee must be willing to assume some responsibility in helping the employer establish policy, administrative guidelines, and daily operating patterns.

The Coalition of Labor Union Women, created in 1974 and recognized three years later by George Meany, then AFL-CIO President, now has 6000 members. At its third national convention, the coalition made plans to establish a National Child Care Task Force to bring together organizations to work for comprehensive child care legislation.[13]

While such legislation is one approach to solving the problem, private sector policy should rightly be the forerunner to solutions. Shared cost arrangements between employee and employer or among a group of employers lower the economic impact upon any individual employee or employer.

Humanizing the work schedule in the twenty-first century has been demanded by women's organizations, and yet it is the private sector employer who stands to gain as much as does the employee. Flexitime, part-time, and shared-job arrangements are at least three options.

In spite of pessimists' fears that a company's work routine would collapse overnight if the work schedule were altered, studies suggest that the positive results outweigh the negative profoundly. What it allows for any parent—in most cases women—is a redefinition of the allowable time to perform child care at home. And for the woman in America who is the head of a household, there is no mate to share the responsibility. Redefinition of work time may be the lowest cost answer, be it in the private sector or in government.

Table 1   Flexitime Usage Rate by Industry, Sector, and Size of Firm in the United States, 1977

Item	Percent of Organizations Using
Industry	
Manufacturing	10.3
Transportation, communications, utilities	17.1
Wholesale, retail trade	14.4
Finance, insurance, real estate	19.3
Services	14.4
All industries	12.8
Sector	
Private	12.9
Profit	13.0
Nonprofit	9.7
Public	17.6
All sectors	12.8
Size of Firm (number of employees)	
50 to 1000	12.5
50 to 499	8.6
500 to 1000	17.1
>1000	13.1
All sizes (>50 employees)	12.8

Note.   Percentages are based on responses from 495 organizations that are customers of the American Management Associations. The figures are adjusted for response bias and are intended to be nationwide projections.

Source.   Stanley D. Nollen and Virginia H. Martin, *ALTERNATIVE WORK SCHEDULES, Part 1: Flexitime,* New York: AMACOM, 1978.

Part-time jobs are a second way in which private industry can restructure the workday in order to increase the labor force.[14] In addition, shared jobs are being explored by the Smithsonian Institution[15] and the Federal Reserve Bank of Boston, with a high degree of success among both professional and clerical workers.

What are the benefits of nontraditional scheduling of work to the employer? The firm that offers part-time and shared job opportunities will likely experience greater productivity and lower unit costs, due to reduced absenteeism, turnover, recruitment activity, and overtime pay.[16] Flexitime studies suggest that the firm benefits in a reduction of casual absenteeism, in work continuity, stronger motivation, and reduced job turnover.[17] Lateness virtually disappears as a problem, since

Table 2   Key Effects of Flexitime for Long-term vs. Short-term Users (Percent Reporting Each Effect)

| | Changes Caused by Flexitime | | | | | |
| | Short-term Users | | | Long-term Users | | |
	Better	No change	Worse	Better	No change	Worse
Usual or Frequent Good Effects						
Employee morale	100	0	0	97	3	0
Employee commuting	77	20	3	77	15	8
Productivity	45	52	3	51	44	5
Turnover	39	61	0	64	36	0
Absenteeism	77	19	4	66	33	1
Tardiness	77	16	7	81	15	5
Recruiting	50	50	0	62	37	1
Overtime	40	60	0	38	60	2
Public relations	37	63	0	46	52	2
Occasional Problems						
Coverage of work situations	43	30	27	36	34	30
Employee scheduling	37	30	33	30	33	37
Work scheduling	30	33	37	25	41	34
Difficulty of management job	0	50	50	5	46	49
Internal communications	3	70	27	8	53	39
External communications	20	67	13	18	56	26

Note. Short-term means less than one year ($n = 31$); long-term means more than three years ($n = 61$).

Source. Stanley D. Nollen and Virginia H. Martin, *ALTERNATIVE WORK SCHEDULES, Part 1: Flexitime.*

a tardy worker usually can make up for lost time at the end of the day. Employees are also more inclined to stay until the job at hand is done, whereas work under a rigid 9-to-5 routine tends to be dropped at the moment of closing.[18]

Work preparation, or training as we traditionally call it, is a much needed ingredient in the work force of women in the twenty-first century. Much of the need is technical and job-related, and much of it is concerned with attitudes about work as a philosophy.

Even given situations of structural unemployment, where skills needed and skills available do not match, training can be a very forceful tool of change for private sector management. This is true regardless of whether the women in question are assembly-line employees or of top-management potential. The need for work preparation pointed out in a recent study is true for almost all women in all varieties of occupations.[19]

Career counseling, skills identification, and opportunities for upward mobility can all serve as powerful management tools. In return, employees can help share the cost of training or indicate to the employer their commitment to undergo training for jobs that will appear in the future.

Direct reimbursement and shared cost of training and education are both viable options for employers. Training on the job is also useful in trades where line production is an important ingredient. Partner-learning—which pairs one woman with a partner to strengthen skills and attitudes necessary for promotion—can be successful.

All parents in the labor force have at least two responsibilities: one to the employer and another to children. Some consistently prefer to honor one above the other, whether we speak of employer or employee. And yet the fabric of society which concerns us all dictates a reasonable amount to be given to each, by both the employee and the employer. If the industrial network takes its role seriously as a force for change, it can, indeed, move society to its advantage, beginning now. And both industry and employee will benefit.

There is yet another American institution that will benefit from the participation of women, and that is organized labor. My prediction is that women will constitute the greatest single source of union membership growth in the future. Women, as a labor pool, are the last major untapped source of membership.

A continuing problem for women in the labor movement is the lack of women represented in top-level union management. There are qualified women who can and will serve at the highest levels of union organization in the United States, and their participation is greatly needed now and in the future.

One woman described the lack of women in union leadership as analogous to a truck carrying union members and the driver always being an Anglo male. "Every time the truck hits a bump, we suffer the consequences."

In many conversations with women in both professional and non-professional jobs, I have been told that women see unionization as their opportunity to present a united front in the labor market. They are in positions ranging from clerks all the way to assistant vice presidents, and unionization is definitely an item on their agendas.

REFERENCES

1. U.S. Department of Labor, Employment Standards Administration, Women's Bureau, "Twenty Facts on Women Workers" (Washington, D.C.: Government Printing Office, August 1978), p. 1.

2. Joint Economic Committee, Congress of the U.S., *American Women Workers in a Full Employment Economy,* "Part-Time Work" (Washington, D.C.: Government Printing Office, 1977), pp. 182–191.

3. U.S. Department of Labor, "Twenty Facts on Women Workers," p. 2.

4. U.S. Department of Labor, Employment Standards Administration, Women's Bureau, "The Myth and the Reality" (Washington, D.C.: Government Printing Office, May 1974), p. 1.

5. U.S. Department of Labor, Bureau of Labor Statistics, "Labor Turnover of Women Factory Workers, 1950–1955," *Monthly Labor Review,* August 1955.

6. U.S. Department of Labor, "Twenty Facts on Women Workers," p. 2.

7. U.S. Department of Labor, Manpower Administration, "Years For Decision," *Manpower Research Monograph No. 24* and "Dual Careers," *Manpower Research Monograph No. 21.*

8. Susan Cheever Cowley, Mary Lord, and Lisa Whitman, "What Makes Sally Run," *Newsweek,* December 6, 1976, p. 81.

9. "When Mothers Are also Managers," *Business Week,* April 18, 1977, p. 155.

10. Betty Burnside, "The Employment Potential of AFDC Mothers in Six States," *Welfare in Review,* July–August 1971, p. 18.

11. Joint Economic Committee, U.S. Congress, "Economic Aspects of Child Care," *American Women Workers in a Full Employment Economy,* (Washington, D.C.: Government Printing Office, 1977), pp. 170–177.

12. California Legislative Analyst's Office, "Publicly Subsidized Child Care Services in California," August 1974, pp. 113–117, 123–125.

13. Linda H. LeGrande, "Women In Labor Organizations: Their Ranks Are Increasing," *Monthly Labor Review,* August 1978, pp. 8–14.

14. Carol Greenwald and Judith Liss, "Part-Time Workers Can Bring Higher Productivity," *Harvard Business Review,* September–October 1973.

15. Robert I. Lazer, "Job Sharing as a Pattern for Permanent Part-Time Work," *Conference Board Record*, October 1975, pp. 57–61.

16. Joint Economic Committee, "Part-Time Work," pp. 182–191.

17. Robert Lawrence, "Flexible Working Hours: A New Key to Productivity," *Best's Review*, p. 100.

18. Lee Smith, "Flexitime: A New Work Style Catches On," *Dun's Review*, March 1977, p. 62.

19. Martha G. Burrow, "A Worldwide View of Their Management Development Needs," *Women* (New York: AMACOM, 1976), p. 1.

CHAPTER 11

Personnel Policies for the 1980s*

Jerome M. Rosow

During the 1970s, the American labor force changed significantly. Some of these changes were reasonably well predicted from the demographic material at hand, but others presented surprises that were grossly underestimated in nearly every responsible forecast. A major part of this data is presented by Harvard economist Richard Freeman in his excellent chapter, "The Work Force of the Future: An Overview," from *Work in America: The Decade Ahead,* edited by Clark Kerr and myself.[1]

Significant changes in the American labor force were:

- A marked shift in employment away from blue-collar jobs, particularly toward professional, technical, and clerical positions. This shift was especially marked among nonwhite workers.
- A near doubling in the governmental share of the labor force. However, this rate of growth declined in the mid-1970s, and the outlook is clouded by the popularity of tax-cutting proposals such as Proposition 13.
- Geographic shifts in the distribution of employment, with a move away from the Eastern and Midwestern industrial regions. The fastest growing regions were the South, Southwest, and—to a lesser extent—the West Coast. The Sun Belt outshone the Snow Belt.
- Decline in private sector unionism, offset in part by the growth of

public sector unions. Twenty-five years ago unions represented 34% of the nonagricultural labor force; now the percentage hovers near 25%.

- Influx of "illegal aliens," primarily from Mexico and Latin America. This represents a new force in the labor market. Experts estimate an infusion of perhaps six million workers. They have been a major source of supply for low-skilled jobs.

Three additional important developments were grossly underestimated in nearly every forecast:

- The massive movement of women into the work force, especially the dramatic rise in the participation of younger women.
- The growth in the number of younger workers was underestimated, despite obvious demographic factors. The reasons relate to the difficulties of forecasting the numbers going to college, the entry of young women, and the influx of illegal young immigrants.
- The marked decline in the participation of older men. In 1947, 91% of men age 54 to 65 were in the work force. By 1977, the participation rate for this age group had declined to 78%. The principal factor has been the Social Security laws, especially for men over 62. However, for those below 62 other forces were also at work. There were voluntary and involuntary early retirements, the effect of the business cycle on layoffs, the influence of age discrimination on reemployment, the growing financial ability of older men to retire early, and the rise in family income as a result of the increase in working wives. The labor force participation for men over 60 has decreased sharply during the past two decades. In the age 60 to 64 group, the decline was 24%. In the age 65 and over group, the decline was 45%.[2] The real issue for the 1980s is whether this decline will continue, level off, or be reversed.

Given this broad sketch of the changing American labor force, what can we reasonably forecast for the decade ahead? I see five shifts in the composition of our work force.

SHIFT 1. THE COMING SHORTAGE OF YOUTH

Because of the low birth rate of the 1960s, the absolute number of young workers is expected to fall sharply in the 1980s. The decline will exceed one million persons between the ages of 16 and 24, a reduction of six percentage points. The problems of teen-age and youth unemployment will ease, but not proportionately for black teen-age youth. In the black community, the birth rate has not declined as sharply as it has for whites. But for the entire population, the only factor that could ameliorate the coming shortage of youth would be a marked increase in young immigrants, legal or illegal.

Although the 1980s will experience an overall decline in the youth population, it will be concentrated among white youth. The 16- to 24-year-old group will drop by 2.8 million between 1980 and 1985, while the nonwhite population will hold steady at 5.8 million. Thus, non-whites, as a percentage of total workers who are 16 to 24 years old, will rise from 15.5% (1980) to 16.8% (1985) and 18.3% (1990).

SHIFT 2. THE MIDDLE-AGE BULGE

One of the most remarkable factors in the decade ahead will be the demographic bunching up of the prime-age work force in the 25 to 44 age bracket. In 1975 there were 39 million workers in this age bracket; by 1990 there will be 60.5 million, an extraordinary jump of 55%. Their share of the total labor force will be 52%, an increase of 10 points over 1975.[3] These are the individuals who are typically competing for promotions, professional recognition, and supervisory responsibilities.

We can look ahead to intense competition for promotions, severe disappointments, and increased pressure on management development and pay policies in most institutions. People of this age group suffered the same bottleneck problem when they were competing for placement in college classes. In their mid-careers their sheer numbers will translate into a blockage in the normal flow upward in the organization. We can be sure these employees will not suffer silently. Some of the major personnel and management problems of the 1980s will revolve around this critical group.

SHIFT 3. THE INCREASING ROLE OF WOMEN

The upward trend of the participation of women in the labor force is expected to continue. Those sectors of the economy that are more prone to favor women are obviously those most likely to grow. Their responsiveness will encourage more ambitious demands. At the same time, the increased participation of women may well come to apply across the work force and result in a rising female share in more occupations and industries. By 1990 it is predicted that 61% of all American women will be working.

SHIFT 4. COMPETITION FOR DESIRABLE JOBS

Competition for the better jobs will be intensified as women successfully enter traditional male occupations and also because of pressure for equal opportunity employment. A sharp rise in the absolute numbers of those competing, combined with increasingly able women and minorities, could lead to fervent competition.

SHIFT 5. INCREASED EMPLOYMENT OF OLDER WORKERS

Although this predicted shift is speculative, the indications are that it will certainly occur by 1990. The recent raising of the mandatory retirement age to 70 was premature so far as the current labor force is concerned. But by the end of the next decade, employers will be more motivated to attract and retain older workers than ever before. This will make necessary a loosening of Social Security restrictions, more flexible working arrangements for older people, phased or gradual retirement, job redesign to adjust to physical and psychological abilities and needs, and a general set of personnel policies that are more responsive to older workers.

New survey data reveal a reversal of recent employee preferences for early retirement; a majority now indicate their desire to keep working past the normal retirement age.[4] New issues in personnel management will focus on the extension of working life: the increase in the labor force participation rates of older men (ages 50 to 64), the transferability of pensions from one company to the next, the relationship of private pensions to Social Security, the escalation of pensions to stay in line with the cost of living, increased incentives to work longer, improved planning for retirement, and new concepts for transiting from work to retirement and second careers.

Beyond the calculable shifts in the composition of the American work force is the collection of new attitudes that are emerging. It is not enough to know who will do the work. We must also try to forecast the spirit in which they will do it. And on this front, the news is not entirely encouraging.

The suspicions of some of the country's best-informed labor experts that job satisfaction among U.S. workers is on the downgrade have been amply confirmed in a recently released national survey on the quality of employment in the United States.

According to the survey, conducted for the U.S. Department of Labor by Robert P. Quinn and Graham L. Staines of the University of Michigan's Institute for Social Research,[5] the decline in job satisfaction between 1973 and 1977 has been "pervasive, affecting virtually all the demographic and occupational subclasses examined." The decline was particularly pronounced among college graduates.

The 1977 survey included 1515 respondents from 74 different geographic areas and was representative of all employed adults, all occupations in the United States, and all industries.

Judging from the responses to general questions such as "All in all, how satisfied would you say you are with your job?" workers apparently are more apt to express dissatisfaction with specific aspects of their jobs than with their jobs in general. Over the eight years from 1969 to 1977, responses to such questions indicated only a small—although significant—drop in job satisfaction. Responses to more specific questions, on the other hand, exhibited a marked and significant decline in job satisfaction, spread rather evenly over five areas: comfort, challenge, financial rewards, resource adequacy, and promotions.

More than half of American workers reported problems related to:

- Desire for improved fringe benefits.
- Exposure to health and safety hazards.
- Work schedules—days and hours.
- Difficulty in getting duties changed.
- Inadequate time for leisure activities.

More than one-third of American workers reported problems related to:

- Inequities in pay.
- Inconvenient or excessive hours.
- The feeling that time drags at work.
- Unpleasant physical conditions at work.
- Interference between work and family life.

For the first time, the Michigan researchers included questions about the relationship between work life and certain aspects of life away from work. They paid particular attention to the relationship between work and family life and work and leisure. Although their analysis of this data is still preliminary, it is apparent that one-third of married workers feel that their jobs interfere with family life "somewhat" or "a lot." These workers are concerned about the amount of time they spend at work, inconvenient work schedules, and uncertainty about work schedules. They report that energy is sometimes lacking for family life, particularly among working wives with children. One-third of all respondents feel that their work and leisure activities interfere with each other "somewhat" or "a lot."

With the work force increasingly composed of workers to whom a balance of work and leisure is important, the relationship between the two may become a basic factor in measuring job satisfaction in the future.

In the earlier years of this century, there was little question about who was in charge in the working environment. Now questions are plentiful, because young people in America have changed their attitudes toward authority. In 1969 almost 70% of the young accepted authority with few reservations. Now a majority say that they need not take orders from a supervisor at work if they disagree with the orders. We have seen this change in attitude in schools, where youngsters openly disagree with and challenge their teachers. In fact, during 1976 approximately 65,000 teachers were physically attacked in their classrooms. We have also witnessed changes in the family, as parents have adopted more open relationships with their children to maintain consent and stability. These more permissive values have carried over into marriage, so the husband-wife relationship is undergoing a major transformation.

It would be peculiar if these changes in authority relationships did not spread to the workplace. But even as younger, more educated workers resent authoritarianism, they are not opposed to the proper exercise of authority. This distinction is quite important. They respect authority—properly exercised with restraint and rationality—but reject authority that is abusive or arbitrary. This poses a challenge to large bureaucratic organizations: can they rationalize their work procedures and learn the art of managing conflict with consent?

The decline in respect for authority is related to a growing mistrust of institutions. Business, government, labor, the church, and the military have all fallen in the general public esteem. This feeling of mistrust is most directed to the presidency and big business, the two American institutions that are believed to possess the greatest power in the country. Big business had seen a rise from 30% mistrust of corporations in 1968 to 70% by 1975.

The decline of the family, the church, and the small community has increased the importance of the workplace as an institution which can provide social support. Employers have an opportunity to provide genuine involvement with other people in a common enterprise and, in general, to make life more meaningful.

Questions of authority aside, we must also confront fundamental doubts about the moral value of work. The work ethic had its origins in the beginnings of Western civilization. The early Greeks regarded work as a curse. It suggested drudgery, heavy-heartedness, and exhaustion. For the Hebrews it was an atonement for the original sin. The early Christians followed this concept, considering work an act of expiation. Calvinism and Lutheranism both reinforced the link between work and religious values, producing the Protestant ethic that has prevailed among Americans.

Yet many people today are not as prepared to tolerate adverse conditions, hard, unrewarding work, and self-sacrifice for the promise of reward in the afterlife. This is not necessarily an antireligious view but is, rather, supported by the increased knowledge of the vastness of the universe and the growing skepticism about the immortality of man. Concern about thermonuclear weapons, dangerous chemicals, and threats to clean air and water add to basic insecurity. Thus, the deferred gratification of pleasure is less acceptable, and hedonism and narcissism are more in vogue. Young and middle-aged alike no longer accept work as a process of atonement or even as a self-contained goal in life.

In 1973, eight out of every ten American students believed that "it's very important to do any job well." Attitude surveys of youth have revealed consistently that the work ethic is strong and alive, despite the revolution in social values.[6] However, youth's appraisal of the traditional rewards of hard work has certainly changed. In 1967, 69% answered "yes" to the question "Does hard work always pay off?" By 1975, 75% of American students answered this question, "No." This view of the world of work is probably a reflection of attitudes at home. It may also be a judgment that many jobs are routine, dull, and boring and do not challenge the talents of the better-educated worker.

Work increasingly competes with leisure. Although the 40-hour workweek has remained relatively stable over the past three decades, people are generally more attracted to leisure pursuits. When work and leisure are compared as sources of satisfaction, only one out of five people state that work means more to them than leisure. The majority say that while they enjoy their work, it is not their major source of satisfaction. The remaining 19% are so exhausted by the demands of work that it is not even a minor source of satisfaction.

Over the past 10 years, there has been a remarkable increase in employees' desire to take part in decisions that affect their jobs. In 1977, 54% of the people surveyed in the Michigan study felt that it was their right to participate in such decisions. Among younger workers, 62% expressed this view. But it is not that employees want a vote in every corporate decision. Their interest is only in those managerial decisions that directly affect the content of their jobs.

Despite this narrow range of decisions about which employees want a voice, most managers are unwilling to share their decision-making power. As managers see themselves, they have too little authority and too much responsibility. Given that view, there is little willingness to divide authority with subordinates.

This poses a dilemma. Employees have moderate demands for participation in decision making, but the modern organization is structured to allow none at all. Sharing decision making is an art form. It requires a genuine belief in the value of the individual and a willingness to share responsibility. It is not necessary for management to give up its ultimate authority.

The era of rising entitlements has created widespread feelings among workers that jobs, incomes, employee benefits, and a higher standard of living are no longer privileges; they are seen as rights. Because of persistent inflation and rising taxes, American workers have been running hard to stay relatively in the same place during most of the 1970s. The Michigan survey confirms a steep decline in satisfaction with financial rewards and reports that the most problems exist in the areas of earned income and fringe benefits. In addition, significant declines appeared in the "very true" responses to the following statements:

The pay is good—declined 33%

Job security is good—declined 21%

Fringe benefits are good—declined 25%

Promotions are handled fairly—declined 28%

I have an opportunity to develop my own special abilities—declined 26%

Three benefits for which wage and salaried workers are most willing to give up a 10% increase in pay are: better retirement (54%), better medical insurance benefits (47%), and more paid vacation days (48%). The first two reflect the strong need for economic protection against the problems of old age and illness. The third, of course, comes from the desire for more leisure.

Beyond the issues about money, there is the question of industrial democracy. The modern organization is a total society in microcosm. Employees hold voluntary membership in these organizations. Living in a free and open democratic political system, the American worker expects conditions in the workplace to be compatible with political and social conditions in other aspects of life.

These expectations include the right to free speech, the right to privacy, the right to dissent, the right to fair and equitable treatment, and the right to due process in all work-related activities.

One disturbing finding in the Michigan survey is the revelation that 28% of American workers feel that their consciences are violated by the requirements of their jobs—the services they perform or the products they produce. The recent Civil Service reform legislation has launched a major experiment in democracy at work by creating a legitimate basis for "whistle blowers" within the federal establishment. This is a major development the private sector should monitor.

Democracy in the workplace does not mean the right of employees to elect supervisors, managers, or executives. The "one man, one vote" concept is unworkable where management and control are confined to the relatively few who have the executive authority and who are responsible for the destiny of the entire enterprise. There are those who would carry the concept of industrial democracy to such extremes, but this presupposes an undesirable change in the present laws regarding private property and the capitalist system.

During the 1980s, American organizations must advance the process of accommodation between economic and political institutions. They cannot grow and meet free-world competition for ideas and products if they repress human needs and expectations within their own ranks. Organizations that do so may survive, but they will not thrive.

More and more Americans want their work to be a balanced part of their entire lifestyle. Work schedules, travel demands, career pressures, and overtime, they believe, should be balanced with their needs and responsibilities for family, leisure, recreation, and self-renewal. For example, career advancement that requires geographical moves can disrupt family and personal stability. The workplace interacts with employees, their families, the community, and the society. It should do so as a positive force—for itself, its employees, and other people and institutions which it affects.

The complex interplay of changing employee attitudes, values, and expectations creates competition between work and other values in our society. The significant drop in job satisfaction cannot be isolated from the steady decline in the nation's productivity growth rate.

As the 1979 *Economic Report of the President* indicates, a large part of the worsening of inflation in the last year stemmed from poor productivity. Last year, America's productivity increased by less than 1%. During the last 10 years, the national productivity rate has fallen to slightly less than one-half of its historic rate of 3.2%. The reasons are complex and not fully understood, but the consequences have a direct effect on American expectations about improved living standards, better medical care, a strong national defense, and the enhancement of the quality of the environment.

The shocking fact is that the goals for the economy to 1983, as stated in the President's *Economic Report,* project shallow gains in productivity, with an average of slightly less than 1.5% per year. The report forecasts a gain of only .4% in 1979 and 1.1% in 1980. These goals set by the Administration may be realistic, but they certainly leave a great deal to be desired and fail to reflect any solution to our declining rate of productivity growth.

The slowdown in productivity growth has been attributed to shifts in the industrial composition of the economy, to changes in the composition of the labor force, to changes in the capital/labor ratios, to the leveling off of research and development expenditures, to the diversion of investment to pollution abatement expenditures, to the maturation of many industries with little new technology, and to changes in attitudes toward work.

Jerome Marks, Assistant Commissioner for Productivity and Technology of the Bureau of Labor Statistics, presented a detailed analysis of these factors at the Work in America Institute symposium in Chicago in 1978. He concluded that several factors often cited as sources of the slowdown, such as the shift from manufacturing to services and the changes in the capital intensity of the economy, have not played a large role. Instead, he singled out the end in the shift in employment from the farm to the nonfarm sector, the impact of additional investment needed to meet tougher government environmental regulations, and finally, the need to invest in energy saving or conversion of facilities because of higher energy costs.

Positive factors that may accelerate productivity growth are an expected increase in the more experienced age groups in the labor force and further improvements in the capital/labor ratio in the private sector. Productivity gains, in Marks's opinion, depend in large part on increased investment in the education and quality of the labor force, the amount and quality of capital stock and material inputs, and the application of new technology.

The human factor in productivity is subtle and usually underestimated, if not ignored. Yet productivity studies show that the human factor contributes from 10 to 25% of the productivity growth and often accounts for more than 50% of controllable costs. In major intensive service industries and government, people may account for as much as 70 to 85% of all costs. The manager who ignores the human side of the enterprise does so at his peril.

The changing nature of the labor force, the higher education and skills of workers, the growing specialization and professionalization of jobs, the shift to labor-intensive service industries, and the rising cost of wages and benefits have all combined to raise the labor stakes in the productivity game.

Labor's role in productivity growth is so fundamental, so obvious that managers often stare right past it. To put it bluntly, capital and technology by themselves produce nothing. A billing machine, a processing system, or even the most advanced computer is no more effective than the people managing and operating them want them to be or know how to make them be.

It has become the fashion to blame the slowdown in U.S. productivity on the decline in the American work ethic. Managers tend to be frustrated by their inability to increase worker involvement and commitment to the goals of the organization. The habit of laying the blame on employees is counterproductive, however. Certainly, employees produce problems of absenteeism, turnover, poor or marginal performance, or inattention to quality. The presence of grievances, slowdowns, overt labor difficulties, and problems of quality are strong distress signals that should alert managers to the need for prompt corrective action. Still, the marginal productivity of any group of workers in any office or factory is, first and foremost, the responsibility of managers.

With the growing tensions between work and society, it will become increasingly important in the decade ahead to develop innovative ways for repackaging work. The interest in and growing attention to alternative schedules are high. The concept includes variations of the 9-to-5 conventional workday. Most significant among these systems are flexible working hours, a shorter workweek, and experiments in work sharing, permanent part-time employment and job sharing, staggered hours, and the task system.

Although the concept of flexitime did not reach the United States until 1972, its growth and popularity have been remarkable. Between 2.5 and 3.5 million employees are estimated to be on flexitime, not counting self-employed people and many professional managers and salespeople who have long set their own hours without considering their schedules as flexitime. Yet, flexitime applies to a small fraction of the work force.

Alternative work patterns will get increased attention at the collective bargaining table. The classic concept of penalty pay for work on overtime, weekends, holidays, and shifts is changing. This is partly in response to the increased concern with occupational stress and the demands for leisure. In Europe we are witnessing a new focus of attention on shift work and its adverse effects on the biological cycles of human behavior. There is growing interest in legislation to bar or reduce shift work. At the same time, the rising capital investment, the growth of the electronic office, the heavy dependence on computers, and the potential energy saving of off-hour usage of this equipment are increasing the attractiveness of shift work to the employer.

We have already witnessed the early signals of a United Auto Workers' demand to supplement overtime premium pay with an added half-day's compensatory time for each day of overtime. This is equivalent to double time for all overtime; however, 50% of the premium would be distributed as increased leisure for the workers and increased employment for the other workers. This demand seeks to combine leisure with work sharing.

Most flexible and responsive work schedules and arrangements will represent a response to social needs without any capital costs, without change in established production techniques or office systems, but with a high potential for sustaining productivity. Probably one of the safest predictions for this decade is that the use of both flexitime and part-time employment will increase sharply.

The changing attitudes toward authority, the decline in confidence in institutions, and the post-religious society have all weakened the ironclad dedication to work as the first and ultimate goal in our society. The radical changes in our mores and folkways during the 1970s have affected society at large, but work organizations have responded much too slowly to these changes. The challenge of the 1980s lies in a more effective accommodation between society and the workplace.

REFERENCES

1. Richard B. Freeman, "The Work Force of the Future: An Overview," *Work in America: The Decade Ahead,* edited by Clark Kerr and Jerome M. Rosow (New York: Van Nostrand Reinhold, 1979).
2. Phillip L. Rones, "Older Men: The Choice Between Work and Retirement," *The Monthly Labor Review,* November 1978.
3. Freeman, "The Work Force of the Future."
4. Louis Harris Survey, January 1979.
5. Robert P. Quinn and Graham L. Staines, *The 1977 Quality of Employment Survey* (Ann Arbor, Mich.: Survey Research Center, Institute for Social Research, The University of Michigan, 1978).
6. Yankelovich, Skelly, and White, "Corporate Priorities, 1976–78."

SECTION THREE

Individual Lifestyles and the Work Environment

L ouis Harris leads this section from the vantage point of one whose business it is to take the American temperature. He reports a pervasive mutation of our social values, a phenomenon so robust that materialism is seriously on the wane as a motivator of human behavior. The new search, reports Harris, is for quality in the human experience. Given the hard choice, Americans would accept a lower standard of living over burgeoning technology and wasteful consumption.

As if in echo, Stewart Brand defends his home turf, Marin County, California. Often described as the headquarters of the new preoccupation with self, Marin is also a laboratory for what Brand calls "textured living," in which people "grow weary of responsibility to stuff and catch on to the pleasures of responsibility to lives." Behind the smokescreen of self-indulgence and fads, Brand insists, is a healthy movement toward attention to self and to others, a desire for control of one's life, and a willingness to take individual responsibility for it.

Ian Wilson introduces his vision of a society in which affluence, technology, and education have combined to produce citizens ready for a post-industrial society. The argumentative students of the 1960s are today's professionals, Wilson says, and they brought their values and desires through the 1970s largely intact. They will profoundly affect the workplace, using the law tactically to enforce equal opportunity, due process, conservation and environmental protection, and worker participation in corporate decision making.

"Raised for roots and permanence," writes Suzanne Keller, "we confront a world of transience and impermanence." There are frequent and glaring differences between what we were taught to believe and the society we are actually building by our behavior. These collisions are evident in the workplace, where worker desire for individual satisfaction and disillusionment with material striving are highly visible.

We also see the rise of new values in our changing perceptions about marriage and the traditional family. In the shift from the goods-producing economy to the service economy, Keller sees a social time bomb. With an even higher premium on education and skill, we may create an underclass of unemployed people who are, perhaps, doomed to perpetual unemployability. What price then will be our traditional view that work and reward are absolutely linked?

Cutting back against the grain of this section, James O'Toole calls us "The Irresponsible Society" and explains that in the assertion of many new rights and entitlements, we have bent the notion of personal responsibility beyond recognition. "Because of the increasing balance of payments deficits and the declining dollar," observes O'Toole, "Ameri-

121

can managers may no longer be able to afford to play golf on company time, and American workers may no longer be able to afford to goof off or sabotage cars on the assembly line."

Although he does not care for adversity as a motivator, O'Toole sees grim economic necessity as the most likely reason American workers and managers will turn back from preoccupation with entitlements to personal responsibility for high-quality work. But there is an intermediate possibility as well. Although taking away worker "rights" is not feasible, O'Toole believes, we could try building new worker responsibilities into the structure of working life. And his suggestions for doing that, we think, sound very like the demands for worker participation outlined elsewhere in this book.

There is much agreement in this section about the shape of our working future. In counterpoint, Theodore Gordon uses his "iconoclast's hunting license" to look beyond observable trends at the long shots in our changing styles of living and working. Among them: a change in the meaning of "retirement," a rise in the birth rate near the year 2000, and the advent of "conspicuous conservation" as one part of the solution to our intractable shortage of energy.

C.S.S.

D.C.C.

CHAPTER 12

Our Changing Structure of Values
Louis Harris

We are in a period of vast and sweeping change, most basically in our structure of values. Many of the values that once were totally accepted in modern life simply are not adhered to seriously by substantial majorities of Americans.

Let me report some of the thinking of our people today and then try to explore some of the implications for life in the twenty-first century:

- By 69–22%, people say they like individual experiences better than group experiences.
- By 73–23%, most Americans want to participate in community decisions that affect their lives.
- By 72–21%, people want to be involved in efforts where people cooperate and don't compete.
- By 89–8%, people seek out those experiences that make them feel peaceful inside.
- By 86–9%, people want to experience life directly, rather than observe it on television.
- By 84–13%, they welcome challenges to their own creative abilities.
- By 73–23%, they would rather live in open country than in the cities or suburbs.
- By 79–14%, they believe most other people are decent and honest.
- By 61–27%, they feel that modern technology has caused as many problems as benefits for people.

- By 71–18%, they would rather live in an environment that is clean than in an area with a lot of jobs.
- By 73–7%, they think the country would be better off if children were educated to find their own inner satisfaction than to get out in the world and be a success by making a lot of money.

Specifically, on the much discussed issue of economic growth, increasing the GNP, majorities feel this way:

- By 59–25%, people think such growth tends to overproduce products, which in turn leads to more waste.
- By 68–15%, they say growth makes us far too dependent on physical resources, which are running out.
- By 60–21%, economic growth falsely makes people want to acquire possessions rather than to enjoy nonmaterial experiences.
- By 56–27%, growth makes everything bigger and more impersonal.

Of course there will be exceptions to the limited potential of growth. The most notable is energy, where by 57–30%, a majority now thinks that expanded non-OPEC production will do more to solve the problem than conservation. Only a few years ago, no more than 41% saw energy relief coming from expanded production.

But growth remains suspect. Thus:

- By 79–17%, Americans say it is more important to teach people to live with basic essentials than to reach higher standards of living.
- By 77–15%, they prefer spending more time getting to know each other better as human beings than improving and speeding up our ability to communicate with each other through more advanced technology.
- By 63–29%, they feel it is more important to learn to appreciate human values over material values than it is to find ways to create more jobs for producing more goods.
- By 66–22%, Americans want more emphasis on breaking up big things and getting back to more humanized living than on developing bigger and more efficient ways of doing things.

Basically, less than a quarter of a century away from the year 2000, our people are far more concerned with the quality of human experience and far less with the unlimited acquisition of physical goods and products.

More than two in every three people admit they are highly wasteful, and 92% think we are going to have to find ways to cut back on the number of things we consume and waste. A substantial 71% think such a cutback will mean a cut in the U.S. standard of living. This subject is no longer an academic matter, for as a nation we are going to have to face the fact that we consume roughly 35% of the world's resources, although we are only 6% of the world's population.

These are radical findings by any measure, for they mean that the age of materialism as we have known it is going to be radically altered. When the choice is posed between changing our lifestyle to have less consumption of physical goods, on the one hand, and enduring the risks of continuing inflation and unemployment due to raw material shortages, on the other, by 71–12%, the American people opt for a change in lifestyle.

If such a cutback in material consumption is to be the order of the new day, then how will we avoid even harder times with people buying less and many jobs disappearing? This is not an easy question. Yet we are further along on this path than most of our leadership realizes today. Indeed, it is forgotten that even today roughly 65% of all employed people are not engaged in turning out physical goods and products. Instead, they hold down service jobs in communications, financial services, health services, education, recreation, transportation and travel, maintenance trades, and government.

In a world short of raw materials, it is not hard to predict that by the turn of the century employment will be 80 to 85% in the service trades. The economy will grow, and will be stimulated to grow, not by expanding our physical production but by expanding our service economy. And there is one very good reason for it: the most renewable resource on earth is the human resource. Turn on human creativity, and what we can produce in terms of services to our fellow man is boundless. Treat humankind well, replenish it and nurture it, and it is well nigh inexhaustible.

We are entering a new era where the human dimension will be the most critical in the minds of our people. Above all, it will be a pluralistic world, for a powerful lesson of Watergate was to teach us just how precious is the right to be different. Dialogue has taken on new meaning. People want "in" on the process, not "out." They want the gates of power opened up to let them in. They don't want to wait for the pearly gates of St. Peter later on.

Over the next 20 years, key segments of our population will struggle to find ways to enter the mainstream. I mean the racial minorities who still feel largely shut out, women who are determined to be part of the work force and to be treated equally on the job and in their career opportunities, older people who want to work until the day they die and to make a contribution to society. This last group, at least, has solid support; by 86–12%, a sizable majority feels that people should work as long as they wish with no restriction due to age, provided they can hold down jobs.

There are also the handicapped, who have been largely dumped into alleys of special confinement and now want to join the rest of the human race, and the young. The problems for the young will be how to obtain ample opportunities to work in the first place and how to advance when older people stay on the job into their 70s and 80s as our population grows older.

Not only are we getting older as a nation, but we are rapidly changing our work force. Most women now work. They make up 41% of the work force now and, being 53% of the population, are going to bid fair to be a majority of those gainfully employed. Women feel discriminated against in the wages they are paid, but men do not think they are. Women feel discriminated against in getting promoted into managerial jobs, but men do not think they are. Women feel discriminated against in getting credit, loans, and mortgages, but men disagree. A basic new fact of life is that women are playing for keeps in the employment arena. Jobs are no longer a short interlude between school and marriage. Women want "into" the economic process, not "out."

We see this desire on the part of the people to participate in the economy when we examine the phenomenon of consumerism. Here is a partial roll call of the worries consumers have these days: 82% are worried about the poor quality of many products, 77% about the feeling that many manufacturers don't care about them, 81% about the failure of many companies to live up to claims made in their advertising, 69% about too many products breaking or going wrong soon after they bring them home. In addition, 63% worry about too many products being dangerous, 67% about misleading packaging or labeling, 65% about inadequate guarantees or warranties, and 73% about the poor quality of after-sales service and repairs.

On every one of these dimensions, the number who feel that way has increased just in the past two years. A massive 85% of the public today say they would support an organized consumer group that was set up locally to put pressure on all retailers who sold products of a certain manufacturer that the group felt were inferior or harmful.

The work we have done in the consumer field indicates clearly that the day when organized consumers sit down to collective bargaining sessions with producers of goods and services is not far off. The next century surely will see bargaining agreements between the producers and consumers, much as we now have collective bargaining between employers and unions.

When we recently asked people about their future lifestyles, 83% saw a big rise in do-it-yourself repairs and construction, 76% in smaller families, 67% in self-service gasoline stations, 65% in fast-food restaurants, and 58% in widespread psychological counseling. Comparable majorities do not see a rise in popularity for long hair for men, wearing jeans, informal manners, and unisex clothing.

One critical value change in this new, less materialistic era is that time and its expenditure will become more precious than material acquisition. More and more, people report to us that there are more options to which they must commit time than there is time to commit. This means that one of the key decision processes people in the future are going to have to go through is how to decide to commit to what is worthwhile. The idea of *saving* time is not of great value to people, but the concept of *gaining* time is one of the higher orders of priority in the emerging world. In the future, people will spend freely of their money to obtain the necessary time to do what they want, much more than they will just to acquire more physical products.

In the area of power and politics, the world is going to have to develop better ways of controlling the proliferation of nuclear weaponry, or there just might not be any world left by the year 2000. Superpowers with overkill in the nuclear area are going to have to give up some of their exclusive prerogatives in this area and will have to form a kind of international joint chiefs of staff to control future nuclear wars or, to put it practically, to find fail-safe ways to avoid them. We are still "between the quick and the dead," as Bernard Baruch told the United Nations in 1946.

Yet, with this development, there is not likely to be a withering away of national identities of countries. It is entirely likely that smaller, conventional wars, stemming from hunger and ideological and religious differences, will continue to take place in the Third World well into the twenty-first century.

There will be radical changes here at home. One will be in the role of cities, which are going to see a resurgence. The crucial fact about cities is that they are hidden from sight: they are *the* hub of employment and economic decision making in this country. For example, when suburban residents go to a movie, 53% of the time they go to a city; when they go to a cultural event, 53% of these trips are to the city; when they buy furniture or a major appliance, 46% of the time they go to a city, not a suburban store; when they buy new clothes, 48% of the time it is in a city store; 50% of the times that they go out for dinner, they go to a city restaurant rather than one in the suburbs; when they attend religious services, 44% of such attendance is at a house of worship in the city; when they visit friends socially, 47% of the visits are in the city, not the suburbs; when they go to a doctor, 52% of the calls are to a doctor in the city.

The implication is clear. Cities are going to have to be financed in the future *not* by a shrinking tax base of city residents but by use of taxes under which people who use city services will have to pay.

In this country, it is entirely probable that the role of government is going to change. This change is likely to find government serving as the mediator between competing and conflicting forces but not as the prime mover or prime initiator of new social and economic programs. Government will still have to be a power of last resort in crises, some of which are likely to center on the suddenly discovered shortage of potable water and in other countries the well-known long-term shortage of food. Ironically, by the turn of the century, we may well be on our way toward energy self-sufficiency, if we can survive the next two decades of insufficiency.

A major change is likely to take place in the way public needs are tied to the private sector. If government is unlikely to grow much bigger, and indeed is likely to level out, as are the social welfare benefits derived from government, then government will be the central pivot in quite another and even radical way. It is possible that with the advent of the six-year single term for our presidents, we will also see the adoption of a kind of national convocation through which representatives of assorted segments of our population will settle on the major objectives for our society. These broad objectives will be quite specific. Today, they would include conservation of energy; containment of inflation; a clean-up of the environment; establishment of better safety standards in employment and in products and services; and equal employment opportunities for racial minorities, women, the handicapped, the elderly, and the young.

Instead of government handing down fiats in these fields, it is likely that a system of incentives will be developed to make it worthwhile for the private sector to see the goals realized. The principle would be that in environmental clean-up, for example, if corporations and institutions live up to certain standards, they receive tax breaks. But if they want to flaunt the standards, they risk increasingly higher taxes, even to the point of confiscation.

This principle will be applied to creation of jobs during times of high unemployment; to raising prices and wages in times of high inflation; to employing minorities and women, the handicapped, and the elderly; to living up to safety standards in products and services and working conditions; and to conservation of energy. To be sure, society will pay for these objectives being realized, but they will be executed largely through the private rather than the public sector. When we have tested this concept, majorities ranged from 2–1 to 10–1 in favor of it. This means, of course, that socialism is unlikely to gain much ground in this country or in other Western developed countries. In more emerging Third World areas, however, state control may well gain.

One area where this incentive system is likely to be employed is in health services. The basic concept of health maintenance organizations, HMOs, now is favored by a 77–10% majority of the American people. Under this system, health care is concentrated in health units that can service nearly all the health and medical needs of people in an area. People pay private insurance fees for this service. When they begin, all will pay the same fee. After one year those who have maintained their health with a minimum of need for special health care will pay a smaller fee, while those who maintain poorer health will pay a higher fee. Again, this is the basic incentive principle at work. Such an alternative now is far more likely to be adopted on a massive scale than either comprehensive national health insurance or the present status quo. This is an idea that should be almost universal by the turn of the century.

Americans have never been really ideological, except to rise up when their basic pluralism and freedom to do their own thing are threatened. The big political divisions of the future are likely to be between those who advocate a higher and higher material standard of living, on the one hand, and those who feel that such a rise in material acquisition is less important and that the quality of human experience is far more important. In this lineup, old-fashioned "New Deal" liberals and old-fashioned materialistic conservatives are likely to find themselves on the same side. Indeed, just such divisions are beginning to shape up in our politics today.

By contrast, those who believe the prime aim of life is to realize a creative nonmaterialistic quality of experience and who reject traditional appeals of economic self-interest are likely to be drawn together in a new coalition, supported by groups of minorities, the elderly, women, the handicapped, and consumerists. Such a coalition will, at one and the same time, be made up of the most and the least privileged in society. This coming conflict could alter radically the present party structures and organizations, albeit we would still elect a congress, a president, and other key officers to man the government.

We are rapidly losing the economic determinism of our politics. In the future, redistribution of the opportunities to partake of quality of life experiences, to join together in new common causes to enhance the living of life instead of simply redistributing wealth, is likely to be the focus of the American scene. In the world, however, the press for redistribution of wealth will probably continue well into the twenty-first century.

What I have reported comes out of my own professional experience, from putting a sensitive ear to the ground to try to pick up in considerable depth what is going on in the minds of our own people and those in the more developed world.

The past surely is prologue, and history may not be a very accurate teacher. Our destiny is largely in our own hands. That is both the most dangerous and at the same time the most hopeful fact of all. The human dimension has taken over from the notion that physical or supernatural forces have decided what our destiny shall be. It does not mean that man can live without faith or religion. It does mean that the essential, critical decisions still remain for man to make.

CHAPTER 13

Texture in Living and Working
Stewart Brand

I 'm assuming approximately what Herman Kahn and friends foresee in *The Next 200 Years*—relative continuity from the present through 2025 for Americans, and somewhat increasing prosperity. In other words, we will lead lives more governed by choice than by necessity.

As a resident of Marin County, the wealthy rural bedroom community north of San Francisco, I'm aware of the grim burden of new affluence and leisure—self-preoccupation, fads, guilt, alcoholism, excessive display, erratic loyalty, the usual lot reported in NBC's "I Want It All Now."

But in the same community, I'm aware of a high degree of commitment to service and considerable innovation in the forms of service. This county has one of the nation's first hospices for home care of the terminally ill, a most subtle and worthy Buddhist monastery (open to the public), and a quite effective organization offering free professional entertainment to local prisons, hospitals, nursing homes, mental institutions, and so on—founded and run by a successful popular singer. All three of these groups have earned national reputations.

Marin County's service and dissipation are not contradictory, or even paradoxical. The one solves the other in each individual life that grows weary of responsibility to stuff and catches on to the pleasures of responsibility to lives.

That's one light on what I'm calling texture. Texture is attention to detail. You can't have it unless you have time and continuity. If you have both, you almost can't avoid it. People in this frame of mind can quit smoking because they can notice the nuances of life that addiction blunts. Beyond a certain point even the profit motive fades and sometimes reverses. Rather than buying, many people focus on making, partly for the fun of it, partly because their new experience of quality suggests that they can make better than they can buy—from harpsichords to service for the car.

Texture in the workplace, at least in my workplace and the ones I ally with, means greater continuity of staff, more familial amenities (in our case daily volleyball and home cooking for lunch), more individual choices of hours and vacation, more individual responsibility for tasks, less supervision from above and perhaps more by peers, more personal service to customers, greater attention to integrity, more casual intimacy between responsibility levels, clearer role definition, more good suggestions, a messier office (with sporadic purges), more gossip, and less politics.

I'd say that texture is good for the workplace. Get all you can. Once begun, it feeds itself.

Texture naturally extends to the community. People who live and work attentively are less patient with poor schools, parks, shops, town administration, and they are dangerously well equipped to do something about it. They are formidable when opposing something, and often effective at the harder task of building something.

One of the driving forces of finely textured lifestyle are elites, in what I claim is a good sense of the word. Elites are people defining for each other what good is by their actions. It is the way humans use each other to surpass themselves. In your case, it is the people you keep an eye on and who keep an eye on you, and whose esteem means more than money.

Besides their value to the members, elites are potent forces for excellence in the community at large. The more the better—then any ill effects from their strengths will offset each other.

What are the drawbacks of textured living? Well, it may be microinnovative, but it's macroconservative—aware of pace and determined to slow down the great brutal swerves of abstract economics, ideas, politics. Personally, for example, I like the idea of space colonies, but the textured readers of *CoEvolution* detest them, doubt their motives, and fear their consequences. Such conservatism may be needed now. It redresses a balance.

The most conspicuous failing of self-conscious living Tom Wolfe accurately needled as the "Me Decade." It will outlast the decade. And people will continue to use it to dismiss the massive healthy movement going on behind its smokescreen. That's fine. Whether or not individuals are Freudian, societies undoubtedly are. Denial precedes acceptance.

And close attention to self, by its very limitations, precedes close attention to others. It leads to responsibility, though by a different route than usual. This responsibility is sought; it is perceived as part of the textured fabric of life and . . . joined.

CHAPTER 14

The Mosaic Society

Ian H. Wilson

With change occurring at an accelerated pace in a highly complex, interdependent world, forecasting is a chancy business. Yet this very change imposes on us the need to venture into the forecasting business if we are to have any chance of managing, rather than being managed by, these forces.

Generally speaking, we would be better advised to think in terms of alternative future possibilities rather than make outright predictions. One prediction that *can* be made with virtual certainty, however, is that the "melting pot society" of the United States, with connotations of unification and homogeneity (always of dubious accuracy), will give way to the "mosaic society," a highly segmented and differentiated pattern of some 260 million individuals in the year 2000.

For the United States, the change starts with the fact that we are experiencing an historic transition in society, the likes of which has occurred only a handful of times in the history of man.

This so-called "post-industrial transition" is truly a systemic change. It is compounded of social, political, economic, and technological forces. It affects both individuals and institutions. In many of its aspects, it is worldwide in reach.

A comparable transition took place when man the hunter and nomad became man the settled farmer; again, when life in cities—civilization, in its literal sense—became the norm; and again when the agricultural society gave way to the industrial society. Now our society is on the brink of becoming something different, a form of society that the world has not seen before.

Although the term "post-industrial" is not very descriptive of the form of society we may become, it does accurately indicate one of its

134

developing features, namely, the relative decline of manufacturing industry as the primary motive force of the economy. From now on, manufacturing's share of employment and gross national product will steadily decline. As early as 1985, for instance, we shall be able to produce all the "things" our society needs—all the food, fibers, and ores (except for what we import); all the buildings; all the machines and consumer products—with less than a quarter of our work force, or less than 10% of our population.

The major growth area of the post-industrial society will be the service sector of our economy—education, communications, health care, leisure and cultural activities, the professions, government, and nonprofit institutions. Small wonder, then, that this basic change in the character and structure of work should be causing some revision of our traditional attitudes toward work.

Predominant among the characteristics of this post-industrial society are increasing levels of affluence, education, and technology. All three have, of course, been features of our society for many years. However, when an established trend continues to have force as an agent of social change, its future implications may still have an element of novelty—even, almost, of revolution. At a critical point, a difference in degree may lead to a difference in kind. These three forces seem now, like a nuclear reactor, to have reached a point of criticality, at which a new chain reaction of attitudes and trends starts.

The first of these newly critical forces—affluence—is a good illustration. As a rough rule of thumb, per capita income has doubled every generation since 1800. Thus, in the five generations from 1800 to the mid-1960s, per capita income has grown from $200 to $400 to $800 to $1600 to $3200 in constant dollars. The quantitative results of this affluence to date are well known. But who can doubt that a *qualitative* difference will ensue if this generational doubling continues in the future, to $6400; $12,800; $25,600. . . . ?

More significant than changes in income levels and consumption patterns are the prospective changes in ways of thinking about one's self and one's world. We can see this in the increasing emphasis being placed on quality rather than mere quantity—the switch from "more" to "better." We can also note some changing attitudes toward work and leisure.

In part, these changes may be due to changes in the character of work—the move from manufacturing to services, for instance—but they are also a consequence of the fact that there is no longer the same grinding necessity to strive for survival and security. We seem to be raising our sights to a higher level, at which we can choose among types of work and consider leisure as a valid activity in its own right. It is this sense of affluence and choice that has contributed to a growing impatience with the progress we have so far made in resolving our social problems. We are impatient with all forms of economic hardship, social injustice, and inequity.

Probably nothing has been more characteristic of the U.S. economy in the past 30 years than the application of technology to industrial systems. It will probably continue to be a distinguishing characteristic of the post-industrial society, so much so that Zbigniew Brzezinski coined the alternative title, the "technetronic age." However, almost certainly the future does not hold simply more of the same in this regard. One might say that the high-water mark of the "old" technology occurred in 1969 with the landing on the moon, while millions around the world watched as it happened. Since that time we have become convinced that nothing is technically impossible.

Yet, at almost the same time as this technical victory, there has been a widespread questioning of the nature, value, and the extent of technological progress. At one level we are developing a heightened awareness of some of the negative environmental and societal consequences of technical developments, insisting that "better" replace "more" as our motto. At another level we ask "Do we *have* to do it, simply because we can do it? Does 'can' imply 'ought'?"

Although it is improbable that society will ever totally reject technology, it is certain that we will experience a redefinition of its aims and purposes and a redrawing of the limits within which it will be allowed to operate. Societal and environmental concerns will not be a passing fad; they are strong and developing forces inherent in the type of society we are building.

The last of these three "old/new" forces is education. Like affluence, it shapes our lives in physical terms (more schools, more courses, rising expenditures, changing curricula and methodology) and changes our attitudes. Rising levels of education, particularly since World War II, have done much to raise the spirit of individualism and the level of questioning of dogmatic thinking and authority. The better educated person of today has more self-respect. He or she wants to be treated as an individual, is far less tolerant of authoritarianism and arbitrary organizational restraints, and has different and higher expectations of what he or she wants to put into a job—and to get out of it.

It was no coincidence that the first clash between the new culture and old institutions should occur on the campuses of colleges and uni-

Table 3. Population by Age Group and Annual Rates Change[a] (Census Series II)

Age Group \ Year	1960	1965	1970	1975	1980	1985	1990
Under 20	69.5	76.3	77.2	74.6	70.5	69.6	72.0
%	3.0	1.9	0.2	−0.7	−1.1	−0.2	0.7
20−24	11.1	13.7	17.2	19.2	20.9	20.5	17.9
%	0.8	4.3	4.6	2.3	1.7	−0.4	−2.6
25−29	10.9	11.3	13.7	16.9	18.9	20.6	20.2
%	1.6	0.7	3.9	4.3	2.3	1.7	−0.4
30−34	12.0	11.1	11.6	14.0	17.2	19.3	20.9
%	−0.8	−1.5	0.8	3.8	4.3	2.3	1.6
35−44	24.2	24.4	23.1	22.8	25.7	31.4	36.6
%	1.1	0.2	−1.1	−0.3	2.4	4.0	3.1
45−54	20.6	21.8	23.3	23.8	22.7	22.4	25.3
%	1.7	1.2	1.3	0.4	−0.9	−0.2	2.4
55−64	15.6	17.1	18.7	19.8	21.2	21.7	20.8
%	1.3	1.8	1.8	1.2	1.4	0.5	−0.9
Over 65	16.7	18.4	20.1	22.4	24.9	27.3	29.8
%	2.8	2.0	1.7	2.2	2.2	1.8	1.8
Total Population	180.6	194.3	204.9	213.5	222.2	232.8	243.5
%	1.7	1.5	1.1	.8	.8	1.0	.9

[a] Levels in millions—Rates of change are calculated for 5-year intervals. The boxed pattern highlights the impact of the postwar baby boom.

Source. GE Economic Research and Forecasting, based on data from the U.S. Bureau of the Census.

versities. Given the onset of radical change, the numbers of the postwar "baby boom" and the effect of higher education on personal values and attitudes, such a clash was inevitable. Since then, the ripple effect has spread downward into the educational system, affecting high schools and junior highs, and outward into the world of work, government, community life, and personal and family lifestyles.

The changing demographics of the U.S. population will be perhaps the most potent social force for changing lifestyles and the work environment. The preeminent fact will be the maturing of our society. The largest growth rates, which were focused on the young 20s in the 1960s and on the 25- to 34-year-old cohort in the 1970s, will occur among 35 to 45-year-olds in the 1980s (and the 45 to 55-year-olds in the 1990s). As a result, the median age of our population, which was 29 in 1977, will increase to 33 by 1990.

The passing of the youth culture will go hand in hand with the maturing of the post-World War II baby boom. The generation of 1946–1965 (the peak period of the baby boom) will be, by 1990, a force of nearly 80 million young adults (between the ages of 25 and 44), nearly one-third of the total population. This is the generation that has already had far-reaching effects—on the growth of suburbia, on schools, on teenage markets, on university and college education—as they moved through successive stages of life. Can we really doubt that they will continue to have profound effects on companies, unions, consumer markets, politics, and public policy as they become fully absorbed into the work force and electorate?

The principal perspective on this generation is to see them for what they will be—the "quiet revolution from within" for many organizations. The students who manned the campus barricades or marched in protest against racism or the Vietnam War in the late 1960s and early 1970s have passed into history. They are becoming, very largely, the career professionals of the 1980s. The tactics of violent confrontation have been laid aside, for now at least. This seeming quiescence appears to be lulling many managers into the mistaken belief that these former agitators have been disciplined by the 1974–1975 recession and the demands of job and family and are now settling down to traditional patterns of organizational behavior and career development.

Nothing could be further from the future truth. The tactics of the 1960s are being replaced by the strategy of legalism, which can lead to confrontations no less traumatic for the institutions against which it may be directed. These young professionals are discovering, for instance, how to play the corporation at its own game, but for their purposes. The tactics are now:

- The leverage of education and professional expertise.
- The strict interpretation of corporate policies, in which statements of good intention can come back to haunt the corporation.
- The stockholder proposal.
- Even so mundane a weapon as the suggestion awards program.
- The political initiative.
- Legal action, including the class-action suit.
- As a final resort, the tactics of peaceful confrontation, including the boycott and sit-in.

And what are this new generation's purposes likely to be? If they are indeed the children of their times, their goals and issues will include equal opportunity; employee rights; the rights of other corporate constituencies; due process; continuing educational opportunities; openness in attitude and in communication; conservation and environmental protection; and, perhaps above all, participation—that forceful trend about which so much has already been written.

Beyond the hard numbers of population growth and mix, we come to the "soft"—but still significant—area of changing personal and societal values. Perhaps because of its subjective nature, this topic has attracted some highly emotional or ambiguous slogans—"erosion of the Puritan ethic," "counterculture" (Roszak), "entitlement ethic" (Yankelovich), "new paradigm" (Harman). Yet it is possible to move beyond the confusion and emotionalism to speculate about what is really afoot. These changes in values are neither illusory nor transitory; they are rooted in some basic structural shifts in our society and the world, including the shifts in affluence, education, and technology already mentioned.

One way of anticipating probable changes in values, attitudes, and behavior is to view them as the consequences of a progression, on a national scale, up Maslow's hierarchy of needs. The late Abraham Maslow postulated that we could arrange man's needs in a hierarchy of five levels:

1 Physiological needs (for food, shelter, warmth, etc.).
2 Safety and security needs (to induce a measure of stability into one's environment; to secure the physiological gains already achieved).
3 Social needs (for giving and receiving love and friendship; for being part of something larger than oneself).
4 Ego needs (for self-respect, independence, achievement, status, recognition).
5 Self-actualization needs (to realize one's full human potential).

This model of human needs is useful as a predictor of attitudes and behavior because progression tends to be upward on the scale—from the first to the fifth level—rather than random. Since man is a creature of seemingly endless needs, we can predict that when one need has been satisfied another will appear in its place. The levels are progressively less essential in terms of sheer survival and more important in terms of living at one's fullest human potential.

History seems to validate the Maslow hypothesis at both the national and the individual levels. It is possible, for instance, to plot the position on the hierarchy of each nation according to the level or levels at which the majority of its people live. Thus, virtually all the populations of the underdeveloped nations exist at the survival or security level, while in the United States the majority of the vast middle class operates on the basis of social or ego needs.

When discussing shifts in national values, some gross oversimplifications have to be made, yet it should be possible to predict major trends and changes in emphasis. In a society as complex and varied as the United States, the population cannot be slotted at one level only, for there are people operating at all levels. A profile of the population makeup, with its various modes of living, will thus be needed to represent the full range of values, and future changes in the profile will be indicative of shifting value systems.

As a start, it is possible to predict that there will be fewer people in the poverty class and so a reduction of emphasis on survival and safety needs. At the other end of the spectrum, increasing affluence, higher education, and the changing composition of the labor force will mean an increase in emphasis on social, ego, and self-fulfillment needs.

Focusing on levels 3 and 4, it is possible to note an upward shift within the range in the recent past and to project further movement in the future. The 1950s might well be characterized as a decade of belongingness and conformity, a time during which perhaps half the adult population operated at level 3. In the 1960s the new emphasis on college education and the growth of professional and technical personnel brought increased emphasis on knowledge, competence, professional recognition, and status. Forces for the future indicate a growth in the level 4 population to a point where it approximates in numbers that at level 3. Combined, these two segments would account for perhaps two-thirds of our total adult population.

If we combine the evidence of impending trends with the deductions that can be drawn from the Maslow thesis, it is possible to construct a profile of some of the more significant value changes that may occur. In our work at General Electric we have attempted to plot some value-shift possibilities in graphic form. This chart should be viewed not as a detailed scientific measurement but merely as a useful way of looking at the future. Its plottings are meant to be indicative, rather than definitive.

Profile of Significant Value System Changes: 1970-1985

	1970	1985	
War (military might)			Peace (economic development)
Nationalism			Internationalism
Federal government			State/local government
Public enterprise			Private enterprise
Organization			Individual
Uniformity/conformity			Pluralism
Independence			Interdependence
Sociability			Privacy
Materialism			Quality of life
Status quo/permanence/routine			Change/flexibility/innovation
Future planning			Immediacy
Work			Leisure
Authority			Participation
Centralization			Decentralization
Ideology/dogma			Pragmatism/nationality
Moral absolutes			Situation ethics
Economic efficiency			"Social justice"
Means (esp. technology)			Ends (goals)

———————— 1970 Values profile

■——————— 1985 Values profile

Source. *Our Changing Business Environment: A Reevaluation, 1969,* General Electric Company

To point up the possible attitudinal changes as dramatically as possible, the chart on page 141:

- Has been made up of contrasting pairs of values. To a greater or lesser extent enhancement of one value implies a diminution of the other—for example, war versus peace; conformity versus pluralism. Each society and generation has tended to seek its own new balance between these contrasting pairs, with the weight shifting from one side to the other as conditions and attitudes change.
- Emphasizes the value changes likely to be most prevalent among the trendsetting segment of the population—young, well educated, relatively affluent, "committed." These are the people organizations recruit for the managerial and professional talent they require.

On the chart are plotted two value profiles, one representing the approximate balance struck in 1970 by these trendsetters between each pair of values; the other indicating the hypothetical balance that might be struck in 1985. It is important to stress that the chart attempts to predict value changes, not events. Even though trendsetters may value, say, arms control agreements, events may lag behind their influence, perhaps because of political thinking of the electorate as a whole, or lie outside their control, as in the case of regional wars among developing nations.

It is important to stress that I am not talking about "new" values. It would indeed be remarkable if, after many millennia on this earth, mankind had truly discovered a "new" value. What we shall be encountering might more accurately be described as a New Reformation —a major re-formation or re-ordering of our public and private value systems. The major elements of this prospective reordering can be discerned in the shifts in emphasis:

- From considerations of quantity ("more"), toward considerations of quality ("better").
- From the concept of independence, toward the concept of interdependence (of nations, institutions, individuals, all natural species).
- From mastery over nature, toward living in harmony with it.
- From competition, toward cooperation.

- From doing and planning, toward being.
- From the primacy of technical efficiency, toward considerations of social justice and equity.
- From the dictates of organizational convenience, toward the aspirations of self-development in an organization's members.
- From authoritarianism and dogmatism, toward participation.
- From uniformity and centralization, toward diversity, pluralism, and decentralization.
- From the concept of work as hard, unavoidable, and a duty, toward work as purposeful and self-fulfilling, and a recognition of leisure as a valid activity in its own right.

There seems, too, to be a general backing away from an automatic acceptance of the presumed benefits of increases in scale, centralization, and standardization. There is substantial evidence of a movement toward the opposite pole—which would suggest, if we believe in some form of social change dialectic, that the future will lie somewhere between these two poles. The signals of this emerging trend can be simply catalogued:

- The new value that is being placed on individualism and pluralism, in lifestyles and political action.
- The growing desire for human scale (in our buildings, our communities, our technical projects), in the face of increasing scale in the real world.
- The growing demand for more control over our personal lives, whether expressed as "participation" in the work environment or "citizen action" in politics.
- A movement away from representative democracy toward participatory democracy.
- Increasing demands for a devolution of political power to regional or ethnic groups within countries (in the United States this shows up in the "new federalism" and in the growing tendency of states to behave as if they were sovereign nations).
- A preference for decentralized projects over centralized, smaller scale over larger scale, "soft" technologies over "hard," labor-intensive projects over capital-intensive.

Some of this evidence is episodic and tentative, but it all adds up to something, I am sure. Whatever name we give it, this development is consistent with certain other, better documented trends in our socio-political environment. It is consistent, for instance, with what we know of public attitudes toward large institutions. The Harris survey has documented over the years the dramatic decline of public confidence in the leadership of large institutions.

It is consistent, too, with the growing popularity of "networking" among individuals and smaller institutions. This would seem to be a rational reaction to the slow crisis of complex institutions, and a clear preference for multicentered flexibility over monolithic structure. Finally, it is consistent with the movement of women into positions of power and responsibility. Women seem to have an innate preference for decentralization and smaller scale, not in any sense of cuteness but as an intuitive sensing of what so often seems to make for better working relationships.

If I am right about the sensing of this trend, there is much that we need to be planning for. We need to think through the implications, systematically looking, for example, at possible changes in organizational structure, the scale of future plants and offices, the individualization of employee pay and benefit programs, the segmentation of consumer markets, new patterns of technological development, and shifts in the nature and focus of business–government relationships.

These are but a few of the pieces in a complex mosaic of interacting trends that are likely to reshape our values, our behavior, our institutions, and our society over the next 30 years. Above all, we must remember that it is not the individual trends but the overall pattern (the complex weaving together of trends) on which we must try to focus. For that is what will make up, as it always has done, the fabric of our lives in the twenty-first century.

CHAPTER 15

Shifting Values: New Choices and Old Dilemmas
Suzanne Keller, Ph.D.

The future is here. And so are prospective lunar resources, space factories, and elaborate planetary networks. New gadgets beckon to the imagination in a cosmic marketplace, and exquisite robots dance across ever less mysterious heavens.

These technological marvels astound and dazzle, to be sure, but what of their human dimensions? What, if any, difference will they make in our lives?

When we scan current futurist writings, it is clear that people are more willing to anticipate a new technology than new social institutions and values. This is true even for such imaginative science fiction films as *Star Wars* and *2001*—where all else is changed, but human passions and foibles stay the same. It would seem that individuals will vault into space and yet retain the social and moral systems of the prespace era, as if major technological changes could occur without changes in human nature and institutions.

Admittedly, it is difficult to anticipate moral and social futures, but there is all the more reason to do so. It is difficult because most of us lack the detachment needed to assess our social arrangements and beliefs. Any discussion about the future must deal not only with external developments but also with the internal barriers to awareness that limit our ability to see the tomorrows in which we will live.

Futurist writings vary greatly as to scope and ideological commitment. Some opt for more and more technology, while others give priority to new and humanitarian values.

This division is clear in three well-known, large-scale scenarios, each attempting to depict the same future but in dramatically different ways.

There is Daniel Bell's post-industrial society, with its sharply altered division of labor, computers, electronic communication, and the predominance of science-based knowledge.[1] Surprisingly, in retrospect, this scenario does not deal with the energy and resource costs of post-industrial society, nor with the idea that growth is limited—the very focus of the second scenario written by the Club of Rome.

In two reports[2], the second less drastic than the first, the Club of Rome carefully reviews the idea of growth, with the conclusion that unlimited growth can no longer be sustained. Report number two would have us distinguish two types of growth processes—(1) undifferentiated growth and (2) its opposite, organic growth, or growth *with* differentiation. The first is undesirable, the second, desirable. A multilevel, regionally diversified world, it is argued, needs a diversified growth policy—with growth for some, no growth for others.

The last proposal to be touched on is that of the late E. F. Schumacher, whose book, *Small is Beautiful,*[3] has become a worldwide best seller.

Largely addressing the Third World, Schumacher argues a radical thesis which would have that world reject Western models of development and their heavy capital investments, advanced technology, mass production, and centralized planning. He would have them follow a different route, reversing the priorities that put production first and human satisfactions later or profitability ahead of spiritual nourishment.

Schumacher opposes bigness for its own sake and abstractions like GNP that ignore the human realities of poverty, alienation, congestion, and ugliness. He would compel us to look at the neglected majorities in the developing countries who continue to live in the premodern world, tasting little of the fruits of industrialism. Although he believes in development, in his view it does not start with goods, with buildings, or with impressive machines, but with people—their education, development, and discipline.

Schumacher thus came to advocate the use of intermediary technologies that would provide work, livelihood, and opportunities for the poor right where they live and with the modest means at their disposal.

What is striking about these three prognoses is that while they disagree on important matters and have different emphases, they agree on certain fundamentals: the world is changing; it is changing profoundly;

it is changing not only its technology but its ways of work and leisure, values, and family life.

In other words, we must take the future seriously and get ready now for our rendezvous with destiny.

One way to get ready is to inform ourselves of the developments ahead, for example, as in the three topics for advanced industrial societies which I have chosen to discuss: (1) changing patterns of work, (2) the changing family, and (3) new values.

As Bell and others have stressed, we are seeing a shift in the prevailing patterns of work—from manufacturing and manual occupations to service, technical, and professional occupations. Services here refer not only to management and business but to health, education, leisure, and self-enhancement activities.

In 1970 for the first time more Americans were employed in business and professional services than in manufacturing. Though the margin was slim (20,143,525 vs. 19,864,209), more people were providing services than were producing goods.[4]

A similar shift at the lower occupational levels shows that between 1950 and 1972 white-collar jobs increased by 70%, blue-collar jobs by only 17%.[5] Incidentally, computer specialists, 254,537 of them, made their formal debut with the 1970 census.

Another trend concerns the hours on the job. There is the four-day workweek, already used by some 10,000 companies, and there is flexitime, which has been quite successful where it has been tried. Each has its pros and cons.

The pros of the four-day workweek are long weekends; the cons are long (10-hour) workdays. Such long hours are too hard for some individuals and groups and do not fit the needs of those such as working mothers who have fixed outside obligations.

Flexitime, which gives workers the right to adjust the beginnings and endings of their workdays, is apparently very successful. It increases the individual's sense of personal control on the job as well as his or her productivity and morale. It also reduces rush-hour traffic. Some 5000 European enterprises employing one million persons have introduced flexitime to date. In America, relatively few companies have done so, but more will be trying it out.[6] While the advantages are obvious, not every firm is sufficiently flexible for such an arrangement.

Perhaps most significantly, we are witnessing a change in the incentive and reward system and in the expectations of what work should mean in one's life. In the future, it seems, there will have to be less stick and more carrot, as workers will demand, along with good pay and agreeable working conditions, opportunities for intrinsic work satisfaction, personal growth, and autonomy to a much greater extent.

While work continues to be a major source of one's personal identity, people are no longer willing to stick to a job at all costs. They are not as resigned to their fate as were earlier generations. Surveys have shown that what current American job holders want most from their jobs are opportunities to grow, the freedom to set their own pace, and the right to influence the decisions that affect them. Even the dissatisfied young, poor, and minority workers are looking to the job to fulfill their strivings for self-respect and autonomy.

Daniel Yankelovich, the attitude researcher, concludes from his own recent survey of work that "concern with the human side of the enterprise can no longer be relegated to low-level personnel departments."[7] He also notes that we will need to rethink our work organization to absorb the new breed of workers, as he calls them. These are better educated, more aware, and more demanding than ever before, and they are eager to make a contribution to the world.

The implications of these developments are varied. The shift to service, professional, and technical jobs will require a general rise in the skills and skillfulness of the work force. This requirement, plus high rates of change, will put a premium on lifelong learning, or as Marshall McLuhan once put it, on learning rather than earning one's way through life.

This then links future work patterns to new educational patterns—to learning focused on integration and understanding, learning by doing and problem solving, learning for change.

There is, however, a bleak side to all this. The rise in skill requirements may create a pool of workers with nonemployable and nonrewarding skills—an underclass that Gunnar Myrdal warned of years ago. If a computerized economy cannot absorb them, how will these workers be supported? Retraining and upgrading skills is desirable but may not be effective for all. Yet, to support people for not working shatters our cultural assumptions about work and reward, work and survival.

Thus I foresee two contradictory developments regarding work. There will rise a super-trained, well-paid, relatively contented class of technicians, service workers, and professionals and an underclass of unemployed and perhaps unemployables.

Robert Jungk, the German futurist, sees the emergence of a new division between "those who do interesting work which is nonroutine" and "others . . . who do not create, influence the course of things, make decisions for others."[8] These people "form a new class of poor people. . . . This causes a deep malaise, which has nothing to do with economic demands. A human being is basically a creative being . . . "[9]

The unemployables may well force us to reconsider our assumptions about the link between work and survival and break the equation between employment and the right to consume, that is, to survive. We may, according to a number of economists, need to find a radically different basis for distributing the products of our economic system. At the same time we will need to maintain the work motivations of those needed to fill jobs at both upper and lower levels of society.

For the society as a whole, then, we need to think our way through the following work-related developments:

1   The gradual elimination of meaningless or degrading work, which can eventually be assigned to computerized robots, accompanied by a general upgrading of skills and the skillfulness needed to participate in a post-industrial society.

2   Continuing high rates of change which should challenge the idea of one job or one occupation for life in favor of the multi-job and multi-career life.

3   A change in the traditional work-for-survival formula which will strain both our cultural and substantive resources.

4   Increasingly, the elimination of work as a basis of gender and sex-role typing. As women continue to participate in the job world, these stereotypes of masculinity and femininity will necessarily change with critical consequences for another major aspect of life—the family.

The anticipated changes in the organization of industry, technology, and work cannot leave the industrial nuclear family unaffected, because work and family are profoundly connected. Always less solid and more vulnerable than myth would have it, the nuclear family currently confronts challenges bound to transform it profoundly.

Very small families and much longer life spans have already altered the priorities and timetables of family life. In 1977, the birth rate dropped to 1.8, or below the replacement level. And the standard model of breadwinner father, homemaker mother, and their dependent children is today characteristic of no more than one out of six households. Singlehood, divorce, and widowhood have swelled the ranks of the nonmarried to a total of 44 million. More than half of all families in the United States currently have two or more wage earners, as women have increasingly combined marriage and motherhood with outside employment. Today in industrial countries, whether socialist, capitalist, or in-between, from one-half to nine-tenths of women are gainfully employed, with obvious consequences for the division of labor in and outside the home. Also, because of rising divorce rates, millions of women find themselves self-supporting heads of their own households. These simply stated developments have a host of complex consequences for marriage, for male-female relations, and for the nature of family life.

Curiously, as the traditional meaning and purpose of marriage decreases, its romanticization is proceeding apace. In the past, when spouses had to exchange work as well as affection, when children were a source of social security for old age, and when the family was a whole world unto itself, romance took second place at best. Emotional fulfillment and sexual bliss were not the primary goals of family life but rare, if fortunate, byproducts.

Also, in the past couples may have married till "death do us part," but the facts of life and death typically decreed otherwise. People live too long to make that rhetoric convenient. Thus, according to French historian Philippe Aries, "adults have had to invent divorce to replace death."[10]

Increasingly also, we find individuals grappling with such recent developments as the househusband, the female breadwinner, open marriage, new modes of child care, and voluntary childlessness. The search for new modes of emotional and erotic togetherness, however, is hampered by a number of deep-seated beliefs that were driven in early in life: that life is not meaningful without children, that motherhood is essential for normal women, and that romantic love is the highest possible good. The result is a tug-of-war between old tradition and new impulse that leaves people ambivalent and confused.

This ambivalence is especially marked for working mothers who are burdened by double duty as homemakers and wage earners and by guilt over their revision of the traditional family code. And yet most of them must work, either to support themselves or to help supplement the family income.

They are not, of course, alone in their divided loyalties. Surveys show most Americans hovering between a staunch upholding of traditional family norms and an acceptance of some experimentation and innovation. Thus, a Virginia Slims poll found couples to be uneasy about the future of marriage, yet convinced marriage was a bulwark of society. And while more than half of the women would choose to combine marriage, children, and a career for themselves, three out of four chose a happy marriage as their primary choice for their daughters.[11]

More recently, of course, we have witnessed test-tube babies as they proceeded from science fiction to reality. Together with genetic cloning, this technology is bound radically to transform the propagation of the species at some future time. In the interim, given the compression of the reproductive span, we may anticipate the decline of motherhood as a full-time and lifetime occupation of women. Indeed the injunction to be fruitful and multiply has already dwindled to a mere decade in a life span exceeding 70 years. Thus lifelong labor and lifelong motherhood, those pillars of a gender-divided society, are falling before the winds of change.

It is hardly surprising, therefore, that the woman question, or the "Sex Role Debate," as the Swedes have christened it, has become one of the most controversial and passionate issues of the late twentieth century. The issues posed by this debate foreshadow a metamorphosis of values we are but little prepared for.

Many people today feel overwhelmed by what they perceive as the unraveling of traditions; they note with dismay the symptoms of decay and decline. Instead of the old virtues of thrift, self-restraint, chastity, and obedience, there is sexual license, ethical relativism, and the violation of powerful erstwhile taboos. The pace of change is too swift, the uncertainty too threatening.

We can, of course, take pride in some of our accomplishments—extraordinary industrial mobilization, a kind of lavish scale of action, and the launching of the space age.

But alongside these notable successes, there are needs and problems that greatly strain our capacities and resources. There are the problems of ecological balance; the problems of hunger, poverty, and inequality; the crisis of values and beliefs; the difficulty of managing large systems; and the imbalances in our psychic economies, including our collective disorientation in the face of change. Raised for roots and permanence, we confront a world of transience and impermanence.

All in all, we will need to reexamine our basic paradigms for living and our attachments to an economic yardstick as the key criterion for the good life. Already we note a growing skepticism about unabashed consumerism, both because it is hard to isolate ourselves on islands of plenty amidst often desperate deprivation and because of growing doubts about the ability of material possessions to nourish the soul. Thus, Ronald Inglehart, a professor of political science at the University of Michigan, notes an increase in "post-materialists" among the nine countries he surveyed. Although the materialists still heavily outnumber the nonmaterialists in all countries studied, among the youngest age-groups, the two are nearly equal in strength.[12]

All this will change not only our lifeways but also the metaphor used to describe them. Nobel Laureate Glenn Seaborg accordingly sees us moving from the "throw-away" culture to the "recycling" culture in which "virtually all materials are used indefinitely," and in which "secondary materials such as waste and scrap become our major resources."[13]

And economist Kenneth Boulding, in somewhat different terms, traces our course as moving from "the cowboy economy" to the "spaceship" economy.[14]

In the cowboy economy—reckless, violent, romantic, open—consumption and production are regarded as good in themselves without regard for what is produced and consumed, or at what cost.

In the spaceship economy, production and consumption are not good in themselves but only in their relation to human needs and to the preservation of people and resources.

So it is not a growing GNP but being well fed, healthy, and safe that become the yardsticks for how well the economy and we are going.

This shift in objectives could revive two tendencies constrained during the era of unbridled consumerism: (1) the quest for personal fulfillment—as in various forms of self-renewal and (2) service to others—the old, the poor, the ill, the lonely.

The first tendency is already evident in the various human potential movements which have sprung up in the last few decades. These have for the most part an ancient and noble aim: self-knowledge and responsibility for one's self in this complicated world.

Thus, the revolution of rising expectations has a psychological as well as an economic dimension. Individuals want more for themselves. They are less willing to suppress their talents and opportunities. This is true for married partners as well as for singles; the desire for autonomy and personal growth is now endemic.

The person is emerging as an entity in his or her own right. And it is the understanding of the total person that is at the heart of pioneering ventures into holistic medicine and biofeedback techniques. If the healthy, aware, productive individual is one emergent ideal, service to others in the form of numerous national and international undertakings is another.

Take, for example, the Hunger Project, which currently has over

200,000 members. Launched by the same Werner Ehrhardt who founded *est*, one of the most popular self-awareness training programs in the country, its aim is nothing less than to eradicate hunger in the world within 20 years. In the very effort to achieve this, a larger, more aware human community may be created.

Where, then, does all this take us? The changes I have touched on will affect all aspects of our lives, the social system that contains them, and the moral order that supplies their meaning.

But we have not yet truly accepted the enormity of these changes. As many have noted, there is a distinct cultural lag between the values we have inherited and the realities we confront. This lag is responsible for much of our current malaise and spiritual unrest. Our attitudes are out of step with our experience, and these experiences—in regard to work, education, family, and sex roles—are changing profoundly.

Understandably, there is considerable apprehension, mingled with curiosity about the future, as it becomes clear that it will not be business as usual in our lifetimes.

The best technical estimates are that there will be no long-range solutions to the problems of air pollution or energy scarcity until well near the end of the century. For Americans, long reliant on technological fixes, this prospect is not only alarming but perhaps even inconceivable. It does not seem possible that we may not be able to count on essentials such as land, food, and water, which we have come to take so much for granted. Indeed there are many who refuse to believe it.

Thus one important question is, Who will respond to these warnings? Who will continue to cling to the ideals of the cowboy economy and who will join spaceship earth?

The data suggest that societies will be divided in their receptivity to these changes along the lines of age, wealth, education, and ideology. The affluent and better educated young, along with the idealistic and the dissatisfied of any age, may abandon consumerism earlier, mainly because they have been there and found it wanting.

By contrast, the less affluent and the newly rich may held on to material ideals far longer. These generational discontinuities will result in shifting attitudes and views and make it virtually impossible to sum up collective opinion as neatly as we might like. Indeed, fluidity, if not disorder, is likely to be the earmark of the society in the making, along with division and controversy.

Such division is already apparent in regard to many important social issues—environmental preservation, abortion, homosexuality, economic growth, and urban decline, to name but a few. This division is one of the consequences of post-industrialism, a development we are quite unprepared for and even afraid of. Everywhere, then, we see a discrepancy between our expectations and our realities, between the lessons of our childhoods and the events of our adult lives. To insist on traditional recipes in the face of an altered reality is a sure recipe for pain. Hence, there is the necessity for new values and alternative models to help us with the problems and prospects before us. This is where the observation of certain off-beat groups might be instructive. They bear watching, I believe, for their experiments in living—communalism, two-domicile marriages, and innovations in work and household arrangements. In struggling to create new worlds, they are forcing us to think harder about the old worlds. Old and new, ambiguity and mystery are the ingredients of the crossroads before us.

REFERENCES

1. Daniel Bell, *The Coming of Post-Industrial Society* (New York: Basic Books, 1973).
2. Donella Meadows, et al., *The Limits to Growth* (New York: Universe Books, 1972); Mesarovic, Mihajlo, and Eduard Pestel, *Mankind At the Turning Point, the Second Report to the Club of Rome* (New York: E. P. Dutton, 1974).
3. E. F. Schumacher, *Small is Beautiful* (New York: Harper and Row, 1973).
4. E. J. Kahn, Jr., *The American People* (New York: Weybright and Talley, 1973), p. 156.
5. Kahn, *The American People*, p. 156.
6. *The New York Times*, November 9, 1977.
7. Yankelovich, Skelly, and White, "A Continuing Study of Changing Work Values and Employee Motivations," *Signal*, 1979.
8. Edward Cornish, *The Study of the Future* (World Future Society, 1977), p. 152.
9. Cornish, *The Study of the Future*, p. 152.
10. Philippe Aries, "Family, Prison of Love," *Psychology Today*, August 1975, 9:52−4.
11. The Roper Organization, *The Virginia Slims American Women's Opinion Poll*, 1974, Vol. III.
12. Ronald Inglehart, *The Silent Revolution* (Princeton: Princeton University Press, 1977), p. 67.
13. Glenn Seaborg, "The Recycling Society," *The Futurist*, June 1974, pp. 110−112, 114−115.
14. Kenneth Boulding, "The Economics of the Coming Spaceship Earth" in Henry Jarrett (ed.), *Environmental Quality in a Growing Economy: Essays from the 6th RFF Forum* (Baltimore: Johns Hopkins Press for Resources for the Future, Inc., 1966), pp. 3−14.

CHAPTER 16

The Irresponsible Society
James O'Toole, Ph.D.

Most recent descriptions of the future of work have been unconsciously utopian. Whether work is to be avoided through automation or to be made more fulfilling through its redesign, it is usually predicted that workers circa 2000 will be much better off materially and psychologically than their counterparts of the 1970s. I say these descriptions are unconsciously utopian because their authors assume several things I am certain they would be embarrassed to defend if raised to the level of conscious propositions. For example, they predicate their forecasts on such assumptions as: unrestrained economic growth, a radical change in social values, mechanisms for change that do not currently exist in democratic societies, and a willingness on the part of citizens of low station and high to sacrifice self-interest to achieve the public interest.

The most transparent failing of these utopian views of work is the inability of their authors to identify the mechanisms by which society will get from here to there. That is, although something surely must happen to move society from where it is today to the shores of utopia, no one can identify the mechanism by which this miraculous transition will be accomplished.

One thing seems fundamentally clear about the future: if American society continues as it is, its destination will not be one inhabited by happy and productive workers. Current trends point to a future in which America resembles not so much utopia as Britain or Italy. And, there is no getting around it, Italy is a future that doesn't work.

The overriding characteristic that distinguishes Italian and British workers and managers from their counterparts in, say, Japan, is irresponsibility. This attitude is best illustrated by what is undoubtedly the most frequently used saying in the British Isles: "I'm alright, Jack." Translated into American, this means: I've got what I need, and if my getting it transgressed your rights or needs, well, too bad.

British labor union leaders frequently express this sentiment by saying that they would rather bring Britannia to her knees than cooperate with management to increase productivity, or cooperate with government to reduce inflation. And U.K. managers complement the union stance with disdain for the fact that all British social classes are, ultimately, in the same leaky tub.

Such attitudes provide a ready definition of worker and managerial irresponsibilities. They are actions that destroy the sense of community and weaken a nation's economy and polity by sacrificing the public interest through single-minded pursuit of self-interest. In short, the kinds of irresponsible acts with which this chapter is concerned are those that lead to a breach in the social contract.

The most significant trend in the workplace of America is probably the irresponsible behavior that has reached full flower in Britain and Italy. Admittedly, the trend is not as readily apparent in this country, but it is obvious that there is a growing sense of social entitlement in the United States. Workers have an expanding sense of what is due them as *rights* of employment or citizenship. From pensions, health care, and long vacations to a high standard of living, the perception by workers of what constitutes their rights is inexorably being enlarged. Concomitant with this spiraling sense of rights has been a declining sense of responsibility.

I will first review some evidence that irresponsibility is increasing in America. Counterintuitively, this evidence is so pervasive that it has gone largely unnoticed. Irresponsible behavior is becoming so ingrained in the fabric of work in America that it is accepted as an integral part of our nature. But occasionally this seldom-noticed trait will manifest itself, as when the postal clerk slams the window in one's face at the first strike of five o'clock, or when an able-bodied individual turns down a job in favor of a welfare check, or when a fireman goes on strike, or when a schoolteacher gives a true-false exam because he or she can't be bothered with correcting essays. Each is acting within the scope of his or her rights as they have come to be defined in the late 1970s. Indeed, one might view the history of labor relations over the last decade in terms of the expansion of rights: affirmative action, protection for whistle blowers, automatic cost-of-living adjustments, and generous unemployment benefits, for example.

According to Gary Bryner, at that time president of Local 1112 of the UAW, the famous 1972 strike at the General Motors plant in Lordstown was over workers' rights: Bryner argues that the young worker on the assembly line at Lordstown

> had to have some time. The best way is to slow down the pace. He might want to open up a book, he might want to smoke a cigarette, or he might want to walk two or three steps away to get a drink of water. He might want to talk to the guy next to him. So he started fighting like hell to get the work off of him. He thought he wasn't obligated to do more than his normal share. All of a sudden it mattered to him what was fair. . . . The reason might be that the dollar's here now. It wasn't in my father's young days. I can concentrate on the social aspects, my rights. And I feel good all around when I'm able to stand up and speak up for another guy's rights.[1]

Fair enough. But what of the worker's responsibilities on the line? Bryner answers this question, albeit indirectly:

> Talking to guys. You get into a little conversation. You watch the guy, 'cause you don't want to get in his way, 'cause he'll ruin a job. Occasionally he'll say, "Aw—It's only a car." It's more important to just stand there and rap. I don't mean for car after car. He'd be in a hell of a lot of trouble with his foreman. But occasionally, he'll let a car go by. If something's loose or didn't get installed, somebody'll catch it, somebody'll repair it, hopefully.[2]

As workers' rights expand, their responsibility for the quantity and quality of their work diminishes, their responsibility for taking initiative on the job decreases, their attitudes toward fellow workers, supervisors, customers, and subordinates grow less considerate. When the workers at Lordstown complained about filth in their plant, GM responded by putting many more trash barrels around the plant. But as a senior officer in the UAW explained to me: "The young workers didn't even bother to throw their trash in the cans. In fact, the area around the cans was littered with garbage."[3] Whose responsibility was it to keep the area policed? The workers'? The managers'? The Union's?

The facile answer to the question of responsibility is that workers are to blame for failing to assume responsibility for their behavior on the job. But this may be a case of blaming the victim. Indeed, my argument leads to the conclusion that *managers* have created institutional structures that make it almost impossible for workers to assume responsibility for the quantity and quality of their work.

Before returning to this critical question of responsibility, it is necessary first to review the source of the expanding notion of rights. Social entitlements can be understood as a part of the ever-expanding quest for equality that has characterized the history of Western society since the French and American revolutions. During this 200-year span, the definition of who has rights has expanded horizontally to include larger portions of the total population. At the time of the Revolutionary War, the only people in the United States with full rights were white males over the age of 21 who owned property. By the Civil War, property qualifications for the right to vote were gradually disappearing, and black males started to become full citizens shortly thereafter. By the mid-part of this century, women had started to achieve full rights. Now, one hears talk about the rights of children, of the handicapped, of prisoners, of homosexuals, and of fetuses. Most Americans view this long-term egalitarian trend as symbolic of progress toward a more civilized society.

But the notion of rights has also expanded vertically, so that every individual is now entitled to a greater number of things that were formerly in the realm of individual obligations. This category of rights is largely economic. In the United States the Depression was the major catalyst for the enlargement of the domain of economic rights. It is significant that President Franklin Roosevelt included an economic right —freedom from want—in his famous "Four Freedoms" inaugural address of 1941. Certainly this was one of the first non-Marxist attempts in America to equate freedom with economic security; the notion that one cannot be free if one is starving had been traditionally rejected in America. But in 1941 the Social Security Administration was already functioning, and it was only a matter of time before food, clothing, and shelter were added to old-age security as aspects of the freedom from want. By the time of the Nixon Administration, a guaranteed annual income had come to be viewed as a right, even by Republicans.

What concerns us here is not so much the fact that many items were added to the list of rights between the Roosevelt and Nixon years, although this fact is important because of the financial costs it has imposed on society. But more significant for the future of work is that the concept of what constitutes a right underwent a radical transformation. In the Roosevelt era rights were tied to responsibilities; by the Lyndon Johnson era the tie between these concepts was broken.

Arthur Okun of The Brookings Institution, who has written a

thoughtful analysis of the economic implications of rights, suggests that it is instructive to look at changes in the old-age benefit laws to understand this transformation. Under Roosevelt, the basic philosophy of Social Security was contributory, "stressing the obligation of people to provide for themselves."[4] But under Lyndon Johnson, the right to Social Security was extended to septuagenarians regardless of whether or not they had contributed to Social Security. Okun writes:

> Since then, the level of minimal entitlements has been increased and the age requirement reduced to 65 through additional programs that supplement the standard system of old-age benefits. Currently, the principle of contribution serves mainly to preserve pride while fulfilling the right to survival.[5]

Contribution—that is, individual responsibility—thus stands as a quaint anachronism, a mere vestige of our former values. And the new values of entitlement, freed now completely from the notion of individual responsibility, have spread from Social Security to many other aspects of working life.

American workers now feel that their employers have responsibility for their economic security, a responsibility that was once the individual's. Significantly, this shift in responsibility affects behavior.

What is controversial about most programs of social insurance is this very fact that they alter or distort behavior. Workers who are members of group life insurance programs, for example, often fail to insure themselves for the time after they retire when their term insurance expires. But the distortions of behavior I have cited thus far are ones that affect only the irresponsible individual himself or herself. Much more common, and much more costly, is the behavior of individuals in no-fault insurance schemes whose irresponsible actions put bystanders, third parties, or society in general at risk. For example, there is evidence that individuals covered by workmen's compensation will behave more irresponsibly on the job than they would if they didn't have this accident insurance or if there were a penalty for fault. And recent studies show that individuals with unemployment insurance are less likely to look for work than those without it.[6]

Similarly, there are individuals with illnesses such as lung cancer, cirrhosis, coronaries—which are thought by many to be caused by smoking or over-indulgent eating and drinking. One *Newsweek* columnist goes so far as to suggest that these irresponsible people should be ineligible for certain health benefits, or should at least be made to pay more for insurance.[7]

To cite these various examples and arguments is not to set the stage for an attack on governmental social welfare programs. The purpose is to call attention to the fact that American society seems to be pointing towards a no-risk state. Through health insurance, unemployment insurance, auto insurance, old-age insurance, and life insurance, individuals today bear very little economic risk. Indeed, they face little economic risk or job insecurity at all in the workplace. For example, because of recent court rulings, it is increasingly difficult to fire even the most undeserving employee. A disgruntled college professor is suing his college on the grounds he was fired because he is an alcoholic. The government is now arguing that it is illegal for colleges to prefer sober professors over alcoholics because alcoholics are considered handicapped persons under the 1973 Rehabilitation Act. Treason seems to be about the only remaining justifiable cause for termination.

And government regulations dealing with affirmative action, health, and safety further reduce the risks to workers. Affirmative action can be viewed as the ultimate in risk reduction: it provides insurance against the bad luck of having been born black or female. Add to these trends the power of labor unions, unemployment benefits, and cost-of-living adjustments, and it is clear that workers are more secure than at any time in America's history.

Of course, the trend toward greater economic security is a generally positive one. Only the most indecent, insensitive, heartless, or greedy individual would advocate a return to the kind of employment conditions and practices that existed in the early part of this century. What is at question is how much *further* America should go toward providing additional worker rights, more economic and job security, and less risk. The price of each further increment of security would appear to be an increment of irresponsibility. The policy question that needs to be asked is this: Can America, or any nation, afford to pay the social price of providing its workers with a totally risk-free state?

If America fails to address this issue, I fear that it will, in one key respect, run willy-nilly down the road to becoming another Italy. Italy presents a case in which the costs and benefits of perfect job security can easily be measured. Italian workers face a risk-free environment in that they all have job security. To fire a worker requires a prohibitive investment of time and expense to show cause in court. The effects on individual workers, organizations, and national economies of maintaining a fully-tenured labor force are striking. Italy is a leader of the industrialized world in such dubious categories as low productivity, labor unrest, managerial sloth, and worker dissatisfaction. In England, where workers still can be fired, they nevertheless face a relatively secure working environment protected by belligerent unions and cradle-to-grave welfare measures. The effects are pretty much the same as they are in Italy.

The growing attitude of irresponsibility threatens the long-term viability of the American economy. As the American economy becomes more labor-intensive as a result of the shift toward service, clerical, and knowledge work, the attitudes of workers become central factors in national productivity. In the industrial sector, uncooperative, recalcitrant, or obstreperous workers can be automated out of the process of production, and productivity will rise as a result. But in a mature, post-industrial economy, the success or failure of the national enterprise rests on the willingness of workers to take responsibility for the quality and quantity of their work. Each must take initiative in those increasingly frequent situations that cannot be routinely handled, and show a real interest in the welfare of customers, suppliers, and fellow-workers—in short, to *care* about one's work.

But this is not to place blame for the dismal state of the economy solely on the shoulders of American workers. Managers exhibit an equal tendency toward irresponsibility. Most managers in large corporations have as much job security as they would if they were members of a union and would as soon behave entrepreneurially as they would give up their company-provided country club memberships. In the hundred largest corporations, there is a cradle-to-grave welfare for all top and most middle managers. Ivar Berg, professor of sociology at Vanderbilt University, has recently argued that these managers exhibit highly irresponsible behavior in their financing, marketing, production, and planning tasks.[8] And Robert Schrank of the Ford Foundation argues that it is mismanagement that is often at the root of the irresponsible worker behavior exhibited at Lordstown and other industrial settings.[9] This state of affairs should not be a surprise to the nation. Managers, after all, are not capitalists or entrepreneurs. They are not the owners of the firms in which they work. They, too, are employees.[10]

This all might be dismissed as trivia if it were not for the mounting evidence that the world will no longer "buy" the behavior of American workers and managers. Because of increasing balance of payments deficits and the declining dollar, American managers may no longer be able to afford to play golf on company time, and American workers may no longer be able to afford to goof off or sabotage cars on the assembly line. The nation can only afford such behavior if it doesn't want oil, bauxite, coffee, French wines, and Japanese radios.

Importantly, the security/irresponsibility connection has causes and effects that extend far beyond the workplace. As noted author Hannah Arendt points out in *Jew as Pariah,* there has been a long-term secular trend in Western society from the individual as *citoyen* ("A responsible member of society, interested in all public affairs") to the individual as *bourgeois* (who "for the sake of his pension, his life insurance, the security of his wife and children . . . was prepared to do literally anything"). While Arendt goes so far as to claim that the behavior of the Nazis was "normal" bourgeois behavior, I wish only to claim that it is possible to create a social structure in which irresponsibility to neighbors, co-workers, and fellow citizens is the norm, and in which the *search for security actually compels such irresponsibility.* For example, union leaders, too, behave irresponsibly to protect their security and the security of their members. To protect the jobs of middle-aged males, unions unquestioningly exclude women, minorities, or youth from the work force. On another plane, unionists actively support the production of dangerous chemicals, polluting products, and unsafe consumer goods, all in the name of job security.

This line of reasoning seems to lead to an unfortunate, even tragic, dilemma: there is an inescapable trade-off between security and responsibility. And since both concepts are held to be socially desirable, one cannot advocate any easy resolution to the dilemma. For to choose one social good to the exclusion of the other will be unacceptable to the vast majority of the citizenry.

But it is important to recognize that America is unconsciously choosing more security at the cost of reduced responsibility. Legislatures and courts may be moving to guarantee security without adequately analyzing the consequences and costs of a risk-free environment. For example, the California Court of Appeals recently handed down the sweeping ruling that "every citizen has the right to practice his profession."[11] Since future actions are justified by reference to legal precedent, it will no doubt soon be claimed that *no* professional worker can be fired. Moreover, if professionals have unlimited rights, does this not mean that clients—the employers of doctors, lawyers, and professors—end up having no rights?

From the perspective of intergenerational rights, the current generation seems to feel that it has unlimited rights to exploit the air, water, land, fossil fuels, and other natural resources of the nation to guarantee its economic security. So society behaves irresponsibly toward subsequent generations to secure the high standards of material consumption that it takes as its birthright.

The expanding standard of living that Americans enjoy is predicated on increasing affluence and economic growth. In the past, there were incentives for Americans to work hard to get their share of the ever-expanding economic pie. And this behavior, in turn, caused the pie to expand. In the future, the material aspirations of the majority of Americans may become sated with affluence. If this is the case, there will be inadequate incentives to promote continued growth and economic efficiency. And this, in turn, will cause the pie to stop growing. While the majority may no longer be willing to work as hard as they did in the past, the demands for a fair share of the pie will doubtless continue to grow—for larger shares of the economic pie have now been transmitted into rights. The crash we may hear in the future is the collapse of our political system into a black hole of unmet and unaffordable expectations. If this pessimistic scenario develops, then the trends I have been describing will turn to poison in the body politic and economic. For it has been economic growth that has permitted the bankrolling of the risk-free workplace and socially secure nation. If growth stops, some sacrifices will have to be made.

And herein lies the rub: The American system offers no mechanism for retrenchment. There is no process by which workers and managers can give up some of the benefits they have won. There is no mechanism for retreating even one step from the levels of security that are presently enjoyed. California's Proposition 13 is a current demonstration of this unfortunate fact. While revenues will inevitably shrink over the next two years in California, politicians have failed to significantly alter a single major public program. Take, for example, the largest single item in the Los Angeles City budget: pensions for police and firemen. They account for about 50% of all property tax revenues. The Los Angeles police and fire pension fund is undoubtedly the most generous in America.[12] The benefits include an uncapped cost-of-living allowance, no minimum age for retirement, and a provision that bases benefits on the salary of the worker on the last day before retirement—a provision that encourages the eleventh hour promotion of patrolmen to captaincies shortly before "retirement" at age 38.

The pension plan could serve as a model of the irresponsibility I have been analyzing. It has created a kind of contempt of the public among those in the uniformed services. It has encouraged law enforcers to behave immorally, if not illegally. But that is not why I cite the case. What is informative is the way the police and firemen are fighting attempts to bring their pension benefits into line with the fiscal realities created by Proposition 13. There is no process of negotiation to establish reasonable pension benefits. Instead, there is only unreasoned conflict. The police are organized in a powerful union, they have a war chest, and they will not give an inch. It is not unthinkable that they will go on strike if they feel their pensions are even slightly threatened.

Thus, when forced to retrench even slightly, this group of American workers, at least, seems completely unwilling to make some sacrifices for the greater good. On the contrary, they are willing to engage in the kind of industrial "warfare" that characterizes modern Britain and Italy. If America is forced into a period of belt-tightening, it could be concluded that its social prospects would be bleak. Since the time of the Depression, the nation has been adopting policies that create the belief that every benefit that workers, managers, and professionals have won, and more, is theirs as a matter of right. Since it is much more difficult to take away a right than it is to take away a privilege, the nation can only hope that there will be no limits imposed on growth.

But even if America continues to grow, there are still risks to the society that come from growing entitlements. For example, it seems impossible, even with growth, for the nation to keep pace with the expectations of the work force. The consciousness of entitlements seems to grow exponentially while the economy seems only to grow arithmetically, particularly in a future devoid of incentives to produce and sacrifice.

America is at the point where a chain of social, political, economic, technological, and demographic trends are interacting in untoward ways, leaving us without the means to afford a risk-free society. In short, that with which we would be satisfied, we cannot afford. Yet we continue to spend as if there were no tomorrow. We behave irresponsibly; as a nation and as individuals, we do not save, we do not invest, we live only for today. Daniel Bell has called this the "cultural contradiction of capitalism."

It is interesting how often Bell illustrates social trends by referring to workplace trends.[13] And in this brief chapter I have been unable to untangle the various strands at play to identify what are the causes and effects of irresponsible behavior. Irresponsible behavior manifests itself in work, at home, and in the public arena. The costs of providing worker entitlements spill over into the national economy, and the costs of social entitlements spill over into the workplace. Moreover, the absence of retrenching mechanisms discussed above would seem to leave our democratic society sorely ill-equipped to alter its potentially disastrous course. In practical terms, this means that no rights currently enjoyed by workers are likely to be rescinded; perhaps they need not be rescinded.

A more positive and realistic way of analyzing the issue at hand is to ask how America might go about *infusing concomitant responsibilities* into the existing and probably inviolable arena of rights. While I have no idea how this might be done at the societal level, I do have some suggestions for encouraging responsibility in the workplace. Recently there have been some interesting experiments in which workers have been *forced* to take responsibility for their behavior. For example, workers have been given financial and technical information and given both the rights and responsibilities for organizing their own work accordingly.[14] In some instances, such information has been given to workers, and they have been free even to set their own salaries.[15] In other instances, responsibility has been encouraged among both workers and managers by adopting a system of worker capitalism.[16] That is, employees have become the owners of the firms in which they work.

In these various experiments, workers have not given up their rights, but they have assumed concomitant responsibilities. The risk of self-management, of setting one's own salary, and of assuming ownership seem to provide a necessary balance to the idea that rights come without responsibility or that zero-risk comes without cost.

There is a widely held belief that people are more likely to appreciate their rights if they are given concomitant responsibilities. In several American corporations—for example, Lincoln Electric, Donnelly Mirrors, Harman International, and hundreds of unionized shops with so-called Scanlon Plans—the theory is being tested by giving workers greater responsibility and then rewarding them according to how they exercise this responsibility.[17] Measured by increases in productivity and job satisfaction, these experiments seem to work. Perhaps even more important, there is suggestive data that the effects of self-management spill out of the workplace and onto other aspects of life.

I argued that no one has identified the mechanism by which America will arrive at a more desirable future of work. Let me now suggest that this mechanism will be adversity. Unhappily, I know of no instance in this country where workers have been willing to accept greater responsibility (and managers have been willing to let them accept it) in which the alternative has not been the closing of a plant or company and the subsequent unemployment of the workers involved.

Let me cite an example: In 1977, Uniroyal, Inc. abruptly announced that it was closing its inner tube factory in Indianapolis. The plant was profitable, but it was plagued by chronic and worsening labor conflict. The company had constantly held the threat of plant closure over the workers' heads, and the workers responded by finding creative ways to reduce their output and make life miserable for the plant managers. When Uniroyal finally decided that it would concentrate its resources on its high-growth chemical business, the workers were forced to make sacrifices to save their jobs. Through their union, they found another owner for the plant and agreed to give up such things as being paid for the time they spent at lunch and at union meetings. They agreed to assume responsibility for helping management find ways to make the plant profitable. In exchange for accepting these responsibilities, the new owner granted the workers the right to two seats on the board of directors and to 50% of all profits. Observers now say that workers deal with the new owner as a partner, not as an adversary.[18]

In other countries, the notion of employee responsibility has been taken further than it has in the United States. In Japan, workers have organized themselves into Quality Control Circles to take responsibility for improving the quality of their work; in Germany, workers have won the right to membership on all corporate boards of directors; and in Yugoslavia, workers are now learning to manage the firms that they own cooperatively.

While none of these examples is without its negative side effects, it is nonetheless the case that Japanese workers have increased the quantity and quality of their output through assuming responsibility to do so; German workers have moderated their wage demands and have created a climate of labor cooperation on a continent characterized by class conflict; and the Yugoslavs have outproduced the workers who have little responsibility (and few rights for that matter) in the centrally planned industrial systems of Eastern Europe.

I am not suggesting that the United States should or could adopt any of these models, because it is culturally, economically, and politically different from Japan, Germany, and Yugoslavia. But we can learn from these nations that it is possible to increase worker responsibilities *without* reducing worker rights. There may thus be an alternative to the tragic trade-off between security and responsibility. The key to realizing this alternative will be the willingness of managers to create organizational structures and incentives that will permit and encourage workers to take responsibility. Since the power to change organizations is in the hands of managers, workers cannot be expected to rise up and assume responsibility on their own initiative.

It seems neither unduly radical nor conservative to assume that workers will behave more responsibly if they assume the risks that are concomitant with their own freely chosen behavior. I would suggest that workers might also become more satisfied and productive in the bargain. One might even posit that a world in which all workers and citizens assumed a fuller responsibility for their own actions would be a passably acceptable utopia. Yet it does seem a shame that the only path to such a utopia that Americans are willing to take is the way of conflict and adversity.

REFERENCES

1. Studs Terkel, *Working: People Talk about What They Do All Day and How They Feel about What They Do.* (Copyright 1972, 1974 by Studs Terkel and published by arrangement with Pantheon Books, a division of Random House, Inc.). Reprinted by permission.

2. Terkel, *Working.* Reprinted by permission.

3. For a fuller discussion of Lordstown see James O'Toole, *Work, Learning and the American Future* (San Francisco: Jossey-Bass, 1977), pp. 97–105.

4. Arthur Okun, *Equality and Efficiency* (Washington, D.C.: The Brookings Institution, 1975), p. 18.

5. Okun, *Equality and Efficiency,* pp. 18–19.

6. "Labor Letter," *Wall Street Journal,* January 16, 1979, p. 1.

7. George Will, "A Right to Health?," *Newsweek,* August 7, 1978, p. 88.

8. Ivar Berg, *Managers and Work Reform* (New York: The Free Press, November, 1978).

9. Robert Schrank, *Ten Thousand Working Days* (Cambridge: M.I.T. Press, 1978).

10. Roger Strang and Roy Herberger, "Privately-Held Firms: Neglected Force in the Free Enterprise Systems," University of Southern California, Los Angeles, 1978.

11. *Ascheman v. Saint Francis Memorial Hospital,* 45 C.A. 30507; 119 Cal. rptr. 507, February 1975.

12. *The Pension Balloon* (Los Angeles: Town Hall of California, 1979).

13. Daniel Bell, *The Cultural Contradiction of Capitalism* (New York: Basic Books, 1976), and Daniel Bell, *The Coming of Post-Industrial Society* (New York: Basic Books, 1976).

14. James O'Toole, *Work, Learning and the American Future,* pp. 158–168.

15. "Firm Finds Pay Scheme That Works: Employees Vote on Each Other's Raises," *Los Angeles Times,* January 10, 1979, Part III, p. 1a, and Edward Laulev, "Workers Can Get Their Own Wages—Responsibility," *Psychology Today,* February 1977, pp. 109–112.

16. Daniel Zwerdling, *Democracy at Work*, 6025 Western Ave., Washington, D.C. 20015, 1978.

17. James O'Toole, *Work, Learning and the American Future*, and James O'Toole, et al., *Work in America* (Cambridge: M.I.T. Press, 1973).

18. Jonathan Kwitny, "Tube Plant, 600 Jobs Saved in Indianapolis—in the Nick of Time," *Wall Street Journal*, March 22, 1978, pp. 1, 28.

CHAPTER 17

Beyond Conventional Wisdom: Lifestyle Long Shots
Theodore J. Gordon

We need to consider the forces for change that could alter lifestyle and work, and, in particular, we need to take stock of those developments that could confound conventional wisdom about the changes in progress. What surprises are possible? What are the long shots? This is an iconoclast's hunting license.

"Conventional wisdom" is a deceptively simple term, particularly in a time of rapid change. What is conventional and obvious to one group is heretical to another. From what base do we begin when we search for a "long shot"? How does one limit the concept of "long shot"? Clearly, a long shot is a prospective development with low probability and high impact, but using only that prescription admits antigravity, teleportation, and travel at speeds faster than light—all of which might be possible some day but seem somewhat beyond our scope today.

When I deal with "conventional wisdom," I simply state expected changes in individual lifestyle and the work environment as assertions. For the concept of long shots, I have limited myself to plausible developments, those that fit within a general framework of reality and nature and those for which there seem to be some evidence, however slender, that these developments could occur within the next two or three decades.

ASSERTION: *New lifestyles are exemplified by new family arrangements that include a continuing low birth rate, fewer children, and multiple wage earners.*

169

There really are very few long shots I can name that meet the test of plausibility. The statistics that document profound changes in the family are well known—the decline in the growth rate of husband-wife families; the surging divorce rate; the decline in first-marriage rate; the rise of one-person and two-person households; the reduction of the average size of families; the soaring rate of births to women who are not married. All of these reflect rather fundamental changes in the family.

As for the future, the pendulum will probably not swing back in the short term, and the trends so well established already will continue to evolve. Numerically, the "family" of today will remain strong compared to other living arrangements, but "household" will have to be defined only as the consumer buying unit. Single households, childless couples, groups of adults living together, single-parent groups—all of these remain realities for the late 1970s and early 1980s.

If forced to name a few long shots I would mention the following:

- An unexpected rise in the birth rate, perhaps near the turn of the century, as perceptions about women's roles change again, possibly triggered by underemployment in the work force.
- Child-rearing as a profession.
- Technology permitting the choice of sex of one's offspring and perhaps some genetic attributes as well.
- A drop in the rate of formation of single-person households as the economic advantages of multiple-wage-earner households become apparent.

These developments would have the effect of making the family even more a matter of choice than it is currently.

ASSERTION: *While changes in the structure of the labor force will be relatively slow, important forces for change include delayed retirement, continued entry of women into the labor force, and increasing automation.*

True on all counts, but the long shot here, perhaps, is associated with the unexpected intensity of these trends.

In studying future medical technology, we get the impression that diseases of middle age and early old age—cancer, stroke, and heart disease—will cause fewer deaths, beginning essentially now. These biomedical technologies would have the effect of permitting more people to live to older ages and, most importantly, to have improved levels of health and vigor at a particular chronological age. Thus, a 65-year-old of the future would be more like a 55-year-old of today. Perhaps the most profound impact of increasing life expectancy at middle age would be on patterns of retirement.

We seem to conclude that retirement age is apt to increase for several reasons. First of all, the system of Social Security now in effect provides an economic inducement to retire, which many people would otherwise avoid. Retirement without productive work often leads to stagnation and feelings of uselessness; these feelings, in turn, apparently may lead to earlier death. Furthermore, many retired people simply would rather be working, and the economic viability of the Social Security system is greatly improved by increasing retirement age by only a few years. Perhaps retirement will not be a discontinuous event but will occur gradually over time. It may become a phasing out of working life and into retired life, with people working part-time as retirement age nears or perhaps even working as volunteers in the interest of society.

The pattern is apt to be one of receiving the first pension at an earlier and earlier age and then using this economic base to pursue work or avocations more enjoyable than a long-term career.

When automation first was introduced, many felt that large-scale unemployment would certainly result. This proved not to be the case; automation brought with it its own demands for employment. Yet progress in electronic technology has been very impressive. Large-scale integrated circuitry provides the means for packing thousands of components into tiny volumes, and as packing density has increased, costs have decreased. Electronic watches, already more accurate than mechanical watches, will move from simple time-telling to true wrist instruments. Very inexpensive microprocessors will give birth to true household computers with enough memory and computing capacity to handle remedies, recipes, bills, taxes, phone numbers, budgets, birthdays, and whatever else needs remembering or estimating. This same technology literally will provide the intelligence required to build smart machines—robots that will be able to sense and adapt to changing environments and to accomplish preprogrammed tasks.

This is the automation that was both feared and hoped for and that almost certainly will be available to us and used in the 1980s. Robots will be used not only on the production line but also in decision-aiding situations in middle management and, most importantly, in providing services in the home and in commercial applications. These will not be anthropomorphic machines speaking in tinny, frightening voices; rather, they will be friendly, interactive, and supportive, and they will do work people now do.

Another trend of unexpected significance is the changing rate of entry of young people into the labor force. Since the World War II baby boom peaked in 1960, now—19 years later—the number of people reaching 19 years of age each year will begin to diminish. This means that entering the labor force will be easier from now on. This, of course, is a favorable trend.

Beginning essentially now, however, the number of births per year is increasing, not only because of the slight rise in birth rate but because the number of women of child-bearing age is now increasing. This is also a result of the baby boom of the late 1950s and early 1960s. Since the number of babies is now increasing yearly and will do so through the 1980s, we can expect to see, some 19 years from now, increasing numbers of people reaching the age to enter the labor force.

Therefore, at about the turn of the century, we are apt to have a very significant clash between the "echo boom" babies seeking entry into the labor force, robot machines, and the increasing number of healthy people over the age of 65 who fear and reject retirement from an economic standpoint. Superimpose on this mix the continued entry of women into the labor force and the culmination of labor's efforts to ensure job security; then the potential tumult of work and work force becomes more apparent.

ASSERTION: *Intermediate, appropriate, small-scale technology is more desirable than its alternatives: technological stagnation or the continued advent of large-scale systems.* *

This is a simplified statement of Schumacher's view of a desirable lifestyle, particularly for people in countries early in their development process. He and others stress quality over quantity and argue that the Western model for development may be a trap for many countries, that the aggregate machine must be secondary to human considerations of the society that employs it. Certainly these arguments are well founded, and enough examples of dehumanization exist to justify serious consideration of this argument and its implications. However,

---

* E. F. Schumacher, *Small is Beautiful: Economics As If People Mattered* (New York: Harper & Row, 1973).

there are at least two areas where reduction in the scale of our activities could result in very serious harm.

The first results from the perception that the burning of renewable resources—wood, biomass, garbage—is better than the burning of nonrenewable resources—coal and oil—and that the burning of nonrenewable resources is better than the use of large-scale systems such as nuclear power plants.

Yet burning involves penalties that eventually may be seen to outweigh the disadvantages of renewable and fossil fuel sources. Burning necessarily adds carbon dioxide to the atmosphere. If the known production of carbon dioxide is compared with the observed atmospheric increase, we find that about one-half of the added carbon dioxide has remained in the atmosphere. If carbon dioxide were to cease being added to the atmosphere, it would take between 100 and 150 years for the already added amount to decay to one-third, according to current estimates of exchange rates between the deep ocean and the mixed-up layers. The ocean is a potentially vast sink, but one with a slow response time. The world's forests also form large sinks, but the question of whether the forests are growing faster as a result of the increased CO_2 or are being cut down for lumber and fuel at a greater rate than they are growing is unresolved. Carbon dioxide concentrations are expected to reach nearly 400 parts per million (ppm) shortly after the turn of the century. This will mean an increase of 1°C in the world average surface temperature, while an increase to 650 ppm by 2050 will raise average temperatures 2 to 3°C. The exact nature of the climate changes that this temperature change will produce is still quite speculative.

Freeman Dyson, a physicist at Princeton University's Institute for Advanced Study, has examined the possibility of reversing the rising level of carbon dioxide by means of a plant-growing program. He suggests rapid-growth plantations for trees and swamp plants. It would be ironic if, after all, we were to burn fossil fuels to promote the growth of food for the 9 billion or so people who will be alive 50 years from now.

The second argument against the "small is better" position is that the demand for affluence will not be stemmed easily. There are some 4.2 billion people in the world today. The world population growth rate is about 1.8% per year and dropping slowly. Even allowing for some further drop in growth rate, the population will almost certainly double by 2025; that means approximately 9 billion people. The number could be higher sooner with breakthroughs in treating the diseases of old age and diminishing mortality.

Even if we were to keep all measures of per capita consumption only at their current levels, essentially everything we have in the world would have to double within the next 50 years. But the situation is far worse. Most of the people who will be added to the world will be in developing countries, and these countries hope to achieve levels of affluence approaching those of the rich countries. Equate affluence with consumption, and you can quickly arrive at an estimate of 5 to 10 times the current world yearly demand for almost everything within the next 50 years: education, roads, shelter, food. Where will it come from? Technology can help a bit. Rather than increasing the number of schools tenfold, for example, communication satellites can help provide the infrastructure for education. But overall, the problems implied by world population growth will be very difficult indeed.

These people will need food. Most probably, labor-intensive, small-scale (as opposed to our capital-intensive, large-scale) agriculture will be used by most people; nevertheless, expanding agriculture to its fullest potential will require liberal applications of genius-level technology matched to the using society for maximum effectiveness.

ASSERTION: *Energy prices are likely to remain high and the supply of some fuels uncertain. This will result in important changes in lifestyle, including decreased mobility, renewed emphasis on mass transit, and reduced urban sprawl.*

That energy prices will remain high and certain fuels in short supply seems almost certain, at least over the next few decades. The long shots here are limited, despite the array of technologies being promoted. Wind power, tidal power, geothermal energy, even solar energy do not seem to be feasible, large-scale solutions, at least for the next few decades. Among the long shots that might produce cheap energy sooner than expected are the following:

- *Tertiary recovery.* Primary recovery of oil (relying on the natural pressure in the oil formation to force the oil out of the ground) can generally recover only 15 to 20% of the oil in the reservoir. Secondary recovery techniques (mainly the injection of water into the oil field) can increase the yield of a well to about 35%. Overall, at current prices and technology, a little more than 30% of the discovered reserves of oil in the United States (about 425 billion barrels) can be recovered.

Enhanced, or tertiary, recovery techniques could increase this yield in the future. These techniques literally squeeze the oil remaining under the ground after secondary techniques have been exhausted. Estimates of the amount of oil that could be recovered range from 15 billion to 110 billion barrels. A technological breakthrough here could significantly delay (for several decades) the eventual depletion of this resource.

- *Growing petroleum on bushes.* Chemistry professor Melvin Calvin and others have been studying the use of plants that produce petroleum directly. The jojoba plant, which can grow in desert soil, produces a seed oil that has remarkable properties. Apparently, the jojoba oil resembles sperm oil in chemical and physical properties, and hydrogenated jojoba oil has properties similar to carnauba wax. The interesting feature of the jojoba plant is that it can grow in desert regions and is found growing wild in the Sonora Desert in Arizona, Southern California, and New Mexico. The possibility of jojoba becoming a commercial crop is high, particularly if high-yield varieties can be developed. Since the crop grows in very marginal lands, there is a chance that it can be produced commercially at low cost in desert regions of the United States and in desert areas of developing countries.

- *Gasohol.* The Brazilians are currently adding alcohol produced from sugar to their gasoline; some reports indicate that as much as 10% of the mix is derived from crops. Their target is to increase this to 20% over the next decade or so. The technology of conversion is relatively simple and might significantly improve in the future. The possibility exists that microorganisms might be designed, using the new science of genetics, which would happily digest waste cellulose and produce methane and residuals from which sugars or alcohol could more easily be extracted. This represents a very exciting possibility because it utilizes a currently wasted resource and applies a new technology—genetics—to an intransigent problem.

- *Political changes.* This is a very unlikely development, to be sure, but nevertheless must be recognized. The prices of petroleum are high because of effective cartel action on the part of OPEC. Should internal conflict develop on the part of member nations, the price of petroleum might again fall and the supply become relatively more assured. However, the effect of this would simply be to expedite the rate of exhaustion of petroleum, on a world scale.

- *New discoveries.* It is not at all inconceivable that large deposits of oil could be discovered in new places in the world. For example, some oil industry experts believe that China's reserves could be as large as some Middle East producers. PEMEX, the Mexican oil company, estimates newly discovered reserves in Mexico's Sound of Campeche to hold at least as much potential as that of the North Sea. Mexican reserves could exceed 60 billion barrels. More intense exploration is now underway in many countries around the world. New discoveries may not lower prices, but may extend the time of ultimate depletion of this resource.

So, while we expect energy prices to remain high and supply uncertain, there are at least a few long shots possible; some simply delay the inevitable, others provide more permanent solutions.

Will mobility decrease? Personal transportation uses petroleum, and imported petroleum is a major energy problem; therefore measures that restrict mobility are likely to increase in intensity. Rising gasoline prices, gasoline taxes, "gas guzzler" taxes, even rationing are examples.

However, recognize that electricity is a prime means of using abundant indigenous fuel: coal and uranium. Therefore, it is plausible to expect that government policy would tend to move the fuel mix toward electricity and away from oil consumption. Inevitably, this leads to the suggestion of electric automobiles. These automobiles would not be competitive with Detroit products—their range and top speeds would be restricted. Nevertheless, they could serve well as second cars, town cars, going-to-school cars, jitneys for transportation from the train station home or to business, and in many other applications.

As for mass transit, people generally have expected that we would soon see large-scale systems replacing personal transportation, since expanding mass transit is another way to diminish petroleum consumption. Mass transit generally is very capital-intensive and requires very long lead times to install. Only one form is relatively cheap and quick: buses. One could imagine the rebirth of buses as a high-quality, patriotic transportation mode: supermachines, club cars, special highway lanes, attendants, perhaps even in-transit movies.

ASSERTION: *High energy prices and government policies will inevitably lead to a more conserving society, and this conserving society* *would result in much slower economic growth and perhaps even economic stagnation.*

We are already becoming a conserving society. Comparing last year's figures with those of 1910, only a little more than half the BTUs were required per dollar of GNP (constant dollars). Several factors help assure that this trend will continue. First of all, higher energy prices seem certain, increasing by 50 to 100% in real terms through the remainder of the century. This will provide an important incentive to utilize energy-efficient technology in buildings, industry, and transportation. Progress already has been made, and more seems likely. American industry has been conserving and can conserve more energy. A recent report by The Conference Board estimates that American industrial companies improved their average energy efficiency by 15% between 1972 and 1976.

Even at that, American industries still generally lag behind their European counterparts. Energy conservation in industry is largely voluntary; targets for improvement have been published by the U.S. Department of Energy. Some of the 1980 targets have already been achieved (petroleum-refining and coal-mining industries have met their 12% goals; nonelectrical machinery manufacturing has met its 15% goal). The chemical industry has already achieved a 9% improvement and transportation a 12% improvement. The progress is real, and the potential for further progress is an important aspect of the emerging energy situation. In the years ahead, improvements will tend to be made as a result of the introduction of new energy-efficient plants and equipment.

The energy efficiency of the economy is also improved by the movement toward service industries. Today, manufacturing, agriculture, construction, and mining account for 30 million out of 90 million workers. Energy efficiency is also increased by productivity gains that are promised by low-cost automation—the direct result of cheaper and, concomitantly, more effective microelectronics. Current technology or technology soon to be available could have important effects on energy consumption in buildings. Solar heating systems and electronic heat pumps serve as examples. Finally, public policy, such as the Energy Policy and Conservation Act of 1975 (which sets miles-per-gallon standards for the automobile fleet), seems certain to accelerate the trend toward improved energy conservation.

The most important consequence of this conservation imperative may be changing perceptions about what constitutes a good life; that is, what it is desirable to consume. Energy-demanding products and activities may be very expensive and, if the ethic gains acceptance, unpopular. I don't mean that people will suddenly become ascetic—I simply mean to suggest that a whole range of new products and services may come into use. These new products and services will be keyed to conservation. The electric automobile, smaller, more efficient internal-combustion engines, motorbikes, heat pumps, windmills, and high-performance insulation are examples. Electronic devices that substitute communications for transportation also qualify. In this time of conspicuous conservation, people will still go places, but will tend, more often, to stay put once they get there. Touring will go down and "soaking up the culture" up.

With such products available, the age of conservation need not imply stagnation, but rather only a shift in patterns of consumption. "Conspicuous conservation" will replace "conspicuous consumption." We will consume new kinds of products tuned to conservation; these will be fun and enjoyable to buy and use and talk about. They will also be profitable for firms that provide them. The economy will grow, but with less energy needed to fire its boilers.

This mix of technology, social change, ambitions, needs, and goals defines the milieu for lifestyles and, in turn, for work in the years ahead. The mix is complex, with elements that interact in ways that are hard to discern. One thing is sure: some part of that mix, perhaps the most important part, will be the long shots—or beyond long shots, those developments not even yet dimly perceived. And from the mix will come a life and a style that will be vital and exciting to those who live it.

SECTION FOUR

America's Quest to Maintain Economic Growth in a Global Society

In the first three sections of this book, we have examined the future of work in the United States largely as if this country were an island, unaffected by developments in the rest of the world. Now we turn to the reality that, as never before, this country exists in a world of interdependent nations. Our aspirations for meaningful work, for participation in decision making, and all the other needs and wants developed earlier depend importantly on the new world economic order that is under construction.

George Vojta opens the section with a powerful reminder that opposition to growth and to the very idea of profitability can throw a wrench into the engine of expansion built by entrepreneurs. Marx was only partly right about diminishing returns on capital, says Vojta, because he missed the perpetual economic revolution provided by entrepreneurs. Vojta calmly warns that we must respect and nurture the innovator. And he provides a fresh insight into the nervousness about multinational corporations: "It has seemed to me that much of the resistance . . . in recent years may be attributable more to fears of strange customs than to the usual cries of commercial exploitation. . . . If the basic problem is not economic, but tribal, if the multinationals are really the new barbarians threatening to contaminate ancient local virtues, then events like those in Iran begin to make more sense. They also raise serious doubts about the future of competition."

Cecilio Morales forecasts a smaller but nevertheless powerful economic role in the world for the United States. After tracing our willingness to rebuild and befriend our World War II enemies, he points to the Third World and Latin America as trading partners and friendly competitors in the twenty-first century. He warns against political attempts to reduce foreign aid budgets and against the rise of protectionist sentiments within our borders. The timing of such regressive notions could scarcely be worse from the viewpoint of our history and our national security. Given our record of support for the national aspirations of former colonies, to turn away now would be inexplicable. The twenty-first century, Morales believes, will be the one in which extreme poverty is eradicated from the earth. America's role in that accomplishment will be major.

Jack N. Behrman points out the confidence and optimism about the future to be found in developing countries and the uncertainty and malaise evident in the advanced, developed nations. He explains our national uncertainty as the result of having pursued material goods rather than the common good. "Mere material growth, we now know, does not solve our problems or provide happiness; in chasing physical wealth, we have lost our sense of mission," says Behrman. To be a leader in the emerging global economic order, he says, we must show the world that our handling of our own problems is an example worth adoption by other countries. Behrman predicts the gradual formation of regional economic blocs and the increased concentration worldwide of multinational corporations. Equity, and not efficiency, will be a strong force in determining where in the world certain kinds of production take place. "It will now be possible," says Behrman, "to design the international economy."

C.S.S.
D.C.C.

CHAPTER 18

Entrepreneurship: Engine of Growth

George J. Vojta

I suspect most of us could agree that the overlooked detail, the random event, the discontinuities that seem to be in the nature of things, are the forces that emerge to control outcomes of one sort or another.

You will recall that the world's first electronic computer, ENIAC, went on line at the University of Pennsylvania in 1946. It had been commissioned by the Ordinance Department of the United States Army, which hoped to use it for calculating the trajectory of artillery shells. But in 1946 the war had been over for a year, and the Army appeared to have acquired a gadget consisting of more than 18,000 vacuum tubes weighing 30 tons for which there was no apparent use. A market research firm was consulted. It concluded, after intensive study, that there might be a market for—at most—1000 computers by the year 2000.

What the market research team did not foresee, and perhaps could not have foreseen, was the invention about two years later of the transistor, which began the process of miniaturization that ultimately reduced the 18,000 vacuum tubes to a chip.

The first bank computer was built for the Bank of America in 1956 by General Electric—after IBM told the bank's planning committee that it was not interested in the job because there would never be a market for more than 10 big computers in the entire country. Once IBM did become interested, of course, it entered the field with such energy and success that it became a dominant force in enterprise.

Consider: less than 25 years ago, IBM itself could not foresee its own competitive future, let alone that of the country. Today, of course, the United States owes much of whatever competitive edge it still has in the world to its lead in computer technology. Similarly, it is almost impossible to find anyone today who can remember any office that ever functioned without the Xerox machine; yet as late as 1950 Xerox was nothing but a small paper merchant.

In short, many of the companies, and even industries, that are today making major contributions in America's quest to maintain economic growth in a global society were either new or totally unknown less than 30 years ago. And what was true then is doubtless true now. It would be foolish to offer many firm predictions about how we will be making out competitively in the next century, or even the next two decades. There are, however, some observable differences between our competitive posture today and our stance of a decade or so ago. One of those differences concerns entrepreneurship and the falling productivity of capital.

One hundred years ago, Karl Marx based his prophecy of the inevitable collapse of capitalism on the "law" of diminishing return on capital. What happened instead in the developed countries with free-market economies was that productivity of capital, except in years of the most severe depressions, continued to rise steadily.

There are many explanations for these non-Marxian developments, but one of them is undoubtedly that Marx overlooked what another European economist, J. B. Say, identified almost 200 years ago as "the entrepreneurial function." The true entrepreneur, as Say correctly observed, is someone who constantly is engaged in moving existing resources from areas of lesser productivity to areas of greater productivity. This does not require discovering or conquering new continents. It consists of discovering new and better uses for existing resources.

In one sense, Marx was correct. Without entrepreneurship, any economy will drift toward steadily diminishing productivity of capital. That is a principal reason why, according to the best available estimates, the same increment of capital investment today produces five to eight times as much additional output in a free-enterprise economy as it does in the Soviet Union or Eastern Europe. Low productivity of capital is inherent in central economic planning because of its impact on the entrepreneurial function. Management consultant Peter Drucker, in fact, goes so far as to say that central planning "can be defined as a system in which control—or the appearance of control—is being paid for by incurably low productivity of capital."

Joseph Schumpeter, another economist who emphasized the entrepreneurial function, coined the phrase "creative destruction" to describe what he believed to be the essential feature of all capitalist enterprise. It is a system in which people are incessantly destroying the old one and incessantly creating a new one. The fundamental impulse that sets and keeps the capitalist engine in motion, Schumpeter said, comes from the new consumer goods, the new methods of production or transportation, the new markets, the new forms of industrial organization that capitalist enterprise creates.

These things do not happen in the same way that the sun rises or the tide comes in, however. They are the end results of the purposive striving by individual entrepreneurs and entrepreneurial organizations toward a simple end: to move capital from less productive to more productive—and therefore more profitable—uses.

This is not easy work. In Schumpeter's words: "To act with confidence beyond the range of familiar beacons and to overcome . . . resistance requires aptitudes that are present in only a small fraction of the population and that define the entrepreneurial type as well as the entrepreneurial function. This function does not essentially consist in either investing anything or otherwise creating the conditions which the enterprise exploits. It consists in getting things done."

From these sentiments comes my main thesis and, hopefully, a modest ring of credibility. I suspect that America's quest for growth in a global society will be described by the relationship between the future public policy environment and the entrepreneurial function in our country. More specifically, economic growth will depend on whether or not the American value system remains supportive to the entrepreneurial spirit and sanctions the associated rewards.

Our basic value system, which conditions our institutions and practices, must have an important bearing on productivity, and there is reason to believe that that value system may be changing. Certainly since the early 1960s there has been an increasingly critical attitude toward economic growth.

For whatever reason, it is a fact that the trend of rising productivity over the past 100 years has been reversed. This is true not only for the United States. There has been a significant deceleration in productivity advance in all of the developed countries since the mid-1960s. There has also been a decline in the communist part of the world, especially in the Soviet Union. From all reports, the already low productivity of capital in the USSR, in both agriculture and industry, has been eroding for at least the past 10 or 15 years.

There is a very important difference, however, between the two situations. In a government-controlled economy, where capital is normally allocated by political fiat, declining productivity only adds to the customary inefficiency. In a free-market economy such as our own, a continuous loss of productivity threatens the system itself. Entrepreneurship consists of finding ever more productive uses for capital; where that is impossible, entrepreneurship perishes, and with it, the free market system.

There is, of course, such a thing as government entrepreneurship. Governments can, and do, initiate new forms of human endeavor. They can mobilize resources and direct them to a specific objective. The U.S. space program is an example. But governmental activities are rarely, if ever, characterized by a careful management of capital. However worthy the purpose, maximizing the productivity of the capital is rarely high on a government's list of priorities. Nor should it be, necessarily. No one wants to jeopardize an astronaut's life by insisting that all the hardware on a spaceship be supplied by the lowest competitive bidder, regardless of quality.

Governments operate on budgets rather than on the basis of results produced by performance. Even the most efficiently run government agency is not capital-conscious in the same way that the private firm or individual is capital-conscious. If the agency is in the business of providing health care, for instance, a more efficient operation may produce more health for the dollar, but it will not result in the agency getting a larger budget next year. It might even have the opposite effect. In the final analysis, all government entrepreneurship is based on political expediency: to placate pressure groups or prevent revolutions, to produce some acceptable degree of consensus among contending parties, to protect the people from foreign invasions.

This does not make government a villain and private enterprise the hero. It means only that they are different institutions with different goals. But to the extent that government entrepreneurship is substituted for private entrepreneurship, capital will cease to flow toward the most productive uses. And the society over which that government presides will find itself with less innovation, fewer new methods of production, fewer new forms of industrial organization, and fewer improvements in the material standard of living. As a result, such a society will also find itself producing less growth with its material wealth.

Internationally, as domestically, government entrepreneurship can always accomplish its short-term objectives without regard for whether it wastes capital. But in the long term this means decreased productivity and a stagnation of living standards. Yet people and nations have shown themselves willing to suffer this condition over very long periods of time. In fact, throughout most of human history they have seemed to prefer it.

According to Herodotus, "the Lydians were the first nation to introduce the use of gold and silver coins, and the first who sold goods at retail." This and a few other clues put the birth of the market economy at about 700 B.C. In all the long history leading up to that time, international trade was essentially a business of intergovernmental negotiations, whether conducted by tribal chieftains or the Pharaoh of Egypt. Domestic trade was a matter of fixed-price exchanges dictated by the palace or the temple.

Those of us who have grown up in free societies tend to regard the rise and fall of prices according to the action of supply and demand as something akin to natural law. It is hard to visualize the economic processes of those earlier times or to recognize them when they reappear today.

The essential feature of the ancient tribal economies was a form of rationing. It was not egalitarian but hierarchical. The primary purpose of consumption was to express rank; you were allowed three strings of beads if and when you were entitled to wear them. The same drive to evade the social consequences of the price system appears time and again throughout history. In England, according to a law of 1363, a merchant with a net worth of £1000 was entitled to the same dress as a knight worth £500, and a merchant worth £200 could dress no more elegantly than a knight worth £100.

The communist nations of today believe themselves to have reverted to an anti-free-market system in reaction to the destructive social effects of *laissez-faire* capitalism. They believe that goods should be allocated on egalitarian rather than hierarchical grounds. But the result is the same; eliminating the free market requires returning the individual to the social rigidities of tribalism.

The tribal society is a closed society, and as we approach the end of the twentieth century, there is every reason to believe that large numbers of people do not find a closed society an objectionable situation. When we say that our Western civilization derives from the Greeks, what we mean is that the Greeks started—for us—the great transition from the closed to the open society. There are many societies for which that transition has only just begun. And many have signaled strongly that they would prefer not to go. Iran is a recent example.

The most powerful cause for the breakdown of the closed society in early Greek times was probably the development of sea communications and commerce, which was also the underlying cause of the well-known war between Athens and Sparta. All closed societies are, like ancient Sparta, essentially hostile to commerce. Internationally, commerce leads to contact with other tribes and customs whose very existence tends to undermine the authority of the local customs and taboos that hold the society together. Domestically, commercial initiative is one of the few forms in which individual enterprise and independence can still assert themselves, even in a society in which tribalism still prevails.

It has seemed to me that much of the resistance to multinational corporations in recent years may be attributable more to fears of strange customs than to the usual cries of commercial exploitation. Economic analysis has repeatedly demonstrated that the host country benefits at least as much as the home country of a multinational, and frequently more. But such demonstrations have rarely seemed persuasive to their critics. If the basic problem is not economic but tribal, however, if the multinationals are really the new barbarians threatening to contaminate ancient local virtues, then events like those in Iran begin to make more sense. They also raise serious doubts about the future of competition.

Bertrand Russell used to say that his Victorian grandmother lived and died with sublime faith that the whole world would eventually learn to live in peace and tranquility, with a bicameral legislature, just like England. Similarly, most of us in the West have lived with the basic assumption that progress and enlightenment would ultimately lead the world in the direction of "modernization" and economic efficiency. We have to be concerned that both convictions may prove to be unfounded.

The form that America's quest to maintain economic growth in a global society finally assumes will depend, obviously, on what kind of global society we end up with. Or whether that society is, indeed, global. The returns on that are still coming in.

It is by no means certain that the flow of the entrepreneurial function over the global marketplace will be allowed by the community of sovereign governments. It is not foreordained that comparative advantage and the dynamics of product life cycles will extend the growth process in the community of nation-states. All too often the revival of ancient taboos and the extension of hostile ideologies drive the entrepreneurial function away. How else can the boom of foreign investment in this country from Western Europe and the troubled countries

in the Third World be explained? What is it, other than entrepreneurial creativity seeking more favorable surroundings?

In this country, the prognosis is mixed. The entrepreneur's goal is always to increase profit. Business firms have a profit incentive to expand or to preserve their share of the market by introducing new and
better products and finding cost-reducing ways and means of production. Widened profit margins tend to be competed away by other firms
which imitate the innovators.

But something new has been added. As we steadily increase the reg-
ulatory burden, as the cost of making an environmental impact study
begins to approach the cost of actually protecting the environment,
profit margins tend to wither away even faster. As a result, the entrepreneurial imagination seeks other fields to conquer—and what it
seems to be finding in our country is the service industry. The same
capital that might once have gone into agricultural or industrial plant
and equipment is increasingly likely to show up as a new computer
software program.

This trend has been reinforced by, and may have contributed to, the
clearly developing changes in the labor force: more than half of our
work force is employed providing some kind of service. But there are
important differences within the service industries. About one-fourth
of the people employed there are sales personnel and clerical workers.
But the others, the fastest-growing sector, are the so-called "knowledge
workers"—technical, professional, managerial, and administrative personnel. With sales and clerical jobs probably growing only moder-
ately, the great increase will be in "knowledge" jobs, which in another
10 years are likely to account for one-third or more of all jobs and for
most new jobs.

This is the labor force with which and for which Americans will be
seeking economic growth during the rest of this century and into the
next. That such growth will be different from the growth of the past 30
years is virtually certain. And that it will be achieved primarily by entrepreneurial activities which increase capital and labor productivity
in the knowledge sector seems, to me at least, equally certain.

Unfortunately, that is about all that is clear. There is little reason to
believe that the knowledge worker's productivity has increased much
during the past 75 years. The present-day teacher, researcher, or manager is not likely to be much more productive today than he was 75
years ago. Yet we have only to look around us at the extraordinary
new tools that are rapidly becoming available, from computers and
satellites to biofeedback teaching techniques, to realize that we are in

the midst of an explosion in the techniques of acquiring and using knowledge. This is precisely the kind of situation that attracts the entrepreneurial genius, which is why the service sector is where I expect his or her efforts to bear fruit.

There is another reason for optimism. The entrepreneur's time must come before the regulator's time—and in this new race to compete in the sale of knowledge services it appears that the entrepreneur has a strong lead. Here is an omen.

On two separate occasions during the past few years, the Federal Communications Commission has attempted to write a legal distinction between "communication" and "computation." The problem is that if one computer in, say, New York finishes a calculation and sends it over the telephone lines or via satellite to another computer in California, then clearly communication occurs and the FCC should regulate it. But what if both computers work on the same problem simultaneously? In this case, the long distance telephone line or the satellite is no different in function than the microscopic printed circuit in your pocket calculator. They are just part of the same calculating device.

The difference is significant, because one definition puts A.T.&T. into the computer business, and another definition puts IBM into the telephone business. The whole matter is presently in limbo because all of the parties, including the FCC, have agreed that no satisfactory distinction has been formulated. Moreover, the experts seem to believe that none is possible at the moment. If so, we have a situation in which a government is unable to regulate an activity because it is unable to define it. I consider that a hopeful sign.

In the final analysis, the themes of globalism and service-related growth opportunities in the United States link. We can be sanguine about America's quest for growth, provided our society remains supportive to structural evolution that accommodates the increasing mix of services in our economic profile and allows the dynamics of comparative advantage to permit our economy to evolve toward higher levels of productivity. And we can also be sanguine to the extent that our neighbors in the global community manage their own economies in complementary fashion. If the net result is the unshackling of the entrepreneurial function over the global marketplace, our prospects can be very bright indeed. We cannot know the outcome, but perhaps we can know what to look for as the process unfolds.

CHAPTER 19

The United States and the Third World in the Twenty-First Century

Cecilio J. Morales

The United States' relative economic weight in the world will become smaller as we move into the next century. We can anticipate that some matters that have been dealt with mostly under national jurisdiction will be gradually transferred to international multilateral organizations which can act responsibly on them.

In several areas this has happened already. Some important economic issues are presently discussed and decided by the OECD: during the last 10 years, an increasing proportion of aid resources has been transferred to multilateral finance institutions; in the same period, increased responsibilities for management of the world monetary system have been assigned to the International Monetary Fund (IMF); the last round of multilateral trade negotiations has done something similar in the field of trade with the General Agreement on Trade and Tariffs (GATT).

None of this dispersal of authority is a sign of weakness on the part of the United States. Rather, it shows an intelligent recognition of the advantages of sharing the burden of international economic responsibilities with other countries that have the experience, ability, and economic capacity to contribute effectively to the common interest.

I disagree with the prophets of doom, many of them in this country, who forecast a ruinous decline of the international presence and role of the United States. Because of the quality of its society, its national and international traditions, its institutions, and its human, natural,

191

scientific, and technological resources, the United States will continue to play a leading international role into the next century, in partnership and cooperation with other nations.

There is no doubt that the United States of the twenty-first century will be quite different from that of the twentieth, just as this one differs from that of the past century. But change will proceed as a gradual historical process and not as a result of trauma or decadence.

One of the basic factors that will continue to stimulate U.S. leadership will be the tremendous set of challenges lying ahead: the social implications of the new scientific and technological revolution, energy, the environment, availability of raw materials, social and political evolution of developed countries, the world economy, and social, political, and economic problems of the developing countries.

This country's rise during the twentieth century as the leading military and economic nation of the world was prompted by World War II, in which the United States participated when it realized it was the only alternative to the defeat of the Allies. The wartime devastation of Europe and Japan led this country to fill the vacuum left by the destruction of the financial, commercial, and industrial capacities of those areas. The United States used a good part of its newly gained economic power to help with the reconstruction of Europe and Japan as strong political partners, as well as economic competitors in the world markets. In addition to the reconstruction of the countries devastated by the war, the United States played a decisive role in the establishment of a number of international institutions, particularly in the economic field. These institutions make up a very sophisticated system of cooperation and joint action, which was almost totally nonexistent prior to World War II. The system includes most of the UN agencies, the IMF, the World Bank group, GATT, OECD, and the regional development banks.

After the war, the emergence of strategic problems with the Soviet Union provided another stimulus for the scientific and technological development of this nation. However, the main engine of the scientific, technological, and economic evolution in the United States has been always internal. Domestic priorities, expressed through the democratic process, always have been the decisive influence in the evolution of the country. Government and the private sector eventually manage to mesh external requirements with domestic priorities.

In spite of the absence of a formal planning system, the nation has, through an informal system of analysis, rationally approached the study of its important problems and their solutions.

It can be anticipated, therefore, that in the twenty-first century, the United States will continue to be the major world power. Its political openness, its economic size, and its scientific and technological development will give it the capacity to maintain a global presence.

In order to support the technological, economic, and social transformations demanded by a democratic population full of vitality and a desire for progress, the United States will have to sustain a process of economic growth. While it is unreasonable to predict growth with total certainty, it is possible to state that since a national will exists and since the ingredients and technical capacity for sound economic policies are also available, it is highly likely that the country will grow at a steady rate.

THE EMERGING THIRD WORLD

The Third World comprises a very large number of extremely heterogeneous regions and nations, with a population that represents 70% of the world total and that, by the year 2000, will reach almost 80%. It includes Asia (except Japan), Latin America (including the Caribbean), Africa, and the Middle East. Great differences in culture, size, resource endowment, and degree of development are evident among regions, within regions, and within nations.

Latin America is relatively more advanced economically than the others. It is followed by the Middle East, Asia, and Africa, in that order. As will be analyzed in more detail later, the economic differences between regions and between countries in the Third World will increase.

Within the regions and across them, it is possible to identify some groups with common characteristics. Brazil, Mexico, Argentina, Colombia, Venezuela, Chile, South Korea, Taiwan, Singapore, and others have reached a relatively advanced stage of industrial development. They have gone through long periods of rapid growth, supported by exports of primary products, both agricultural and mining, and, increasingly, of manufactured goods. These countries are in the midst of a rapid transition to self-sustained growth but are still highly vulnerable to external economic fluctuations. All of them need expanding world markets for their exports and large amounts of external financing for their development.

The oil-exporting countries, most of them members of OPEC, constitute a very heterogeneous group. Some, including Saudi Arabia, Kuwait, Libya, and the Arab Emirates, have accumulated large financial surpluses. Venezuela has been reabsorbing its surpluses in the financing of far-reaching development programs. Others, such as Nigeria and Indonesia, are still in a backward stage of development.

Another group, in Southeast Asia and sub-Saharan Africa, includes countries with more than 1.3 billion people, of which more than half live in extreme poverty.

The communist countries of Asia, including China, North Korea, and Vietnam, also belong to the Third World, even though their politics usually cause them to be grouped with the more advanced Soviet bloc countries. Vietnam, with 48 million people, is estimated to have a per capita income of less than $200. The corresponding figures for China are 840 million people and $410, and for North Korea, 16 million and $470.

In recent years, Third World countries have been active as a group in several international forums and organizations trying to promote an increased and more effective program of international cooperation to accelerate their development. These actions have taken place principally in the United Nations, where a commitment to support the establishment of a New International Economic Order was recommended by the General Assembly; in the UN Conference for Trade and Development (UNCTAD), where the less-developed countries (LDC's) have tried to promote agreements for cooperation in the fields of development financing, international trade, and stabilization of commodity prices; in the International Monetary Fund in relation to monetary reform; in the World Bank and the regional banks in pressing for increased resources for multilateral financing; and in the Multilateral Trade Negotiations, in trying to obtain better access to the markets of the industrialized countries.

So far, most of these efforts have not gone beyond the stage of rhetorical declarations or recommendations. Perhaps the best of the limited successes were achieved in obtaining periodical increases of resources for the multilateral finance institutions, the World Bank, and the regional development banks. In fact, these institutions have been able to offer more tangible indications of actions and achievements in project development. But, even here, there has been a decline in relative terms of public financing in relation to private financing.

ISSUES FOR THE TWENTY-FIRST CENTURY

The world will start the new century with a structure that will determine much of the evolution that will take place during the subsequent hundred years.

The OECD countries and the Soviet bloc will have become more like each other in technological and economic development and will control a very large proportion of world resources, technology, and economic capacity.

According to *The Future of the World Economy*,* a study prepared by a team of economists headed by Nobel prize winner Wassily Leontief, the industrial countries, which in 1970 had 30% of world population and produced 84% of world GNP, will have 22% of world population in the year 2000 and will produce 70% of world GNP. The average GNP per capita in 1970 was $2486 for the industrial countries against $200 for the Third World. In the year 2000 the corresponding figures are estimated to be $6550 and $801, respectively. These figures are presented in Table 4.

Table 4.   Population and GNP: Industrial Countries and the Third World
(Years 1970 and 2000)

Years	Areas	Population		GNP		GNP per capita
		Millions	%	Billions	%	(U.S. $)
1970	Industrial countries	1071	30	2662	84	2486
	Third World	2512	70	503	16	200
2000	Industrial countries	1370	22	8979	70	6550
	Third World	4961	78	3974	31	801

Source. Based on data from Leontief, Wassily, et al., *The Future of the World Economy: A United Nations Study* (New York: Oxford University Press, 1977).

The forecasts for the year 2000 show a world in which the industrialized countries—with one-fifth of the world population—provide more than two-thirds of production and nearly 80% of world trade. This group is also endowed with a similarly large share of the world's natu-

* Wassily Leontief, et al. *The Future of the World Economy: A United Nations Study* (New York, Oxford University Press, 1977). This study is one of the most comprehensive exercises in forecasting conducted in recent years. It was supported by several institutions of the United Nations, the OECD, the research staffs of Brandeis and Harvard Universities, and a number of consultants.

ral resources: arable land, minerals, forests, fuels, and seas. But the more important advantage this group will have is the concentration of practically all the infrastructure and knowledge in technology, practically all the research and development capacity, and all the scientific foundations needed to support technological progress. This is, in my view, the real meaning of the frequently mentioned gap between industrial and developing countries.

The process of technological development will become more and more homogeneous throughout the industrialized countries. The level of technological development in the Third World will lag far behind that of the industrial countries. Within the Third World there will be great heterogeneity among different regions.

Latin America will be the more advanced developing area in terms of technology and economic development, but it will still be far from reaching the level of autonomous technological development. However, it is highly probable that this level will be reached by Latin America before the middle of the twenty-first century.

Technological development will be a decisive factor in the maintenance of an adequate economic growth into the next century. To achieve this steady growth, the world will have to face a formidable challenge, particularly in the areas of energy, first, and then food production and industrial development.

In spite of all current warnings and crises, the world is moving too slowly to adapt itself to the decline of oil as its main source of energy. We need a vast effort of exploration and development of new reserves of fossil fuels; of utilization of lower grade, more expensive known reserves such as shale oil; and of enhanced recovery in existing oil deposits.

The exploration and development of new sources of fossil fuels will have to take place mostly in developing countries, principally in those which import oil. But that can be done only with massive technical and financial support from industrial countries.

It is clear that the most immediate alternative to oil and natural gas will be coal and nuclear energy. The currently known world reserves of coal are located mainly in North America, the Soviet bloc, and China. Something similar is true of uranium. For the Third World countries, except China, to discover and find enough resources will be an expensive undertaking. They will need to adopt technologies from the industrial countries for the efficient exploitation of these resources. Some of these technologies, such as coal gasification and nuclear fusion, are not yet fully developed in the industrial countries. Other complex problems to be solved include the control of the environmental impact of new energy production techniques, which also pose serious questions such as nuclear waste disposal.

While the prospective evolution of the energy problems is of great concern for the world as a whole, developing countries will face critical uncertainties. They lack an inventory of resources supported by sufficient exploration and evaluation, and they do not possess adequate access to the capital and technology needed to investigate and develop them.

Latin America and China may constitute two exceptions because of the importance of their already-known resources and their possibility for further exploration and development. Both areas, however, will also face technological and capital constraints.

In the next 20 years, the population of the Third World will increase by nearly two billion. This will add to the present population of nearly three billion, of which around one billion is severely undernourished.

As is true of other resources, food surpluses occur in the industrial countries, while most of the developing countries need to supplement their domestic production with food imports.

Population growth, coupled with economic development, will increase substantially food demand in the Third World. Given the limited import capacity of these countries, they will have to face this demand by increasing domestic production. This can be done, provided that adequate financing and technical assistance are made available. To provide an example of the size of the resources needed, Leontief estimates that the total investment necessary to bring the average rice yield in Asia to 4 tons per hectare would amount to more than $60 billion. That yield is only half of what is technologically possible.

In order to achieve adequate levels of food production and to improve the consumption levels of all sectors of their population, developing countries will also have to undertake sociopolitical reforms toward systems more participatory and equitable than those presently prevailing in many of them. Without these changes, problems and crises will only become more acute.

High levels of unemployment and underemployment exist throughout the Third World. The task of providing productive employment for the burgeoning labor force of the Third World is staggering. Because of the social and human elements involved it is also extremely complex, but the failure to succeed may prove extremely dangerous. In spite of the fact that a problem like this is much more difficult than those problems related to energy or food, the research devoted to solving it is practically nonexistent.

World population will continue to concentrate increasingly in urban areas, in industrial countries, and in the Third World. Large urban agglomerations will require heavy investments in transportation, housing, and services. Industrial development will have to supply the needs of these populations for capital and consumption goods and will be the main factor in economic growth and employment in the Third World.

By the year 2000, the differences in economic levels among developing regions will increase notably, as reflected in Table 5.

As can be seen, the Middle Eastern and African oil-producing countries will have reached a substantial average income. The average, however, will hide huge disparities among the members of the group and will not be an adequate reflection of the type of development that these countries will have achieved by that time.

Latin America will have a size—in population, GNP, and GNP per capita—similar to that of Western Europe plus Japan in 1970. The level of development of Latin America at that time will put the area above the traditional economic level of the Third World and on a self-supporting path of development. However, the area may continue to share with other developing regions some common approaches to international political and economic relations. It may also be highly possible that the area will become partially or totally integrated with the OECD group.

Centrally planned Asia, which includes China, North Korea, Vietnam, and Mongolia, will grow much faster than the rest of the continent. It will reach an average per capita income above that attributed to Latin America for 1970. Because of its resources and institutional organization, it may be one of the fast-growing regions of the twenty-first century. The rest of Asia and Africa, with close to three billion people, will remain very backward and will continue to be an extremely serious challenge for international cooperation.

THE UNITED STATES AND THE THIRD WORLD

Soon after World War II, the United States directed its attention to the less developed countries. The Point IV Program established by President Truman started a long and important effort to provide financial and technical assistance to developing countries. It achieved its maximum significance between 1960 and 1966 and declined in relative

Table 5 Selected Regional Indicators, 1970 and 2000

	Industrial Countries				Third World					
	North America	Western Europe/Japan	Soviet Bloc	TOTAL	Latin America	Middle East Africa[a]	Africa	Asia	Centrally Planned Asia	TOTAL
Population 1970 (millions)	229	494	348	1071	281	127	273	1023	808	2512
Population 2000 (millions)	300	623	447	1370	621	318	640	2156	1226	4961
GNP 1970 (billion $)	1059	1004	599	2662	154	36	51	123	135	503
GNP 2000 (billion $)	2720	3582	2677	8979	1217	989	172	761	835	3974
GNP per capita 1970 ($)	4622	2031	1723	2486	546	286	186	119	167	200
GNP per capita 2000 ($)	9067	5754	5986	6554	1959	3111	268	353	681	801

[a] Oil-exporting countries.

Source. Based on data from Leontief, et al., *The Future of the World Economy: A United Nations Study* (New York: Oxford University Press, 1977).

terms from then to the present. Net official development assistance from the United States to developing countries and multilateral agencies amounted to an average of $3.3 billion or 0.41% of GNP in the period 1966–1968. In 1977 it amounted to $4.2 billion or 0.22% of GNP in 1977. U.S. aid was channeled bilaterally through institutions such as the Agency for International Development (AID) and the Export-Import Bank, and multilaterally through the World Bank group, the International Bank for Reconstruction and Development (IBRD), the UN Development Program, and the regional banks.

Without any doubt, the U.S. aid effort has been the largest of its kind, in absolute terms, to have been launched by any nation during this century, and it contributed significantly to the acceleration of development of many of the beneficiary countries.

At the same time, the United States supported actively the processes of decolonization all over the world. This process created a number of independent nations that today represent a large part of the Third World.

Economic and political relations with the countries of the Third World never represented a high priority issue for the United States, in spite of the concern repeatedly expressed by statesmen, scholars, leaders of the churches, and civic groups.

Some developing countries have been of interest to the United States from a strategic point of view, Taiwan, South Korea, Turkey, and Iran among them. Many countries have been suppliers of materials of strategic or purely economic importance. In most of these countries, the U.S. companies have made investments which have sometimes run into legal or political problems.

In the allocation of economic aid resources, strategic and economic considerations always have had considerable weight. Frequently, the aid program was presented as a way to stem advance of communism in developing countries, and in many cases this proved to be a real danger. Aid was also thought of as a means to create and maintain a favourable climate for U.S. investments in developing countries. On several occasions, the flow of aid to a specific country was suspended when conflicts arose about U.S. investments.

At the same time aid was always tied, in varying degrees, to procurement of goods and services in the United States and as such represented, to a great extent, an export financing instrument.

Finally, the principles of international solidarity, cooperation, and humanitarian assistance were always important in the orientation of foreign aid policies and programs.

In recent years, however, criticism of the foreign aid programs has increased. Aid has frequently been presented by its critics as a waste of taxpayers' money, while its impact in export promotion has been ignored. Persistent problems of the domestic economy and increases in oil prices have stimulated negative attitudes to foreign aid. These attitudes have coincided with the resurgence of protectionist pressures in foreign trade.

If the international cooperation programs of the United States are evaluated with objectivity, one must conclude that they have made a very valuable contribution to the progress of many developing countries. They have helped to establish a climate of international understanding and have brought to the United States not only economic benefits, but also a better knowledge and comprehension of a sector of the world which in spite of including 80% of total population has received scant attention.

The Third World will become increasingly important to the United States throughout the next century.

OPEC has been the first initiative of a group of Third World countries. This organization has had a profound impact on the international economy and on the industrial countries, the United States in particular.

Latin America will clearly emerge in the next century as a new group of industrialized countries. As a region, it can become self-sufficient in energy and in food. It has a large store of natural resources, still undeveloped, and a strong infrastructure to support its progress toward an advanced stage of industrialization. The size of the markets in the region can help to increase its participation in world trade.

Latin America will not require assistance from the United States in the next century in terms of traditional aid terms, but both the United States and Latin America will benefit mutually by an effective relationship of economic cooperation.

Because of its cultural, political, and economic characteristics and its location, it would seem logical for Latin America to evolve into full partnership in the OECD club. If this happens, the relationship between the United States and Latin America will become stronger and more stable, as it will be free of the still existent prejudices and suspicions. This new era of trust will stimulate flows of trade, investment, and financing.

Some of the issues that can be anticipated in United States–Latin American relations will be:

1   If both the United States and Latin American countries adhere to
    liberal trade policies within the spirit of GATT, trade in manu-
    factured goods in both directions will expand considerably. For
    Latin America, this may entail the elimination of some un-
    economical industrial sectors. For the United States, an adjust-
    ment will also be necessary to shift from some of its own
    industries as they cease to be competitive into others that offer
    more advantages. This will be a time of frictions and negotia-
    tions, and unions in the United States will have a strong influ-
    ence in the final outcome. U.S. multinational corporations will
    continue to have an important role in this field, and it can be an-
    ticipated that more and more Latin American corporations will
    aggressively enter the international field.

2   Because of the importance of external financing to its economic
    activity, Latin American presence in world money and capital
    markets will grow, as will partnerships among U.S. and Latin
    American financial institutions.

3   Energy will be the subject of far-reaching and mutually beneficial
    cooperation. The use of U.S. capital and technology to explore
    and develop new fossil fuel resources in Latin America may con-
    tribute substantially to an increase in world supply, probably
    above present expectations. This will require a less fearful atti-
    tude on Latin America's part in openly entering a joint effort. It
    may bring additional benefits such as a more open and effective
    U.S. involvement in the development of nuclear energy in Latin
    America.

Without prejudice to the important presence of Japan in the area,
China will tend to expand and strengthen its economic relations with
the United States. If its democratization process advances in the next
century, China may become another candidate for membership in the
OECD club.

It is still uncertain how the Islamic countries—and within them the
Arabs—will evolve. If the peaceful coexistence of Israel with the Islamic countries is finally achieved, the emerging group may have considerable economic strength. They may use their oil and gas resources,
while they last, to build a technical and economic infrastructure to
support further stable and self-supporting growth. While the United
States must share an economic presence in this area with Western Europe and the Soviet bloc, it will be nevertheless of considerable impor-

tance both for the United States and for the Islamic countries. The Islamic countries may complete the establishment of their basic industries in the next 20 years and begin to develop an advanced and diversified industrial sector and a more productive agriculture. At that time, U.S. investments, technology, and exports may have an edge over Western Europe and the Soviet countries.

The more important remaining area in the Third World will be the vast regions of extreme poverty of Asia and sub-Saharan Africa, which will start the new century much behind the rest of the world. The 2.5 billion people of those regions, most of them submerged in poverty or extreme deprivation, will constitute another formidable challenge to the industrial countries. By that time, it can be anticipated that all the capacity for humanitarian cooperation in the world can be concentrated there in order to make the twenty-first century the period of history in which the international community achieves the eradication of extreme poverty.

The more important unanswered question that remains is the type of society that will characterize the new century. I believe the world of this next stage will offer a paradox. There will be shrinking distances for communication, and increasing psychological similarity among individuals around the world. At the same time, the contrasting force will be more jealously political, autonomous communities of all sizes.

And the less analyzed subject is still that of the subordination of the fantastic infrastructure—through which mankind will navigate into the future—to the preservation of the essential values of the human being. These, I believe, will continue to be cherished for the next hundred years and more.

CHAPTER 20

Global Challenges in the Twenty-First Century

Jack N. Behrman, Ph.D.

There is little in the affairs of nations and humans that is truly new. The challenges of the twenty-first century will likely be those that faced most civilizations in the past and those that face us today. Without trying to characterize each challenge in detail, I have isolated 12 that will almost certainly fix our attention in the next century:

1 *Achieving global unity while maintaining cultural diversity.* This is the challenge of achieving peace for all nations with autonomy for each. It means the development of a sense of global community without the loss of national individualism that permits each country to seek its own destiny. Can a country become economically specialized and yet retain its national self-reliance?

2 *Achieving a competitive, yet cooperative, society.* How do we cooperatively maintain the dynamism of capitalism and thus avoid stagnation?

3 *Producing at an adequate level with an acceptable distribution of the benefits in the form of income or happiness.* This challenge requires that we solve the problem of motivation. Does it conflict with the principle of equality? Can we increase productivity, as we must, and yet allow a greater degree of worker participation in the conduct of business? If we can do that, how shall we make sure that some people are not forced to bear the burdens of others?

4 *Achieving political, economic, and social order while allowing the flexibility for change.* Here, the question is one of achieving stability with progress and of deciding what we mean by "progress."

5 *Providing appropriate opportunities for labor, with respect given to all forms of work.* The question is how to use labor without making it a commodity so devoid of humanity that each worker is boxed into his "place" in society. And how, finally, do we end discrimination in employment?

6 *Achieving technological advancement while maintaining acceptable levels and types of employment.* This is the question of the use of technology and its relationship to man's purpose in working.

7 *Gaining social and geographic mobility without a loss of social and economic values.* Here we have the role of the family, its responsibilities to the extended family, and its relationship to the community. With new kinds of cities and satellite towns, how does the family pass culture and tradition from one generation to the next? Can it provide stability for an individual and yet encourage evolutionary change?

8 *Carrying out the responsibilities of government while maintaining an adequate role for private initiative.* How do we reconcile regulation for social purposes with legitimate private interests? We must keep in mind the rigidity of bureaucracy and the comparative responsiveness of market decisions. How do we maintain participative democracy while protecting the privacy of the communication of ideas?

9 *Achieving personal freedom while developing social responsibility.* As we strive for equity in the social development of individuals, what legitimate constraints may we place on individualism?

10 *Achieving justice with mercy in juridical and penal matters.* How do we achieve an equitable society? These are the questions of how to determine the responsibility of an individual, how to rehabilitate people with antisocial personalities, and whether to employ behavior modification techniques.

11 *Using natural resources while maintaining the environment.* How free is man to alter the environment? Is our species evolving under rather tight constraints of our environment, so that our ability to command nature is largely illusory?

12 *Accelerating spiritual evolution while carrying out the neces-*
sary earthly roles. There are questions here of how to integrate
the emotional, physiological, mental, and spiritual aspects of
man. At the individual level, it begins with the maintenance of
healthy minds and bodies. At the social level, it starts with the
formation of values and the application of ethics in everyday
life.

These 12 challenges for the future reflect many of the problems posed
by Plato in *The Republic.* That they are ancient and still unsolved
should not mean that we can ignore them. While we cannot expect
utopian responses to these challenges between now and the year 2000,
we can be sure that in the twenty-first century some significant shifts
will have occurred in the way we respond to them and the way we
think about them.

The term "progress," for instance, will probably not be defined as a
continued growth of material goods and services. Even if we are still
counting goods and services, what we will call a "good" will be very
different. It is likely that we will be counting nonmarket goods in a
new conceptualization of GNP as "gross national progress." We may
even assign values to intangibles as we calculate "gross national happiness."

The first index would mean that we deduct all expenditures, including health maintenance, that merely keep us where we are. The second
would stretch to include psychic income. Under either calculation, we
will substantially reduce the resources now used to produce "goods,"
and there will be a relative shift of material goods to the "have-not"
nations.

Progress in the advanced nations will mean the encouragement of
each individual to develop on his unique path, but without the social
separateness implied in our present-day individualism. Our vision of
"basic human needs" will expand greatly, yet they will be met. The
term will mean much more than material support. It might include
filial love or place in the community. Greater attention will be paid to
those items that permit self-actualization of the individual without
damage to the society. The mix of foods we eat will shift toward those
that provide greater nutrition to the mind and body. Growth may well
be measured by the sum of all individual development, including cultural, intellectual, emotional, and spiritual growth.

The emphasis on individual growth will be paralleled by a much
greater recognition of the interdependence among nations. A philo-

sophical shift is likely, from the concept of "competition to win" over others to a "competition in ideas" within cooperative enterprises, whether corporations or countries. This acceptance of the idea of interdependence will begin to extinguish adversary relationships, including the one between labor and management. This may very well lead to the demise of collective bargaining.

With fewer adversary relationships, income distribution will not be a matter of bargaining and strikes, but of agreed-upon rules for matching talents, tasks, and rewards. Our present inability to find such an acceptable procedure costs us dearly. It is a major cause of inflation, and labor-management conflict tears at our social fabric. It is not conceivable that society could suffer with our present form of wage-setting without realizing that other procedures are required to maintain social stability in the twenty-first century.

Capital will no longer be seen in the next century as the residual element among the factors of production and therefore the rightful recipient of the profits. Recognition will arise that all parties to an enterprise bear the risk, to the extent that the private sector involves risk in the future. There will be greater stability of employment; flexibility in the use of capital equipment and labor will mean fewer plant closings. The flexibility within the labor force will come in part from training in multiple skills; capital equipment, more wisely deployed, will mean less waste in investment. Profit sharing will occur on a wider scale, if what remains after all the bills are paid is called "profit" at all.

With greater cooperation between labor and management and a heightened awareness of the social impacts of business activity, a reduction of governmental regulation is a possibility. It will be supported by greater self-discipline among individuals and groups. It is, after all, only through acceptance of responsibility that the rights of individuals, so often asserted today, can be truly gained.

Will the United States have a leadership role in such a system? The answer remains what it is today: in a peaceful world, leadership falls to those who have shown they know how to meet their own problems. Developing nations are constantly looking for ways to maintain unity with diversity, to progress without fouling their own nest, to give opportunity to all, to meet change without disruption, and to humanize labor. American solutions, to the extent we can provide them, can be imported by those who find them appropriate.

Currently, there appears to be a greater optimism in the developing nations that they know best how to proceed into the twenty-first century and a loss of confidence in the advanced countries. In my mind, this loss of confidence proceeds from the fact that we have placed pursuit of goods above pursuit of "the good." Mere material growth, we now know, does not solve our problems or provide happiness; in chasing physical wealth, we have lost our sense of mission. Material progress by itself is not wrong, until it becomes an end in itself and not subordinate to higher values. This condition, unfortunately, characterizes our society today, and we have only 20 years to come right with ourselves before we step into the twenty-first century.

Twenty years may seem a short time to prepare, but it is the same period over which the multinational corporation has risen to preeminence on the world economic scene. A similar sea-change in the international economic order is entirely possible in the next 20 years, and it will be the prologue for even more rapid evolution in the twenty-first century.

By making certain assumptions, we can paint the picture of the next 20 years in broad strokes, at least. The assumptions are: a slowing of population growth, no radical weather shifts or natural catastrophes, no significant wars, continued concern about poverty in the least developed countries, and continued technological advancement. If these assumptions are granted, I think we will see five major shifts taking place before the turn of the century.

First, there will be a new international economic order, and it will profoundly change the way business is organized and responds to markets. It will not be a world order based on overt agreement about the rules of the economic game but a tacit agreement that permits a considerable amount of jockeying and positioning among nations and groups of nations. The politicoeconomic structure of this world order will be built of regional blocs.

Some of the developing countries of the world will become what are now called "newly industrialized countries," with economic needs and demands more similar to advanced countries than to the remaining developing nations. In the Fourth World, a strong demand for "basic human needs" will arise and will be met in the next 20 years. Governments will enter the market with cooperative multigovernment projects in areas unattractive to private interests: regional development, space exploration, communications and transportation, and development of the seabed.

The location of natural resources around the world suggests that much more of their processing and use will take place in developing countries, with consequent changes in trade patterns, pricing, and inflation in advanced countries.

Political and economic realignments will alter the setting of international business. Accommodations between Japan and China will allow the formation of a regional bloc that includes Southeast Asia; it will be primarily commercial. The Middle East will likely remain unstable, but a bloc will form among the Islamic countries, primarily political with some commercial ties. Europe will expand its political ties and, with Israel and Greece, will likely form a loose economic association with Eastern Europe and Russia. North and South America will begin formation of a bloc, which will be only economic in nature at first. African countries will also make agreements, although the formation of a bloc will be a slow process. These new alliances will lead to changes in the structure and role of the United Nations as a greater concern for interregional affairs becomes apparent.

Science and technology will open up new energy sources, new techniques for communication that substitute for the physical movement of people, and new production techniques. Some industries will move out of developing countries back to the advanced nations. Wholly new product lines will arise.

Given these massive economic changes, the mission and character of transnational corporations will change. There will be increased concentration worldwide, with a few large companies dominating an industrial segment by means of satellite companies in each region. Consortia will form on a scale sufficient to match worldwide problems and opportunities that require massive managerial, technical, and human resources.

The second major shift I see for the next 20 years will bear on the activities of governments and of transnational companies. As a political matter, there will be a change in priority—away from efficiency in production toward equity in the distribution of benefits. This changing priority will include such matters as where production takes place. Greater emphasis will be placed on participative decision making in companies and governments, leading to the chance of conflict between the goals of job security and innovation. Innovation will take place most easily where recombinations of labor and capital, plus retraining of the work force, take precedence over closed plants and lost jobs.

Concurrent with this second shift will be the third: industrial concerns will relocate around the world, with some shifting into developing countries in pursuit of natural or politically contrived comparative advantages. Some relocation will also take place in advanced regions because of government policies, changing company structures and objectives, changes in exchange rates, and similar factors. It will now be possible to design the international economy, and it will be apparent that inefficiencies result from conflicting efforts to achieve national advantage. This will lead to greater regional cooperation. It will become clear that we have no criteria for determining the location of industrial activity—that is, who should produce what, where, and sell to whom. Criteria will emerge, although agreement about them will be easier within regional blocs than between them.

The impact of these first three shifts will demand considerable adjustment on the part of national economies and governments. The increasing significance of agriculture in the world will move more agricultural production into the United States, because of its technological lead in the field. Although ever more sophisticated technologies will push the growth of the advanced countries, they will continue to have problems with employment, appropriate utilization of labor, demands for leisure, continuing education, and training of labor to maintain productivity. Efforts to raise respect for all work in our society will heighten the belief that equity has been achieved; the result will be increased productivity.

Finally, business managers will need to develop more complex techniques for dealing with systemic problems. Companies will have to communicate effectively to make clear their acceptance of a more complex and responsive role. The proliferation of academic courses and literature about the social role of corporations is a beginning of this trend. In addition, managers will have to develop people with many skills and the ability to deal with the varied cultures they meet around the world. Management, therefore, will be using these next 20 years to learn how to become attuned to multiple pressures in multiple markets and settings.

As I look at our ability to respond to these coming shifts in the world order, I see at least four shortcomings in our preparedness. They have to do with education, inequalities of opportunity, the concept of evolution, and the direction of technology.

The challenges we face call for a return to holistic instruction. The separation of academic disciplines has run its course, and we need now to reintroduce more systemic approaches to learning and its application. The idea of the unity of all knowledge has been lost, as has the old debate about the distinction between science and religion and the intellectual separation of man and his environment. More attention must be given to complexity and interrelation.

Also, more attention needs to be paid to continuing education. Our practice is to halt education before the student has a chance to experiment with what he has learned. Experience is still the best teacher, but it would be desirable to provide continuing education for the development of new skills, preparation for new roles, and even for opening avenues to new perceptions of individual, social, and economic progress.

Democratic societies have long called for equality of opportunity. Now, the urgency to achieve it has more than a moral basis. If we are to meet the challenges ahead, we will need all the human resources available. We must be certain that educational and career opportunities are as open as possible, while making sure that individuals moving into new jobs possess adequate skills and concepts, including an understanding of the rights and responsibilities of individuals. Equality of opportunity will necessarily lead to unequal benefits because of unequal contributions, so we will need to devise a system of selection, work, and rewards that is understood and acceptable.

All of us will need better preparation for the shifting sociocultural relations that will arise from this global evolution. We need an understanding of evolutionary change in individuals and societies. Too much emphasis has been placed on satisfaction of the individual's material wants and not enough on his evolution and that of the society.

Technology must be turned away from military activities. We have as an example the technological advance of Germany and Japan without benefit of military technology. We must bring our technological effort to bear instead on the problems of urbanization, rural-urban balance, dispersion of industry, agricultural production, health maintenance, and communication.

In sum, we will continue our evolution toward a world society based on democracy and individualism, but with some detours and regressions as each nation tries to solve its own problems independently. Cooperative solutions will come slowly but surely, as we recognize that we are in a world together and that only together can we reach our goals, which will preclude a continuation of our tearing at each other and tearing up the environment.

EPILOGUE

Ours Is the Power to Choose
James C. Lehrer

O ur search into the future began in Richmond with a film. The images of the twenty-first century flashed on: spaceships soaring off into the stratosphere, machines whirling around and around, far-off planets fading in and out of focus. The sounds, musical and natural, were boomy, jarring, and loud.

Then, suddenly, a silent, peaceful shot of a small boy drinking from a water fountain. He was dressed in the clothes of the twentieth century but his face, his very being, said all that need be said about the twenty-first century. It will be his. Not ours. Most of us won't be around for enough of it to be affected one way or another.

But we are around now—and that's the problem. We're in a position to foul up the future for that young boy and his friends. As W. W. Rostow said: "Decisions in the short run control the long run."

What we do in our literal tomorrows can and will affect the way our young friend lives and works in his literal tomorrow—the tomorrow of the twenty-first century. We can decide how the computer-dominated world of that boy's future will really work.

The experts in this book have laid out the prospects. Ordinary work, as we now know it, will cease to exist. Computers and other machines will make mail deliverers, bank tellers, store clerks, bus drivers, and most similar workers obsolete. Most sales and other business transactions will be done on TV monitors at home. Newspapers and magazines will be delivered the same way. No printers, no pressmen, nothing left to wrap fish in.

All of this is great and flows naturally out of that thing we call progress. But tragedy and disaster for the human beings involved can flow as well. The experts laid out those prospects just as vividly. The element of challenge could be eliminated from the workplace. The result would be boredom, a boredom so strong and pervasive that a kind of listlessness could permeate our young man and his society. Education would no longer be important. Drugs and alcohol would be. We could very well create a world where only machines are vital, where people are only obsolete and turned off.

It doesn't have to be that way.

Isaac Asimov and others see a different vision of the twenty-first century. They see it as a time of creativity, when people, freed of the workplace rigors of our time, turn to satisfactions of the mind and soul. Music and literature, art and ideas will dominate life in the twenty-first century.

No longer required to use his mind to make change for a $5 bill, our young friend will use it to compose sonnets and symphonies.

It can be that way.

We human beings *do* have the ability to make the right decisions for the future. But we won't unless some of us lay aside the baggage of the twentieth century.

And there is a lot of baggage to be discarded. It's the baggage of self-interest and conflict, myopia and tunnel vision, among many other things.

That boy at the water fountain will be watching us as we make our short-run decisions. He'll be watching to see what we're doing to his long run—his life in the twenty-first century. He's what it's all about, remember. Not us.

BIOGRAPHICAL NOTES

THE AUTHORS

ISAAC ASIMOV, Ph.D., Author, Scientist, Futurist: Dr. Asimov is one of contemporary literature's most prolific writers and a stimulating speaker on "The Future of Man." The associate professor of biochemistry from Boston University has celebrated the publication of more than 200 books. He has averaged better than seven books annually—as many as 15 in one year—since his first was published in 1950. Among Dr. Asimov's well-known best sellers are *The Foundation Trilogy, Asimov's Guide to Science,* and *The Collapsing Universe.* Additionally, hundreds of Asimov articles have appeared in publications including *Esquire, Harper's* and *Saturday Review.* He also edits his own magazine called *Isaac Asimov's Science Fiction.* Dr. Asimov was born in Russia and came to the United States in early childhood. He earned his bachelor's, master's, and doctoral degrees at Columbia University.

JACK N. BEHRMAN, Ph.D., Luther Hodges Distinguished Professor, University of North Carolina Graduate School of Business Administration: He is also an advisor to the U.S. Department of State and the UN Centre for Transnational Corporations as well as Senior Research Advisor to the Fund for Multinational Management Education. He is currently writing for the Council on Foreign Relations on the role of multinational enterprises in international industrial integration, and conducting a study on overseas R&D activities of international companies. Dr. Behrman is a frequent member of research panels for the National Research Council, the National Academy of Science, and the National Academy of Engineering. He has written over twenty books and monographs on international economics.

WILLIAM E. BONNET, Ph.D., Vice President–Environmental Assessment, The Sun Company, Inc.: With Sun since 1950, Dr. Bonnet has been Manager of Economics and Planning in its Commercial Development Department, Director of Technical Economics, Director of Science and Technology, Director of Corporate Development, and President of Sun Ventures, Inc. He is a member of the American Institute of Chemical Engineers, the American Chemical Society, and the American Petroleum Institute. Dr. Bonnet is also a trustee of the Midwest Research Institute and the Philadelphia Academy of Natural Sciences.

STEWART BRAND, Editor, Publisher, and founder of the *CoEvolution Quarterly, Whole Earth Catalog,* and *Whole Earth Epilog:* A biology major at Stanford, Mr. Brand was a leading force in the back-to-the-land movement of the 1960s. His *Whole Earth Catalog,* published from 1968 to 1971, was a bible for many young people striving for self-sufficiency. Mr. Brand has been an organizer of many events, including the "Whole Earth Jamboree" and the *Catalog's* widely publicized "Demise Party." He has also been a part-time consultant to Governor Jerry Brown of California and is at present Chairman of the California Water Atlas Advisory Board. Mr. Brand is author of *Two Cybernetic Frontiers* and the recipient of a National Book Award for Contemporary Affairs.

PAT L. BURR, Ph.D., Associate Professor of Business, The University of Texas at San Antonio, and former Associate Administrator for Management Assistance, Small Business Administration: As the first woman appointed to SBA's Management Board, Dr. Burr was responsible for the policy areas of training, counseling, publications, the Small Business Institute, Small Business Development Centers, international trade, the Service Corps of Retired Executives and Active Corps of Executives (SCORE/ACE), and audio-visual aids. She served on the Carter-Mondale transition team, helped create the National Women's Business Ownership Campaign, and designed a national outreach program to attract more women to the business arena.

THEODORE J. GORDON, President, The Futures Group, Inc.: Mr. Gordon has authored more than one hundred reports at The Futures Group. He also helped establish the Institute for the Future, where he studied the future of employee benefits, computer risk, relationships between business and society, problems of technology assessment, and the development of cross-impact analysis. He has assessed geothermal energy resource development and life-extending technologies for the National Science Foundation, and has researched U.S. power needs, lifestyles of the future, future computer developments, new business strategies, and the social responsibility of business. Mr. Gordon was Chief Engineer of the Saturn Program for the McDonnell Douglas Astronautics Company, and was responsible for the design of Douglas' space station, boost vehicle, and interplanetary programs.

WALTER A. HAHN, Senior Specialist in Science, Technology, and Futures Research, Congressional Research Service of the Library of Congress: Mr. Hahn has served as Director of Policy Analysis for the U.S. Department of Commerce, Senior Research Associate on the White House National Goals Research Staff, Deputy Assistant Secretary of Commerce for Science and Technology, head of policy planning for the Environmental Science Services Administration, and Director of Management Analysis for NASA. He was a Visiting Professor at the University of Washington and the founding president of the International Society for Technology Assessment. Mr. Hahn is active in The Institute of Management Sciences, National Conference on the Advancement of Research, American Society for Public Administration, and the World Future Society.

LOUIS HARRIS, President, Louis Harris and Associates, Inc.: Mr. Harris is one of America's leading analysts of public opinion and the author of *The Harris Survey,* a syndicated column which appears in over 200 newspapers twice weekly. His firm has conducted more than 1800 surveys since 1956, including polling for over 200 political candidates, and surveys for *Newsweek, Life,* and *Time.* Mr. Harris, who pioneered election night early projections, was the first to apply sophisticated computer techniques to survey data. He has a long-term contract with ABC News to analyze elections and surveys of public opinion, and he appears frequently on the ABC Evening News. Mr. Harris is also Chairman of the Board of the American Council for the Arts.

JAMES H. JORDAN, Ph.D., Vice President—Employee Relations, ICI Americas Inc.: Dr. Jordan handles employee relations in North America, Canada, and Latin America, specializing in labor and industrial relations, personnel administration, public employment disputes, business organization and management, and manpower development and training. He is an adjunct professor at The Wharton School, and a member of the Industrial Relations Research Association, National Labor Panel of the American Arbitration Association, American Management Associations, and other professional associations. He is the author of numerous papers on industrial and labor relations.

SUZANNE KELLER, Ph.D., Professor of Sociology and Architecture, Princeton University: Dr. Keller has taught courses on social stratification, the family, social theory, sex and society, urban planning, and futurism at the Athens Technological Institute, CCNY, NYU, New York Medical College, Vassar, and Brandeis. Fluent in French, German, and Greek, she has lectured extensively abroad. She was the recipient of a Fulbright Fellowship and a Guggenheim Award. Dr. Keller has been a member of the National Advisory Council for the National Institute of Mental Health and has been Vice President of the Eastern Sociological Association and the American Sociological Association.

THEODORE W. KHEEL, Esq., Lawyer, Arbitrator, Mediator of Labor Disputes: Mr. Kheel is a director of the American Arbitration Association, Athlone Industries, Inc., UV Industries, Inc., Western Union Telegraph Co., Western Union Corp., and Combustion Equipment Associates, Inc. He is also Administrative Director of The Institute of Collective Bargaining and Group Relations, Inc. In the past, Mr. Kheel has served as an advisor to former New York Mayor Beame, a member of the President's National Citizens Committee for Community Relations, the President's Maritime Advisory Committee, and has been on Presidential Boards for various labor disputes. Mr. Kheel has also served as Chairman of the Mayor's Committee for Job Advancement, Special Consultant to the President's Committee for Equal Employment Opportunity, and President of the National Urban League.

JAMES C. LEHRER, Associate Editor and Washington Anchor for The MacNeil/Lehrer Report: Mr. Lehrer has moderated or anchored many special television reports, including "Washington Straight Talk," "Washington Connection," "America '73," and the House Judiciary Committee's impeachment inquiry. His coverage of the Senate Watergate Committee's investigation won his station (Washington's WETA/ 26) an Emmy and the 1974 George Polk Award for excellence in television reporting. He has also worked on productions which have earned the American Bar Association Silver Gavel Certificate of Merit, and the 1974 George Foster Peabody Award for overall broadcast journalism excellence. Prior to joining the National Public Affairs Center for Tele-

vision (now merged with WETA/26), Mr. Lehrer was Public Affairs
Coordinator for the Public Broadcasting Service and a member of the
PBS Journalism Advisory Board.

IRVING LEVESON, Ph.D., Director of Economic Studies, Hudson Institute: Dr. Leveson has spent 18 years in economic research and planning. He has directed projects for the Hudson Institute Corporate
Environment Program, the U.S. Economic Development Administration, the State Department, and other federal agencies. He has also developed studies of consumer markets, leisure, and lifestyle trends for
corporate clients. Prior to joining the Institute, he worked for the National Bureau of Economic Research, the RAND Corporation, and the
New York City Planning Department, and established the Office of
Health Systems Planning in New York, which he headed for three
years. Dr. Leveson's numerous publications include the forthcoming
book, *The Economic Future of the United States.*

WILLIAM LUCY, International Secretary-Treasurer, American Federation of State, County and Municipal Employees (AFSCME), AFL-CIO:
Mr. Lucy, a civil engineer, is also a Vice President of the AFL-CIO Industrial Union Department and The Maritime Trade Department. He
serves on the board of directors of the African-American Institute, the
National Urban League, Americans for Democratic Action, and the National Black United Fund. Mr. Lucy is also a member of the National
Leadership Conference on Civil Rights. He was a founder and the first
president of the Coalition of Black Trade Unionists (CBTU) which fo-
cuses on the needs of black and minority group workers. *Ebony Magazine* has listed Mr. Lucy among "the 100 Most Influential Black
Americans."

CECILIO J. MORALES, Manager of the Economic and Social Development Department, Inter-American Development Bank: Mr. Morales
had been a Regional Representative in La Paz and Lima and Deputy
Program Advisor for the Inter-American Development Bank before becoming Manager of its Economic and Social Development Department
in 1968. Prior to joining the bank, Mr. Morales was Executive Vice
President of the Atlantic Community Development Group for Latin
America (ADELATEC), Director of the Department of Economic and
Social Affairs of the OAS, and Executive Secretary of the Inter-American Economic and Social Council. A native of Buenos Aires, he was

also Economic Counselor of the Argentine Delegation to the UN and Chairman of the International Commodity Trade Commission.

JAMES J. O'TOOLE, Ph.D., Associate Professor of Management, University of Southern California Graduate School of Business: Dr. O'Toole is also Director of USC's Twenty Year Forecast project and is a member of the Board of Directors of the American Association for Higher Education. He has served as a Special Assistant to the Secretary of HEW, and as Chairman of the Secretary's Task Force on Work in America. He has been a management consultant with McKinsey and Company and Director of The Aspen Institute Program on Education, Work, and the Quality of Life. Dr. O'Toole, a Rhodes Scholar, has written five books and numerous articles. In a recent American Council on Education survey, he was selected among "one hundred most respected emerging leaders in higher education."

A. H. RASKIN, Associate Director of The National News Council: For many years Mr. Raskin was a labor correspondent and columnist for *The New York Times* and a member of its Editorial Board, specializing in labor and national affairs. He has also been an adjunct professor at the Columbia University Graduate School of Business and at Pace University. Mr. Raskin is the recipient of numerous awards including the Columbia University Journalism Award for distinction in the field of journalism, the Pace University award for distinguished service in labor-management relations, and awards presented by the Labor Press Council of Metropolitan New York and the Institute of Collective Bargaining and Group Relations. He is co-author with David Dubinsky of *David Dubinsky: A Life With Labor,* and his appraisal of labor's history since the New Deal will be published soon by W. W. Norton & Co., Inc.

JEROME M. ROSOW, President and founder of Work in America Institute, Inc.: Mr. Rosow is also Chairman of the President's Advisory Committee on Federal Pay, an advisor to the Committee for Economic Development, a member of the U.S. Business and Industry Advisory Committee of the OECD, and President of the Industrial Relations Research Association. Prior to setting up the Institute, he was Public Affairs Planning Manager for Exxon Corporation. Previous government positions include Assistant Secretary of Labor for Policy, Evaluation and Research and Vice Chairman of the National Productivity Commission. He edited *The Worker and the Job: Coping With Change* and is a co-editor of *Work in America: The Decade Ahead.*

W. W. ROSTOW, Ph.D., Professor of Economics and History, The University of Texas at Austin: Dr. Rostow, a Rhodes Scholar and doctorate recipient from Yale, has also taught economics and history at Columbia, Oxford, Cambridge, and M.I.T. During the 1960s he served as an advisor to Presidents Kennedy and Johnson. In 1969 he received the Presidential Medal of Freedom with distinction. A professor of economics and history at The University of Texas at Austin since 1969, Dr. Rostow is the author of several books including *How It All Began: The Origins of Modern Economic Growth, The World Economy: History and Prospect,* and *Getting from Here to There, America's Future in the World Economy.*

GEORGE J. VOJTA, Executive Vice President, Citibank, N.A.: Mr. Vojta is in charge of Strategic Planning for Citicorp/Citibank. He joined Citibank in 1961 and has served in Singapore, the Philippines, and Kuala Lumpur. In 1968 Mr. Vojta was made Resident Vice President for Malaysia. A year later he became Resident Vice President for Pakistan in Karachi and Vice President and Senior Officer in Japan and Korea. Mr. Vojta returned to the United States in 1972 to serve as head of the Corporate Planning Department. He was then named Senior Vice President and General Manager in charge of the International Banking Group and later Executive Vice President. Mr. Vojta headed the International Banking Group until 1977.

IAN H. WILSON, Consultant, Public Policy Research, General Electric Company: Mr. Wilson is responsible for analyzing the interrelationships between GE's corporate strategies and future public policy issues, and for recommending company policy and action on these issues. Prior to his work in Public Policy Research, he helped establish a Business Environment Studies program for GE which identified long-range social, political, and economic trends. Originally from England, Mr. Wilson is the author of two books about the business environment of the future. He has also written numerous articles for the *Michigan Business Review, Long Range Planning,* and *The Futurist.*

WILLIAM W. WINPISINGER, President, International Association of Machinists and Aerospace Workers: Since assuming IAM leadership, Mr. Winpisinger has substantially expanded the union's civil rights, community services, job safety, public relations, and organizing programs. He joined the IAM as an auto mechanic in his native Cleveland, where he was soon elected local lodge president. In 1951 he became one of the youngest members ever to be appointed to the IAM's national field staff. Shortly thereafter, Mr. Winpisinger joined IAM headquarters in Washington and in 1977 became International President of IAM and a Vice President of the AFL-CIO. He is also President of the Institute of Collective Bargaining and Group Relations, Inc.

THE EDITORS

DONALD C. CARROLL, Ph.D., Dean and Reliance Professor of Private Enterprise, The Wharton School, University of Pennsylvania: Described as "Wharton's Master of Growth" by The New York Times, Dean Carroll has developed the School's research activities and led the effort to expand the study of management in the public sector. He was the first dean to be selected from outside the University. As a professor at M.I.T., he headed its Management Information Systems Group and Operations Management Group. Dean Carroll later co-founded TMI Systems Corporation, where he continues as Chairman. He serves on the board of directors of Monsanto Company, Morse Shoe, Inc., Vestaur Securities, Inc., Franklin Mint Corporation, National Railway Utilization Corporation, and Arlen Realty.

C. STEWART SHEPPARD, Ph.D., Dean and Tipton R. Snavely Professor of Business Administration, The Colgate Darden Graduate School of Business Administration, University of Virginia: Born in Wales, Dean Sheppard came to the U.S. in 1940 to complete his M.B.A. and Ph.D. He has been a professor at The Colgate Darden School for 18 years, and Dean since 1972. His prior academic posts include Dean and Professor of Business Administration at Cornell's Graduate School of Business and Public Administration and Professor of Economics and Associate Dean of New York University's School of Business Administration. Dean Sheppard is a trustee of The Financial Analysts Research Foundation and The Institute of Chartered Financial Analysts.

SELECTED BIBLIOGRAPHY

BELL, DANIEL. *The Coming of Post-Industrial Society.* New York: Basic Books, 1973.

BELL, DANIEL. *The Cultural Contradictions of Capitalism.* New York: Basic Books, 1976.

BOULDING, KENNETH. "The Economics of the Coming Spaceship Earth" in Henry Jarrett (ed.), *Environmental Quality in a Growing Economy: Essays from the 6th RFF Forum.* Baltimore: Johns Hopkins Press for Resources for the Future, Inc., 1966, pp. 3–14.

BRAVERMAN, HARRY. *Labor and Monopoly Capital.* Monthly Review Press, 1974.

CALLAHAN, DANIEL. *The Tyranny of Survival.* New York: Macmillan, 1973.

CORNISH, EDWARD. *The Study of the Future.* Washington, D.C.: World Future Society, 1977.

D'APRIX, R. M. "Blacks, Women and the Conscience of a Company Man." *Business and Society Review* (Summer 1976), 18:55.

DEUTSCH, KARL W. *Tides Among Nations.* New York: The Free Press, 1979.

DEUTSCH, KARL W. and FRITSCH, BRUNO, eds. *Problems of World Modeling: Political and Social Implications.* Cambridge: Ballinger, 1977.

DICKSON, PAUL. *The Future of the Workplace.* New York: Weybright and Talley, 1975.

DRUCKER, PETER. *The Unseen Revolution: How Pension Fund Socialism Came to America.* New York: Harper and Row, 1976.

FEINBERG, GERALD. *Consequences of Growth: The Prospects for a Limitless Future.* New York: The Seabury Press, 1977.

FERKISS, VICTOR C. *The Future of Technological Civilization.* New York: George Braziller, 1974.

FREEMAN, CHRISTOPHER and JAHODA, MARIE, eds. *World Futures: The Great Debate.* New York: Universe Books, 1977.

GINZBERG, ELI, ed. *Jobs for Americans.* Englewood Cliffs, New Jersey: Prentice-Hall, 1976.

HEDGES, J. N. "Flexible Schedules: Problems and Issues." *Management Labor Review* (Fall 1977), 100:62–65.

INGLEHART, RONALD. *The Silent Revolution.* Princeton: Princeton University Press, 1977.

JONAS, HANS. *From Ancient Creed to Technological Man.* Englewood Cliffs, New Jersey: Prentice–Hall, 1974.

KAHN, E. J., Jr. *The American People.* New York: Weybright and Talley, 1973.

KAHN, HERMAN, et al. *The Next 200 Years.* New York: William Morrow and Company, 1976.

KAHN, HERMAN. *World Economic Development.* Boulder, Colorado: Westview Press, 1979.

KERR, CLARK and ROSOW, JEROME, eds. *Work in America: The Decade Ahead.* New York: Van Nostrand Reinhold, 1979.

LAWRENCE, R. "Flexible Working Hours." *Credit & Financial Management* (January 1977), 79:12–13ff.

LECHT, L. A. "Women at Work." *Conference Board Record* (Spring 1976), 13:16–21.

LEGRANDE, LINDA H. "Women In Labor Organizations: Their Ranks Are Increasing." *Monthly Labor Review* (August 1978), pp. 8–14.

LEONTIEF, WASSILY, et al. *The Future of the World Economy: A United Nations Study.* New York: Oxford Press, 1977.

LEVESON, IRVING. *The Economic Future of the United States,* to be published by Westview Press, Boulder, Colorado.

LEVESON, IRVING. *The Modern Service Sector.* Washington, D.C.: Joint Economic Committee, U.S. Congress, forthcoming (late 1979).

MASLOW, ABRAHAM. *Toward A Psychology of Being,* 2nd edition. New York: Van Nostrand Reinhold, 1968.

MEADOWS, DONELLA, et al. *The Limits to Growth.* New York: Universe Books, 1972.

MESAROVIC, MIHAJLO and PESTEL, EDUARD. *Mankind at the Turning Point, the Second Report to the Club of Rome.* New York: E. P. Dutton, 1974.

NATIONAL COMMISSION FOR MANPOWER POLICY. *Job Creation Through Public Service Employment: An Interim Report to the Congress.* Washington, D.C.: The Commission, 1978.

NICHOLSON, N. and GOODGE, P. M. "Influence of Social, Organizational and Biographical Factors on Female Absence." *Journal of Management Studies* (October 1976), 13:234–54.

NOZICK, ROBERT. *Anarchy, State and Utopia.* New York: Basic Books, 1974.

OKUN, ARTHUR. *Equality and Efficiency.* Washington, D.C.: The Brookings Institution, 1975.

O'TOOLE, JAMES. *Work, Learning and the American Future.* San Francisco: Jossey-Bass, 1977.

OWEN, J. D. "Flexitime: Some Problems and Solutions." *Industry and Labor Relations Review* (January 1977), 30:152–60.

PASSMORE, JOHN. *Man's Responsibility for Nature.* New York: Charles Scribner, 1974.

PEAL, E. "What's a Woman's Job Worth?" *Personnel* (January 1977), 54:6–7.

PEAL, E. "Women in Business" (special report). *Masters in Business Administration* (Fall 1977), 11:21–39.

ROSOW, JEROME, ed. *The Worker and the Job: Coping With Change.* Englewood Cliffs, New Jersey: Prentice-Hall, 1974.

ROSTOW, W. W. *Getting From Here to There.* New York: McGraw-Hill, 1978.

ROSTOW, W. W. *The World Economy: History and Prospect.* Austin: University of Texas Press, 1978.

SAWHILL, I. V. "When Mothers are also Managers." *Business Week* (April 18, 1977), p. 155–56ff.

SCHRANK, ROBERT. *Ten Thousand Working Days.* Cambridge: M.I.T. Press, 1978.

SCHUMACHER, E. F. *Small is Beautiful.* New York: Harper and Row, 1973.

SCHURMANN, FRANTZ and CLOSE, SANDY. "The Emergence of a Global City, U.S.A." *Progressive,* Vol. 43 (January 1979) 1:27.

SEABORG, GLENN. "The Recycling Society." *The Futurist* (June 1974), pp. 110–112, 114–115.

SMITH, LEE. "Flexitime: A New Work Style Catches On." *Duns Review* (March 1977), 109:61ff.

Special Task Force to the Secretary of Health, Education, and Welfare. *Work in America.* Cambridge: M.I.T. Press, 1972.

TERKEL, STUDS. *Working.* New York: Pantheon Books, 1974.

THEOBALD, ROBERT. *An Alternative Future for America II.* Chicago: Swallow Press, 1970.

WAES. *Workshop on Alternative Energy Strategies. Energy: Global Prospects 1985–2000.* New York: McGraw-Hill, 1977.

WALLACE, M. R. "Earnings of Men and Women." *Monthly Labor Review* (January 1977), 100:2.

WALLACE, M. R., "Reflections on Women at Work." *Across the Board* (November 1976), 13:39–42.

WALLIA, C. S., ed. *Toward Century 21: Technology, Society and Human Values.* New York: Basic Books, 1970.

Index

Affirmative action programs, 156, 160
Affluence, 163, 173-174
  and post-industrial society, 135-136,
    139, 142
  see also Wealth
AFL-CIO, 56, 75
Africa, 193, 199, 203, 209
Aging society, 3-5, 8, 47-48
Aiken, Howard, 31
Alienation, 15, 146
  increased, 83-85
  and individualism, 61-62
Alternative work schedules, see Work
    schedule alternatives
American Federation of State, County
    and Municipal Employees, 80
American Federation of Teachers, 56
Anti-unionism, 84-87, 92
Arendt, Hannah, 162
Aries, Philippe, 150
Asia, 193-194, 197-199
Attitudes and behavior, 135
  in conflict with experience, 153-154
  distortion of, 157-161, 165
  value changes and, 139-144
Authority relationships, 111-113, 118, 136
  shift to participation, 142
Automation, 15, 23, 26
  employment trends, 171-172
  impact of, 45, 93
  see also Compunications;
    Electronics

Babbage, Charles, 31
"Baby boom" generation, 121, 137-139,
    172
Balance of payments deficits, 161-162
Baruch, Bernard, 127

Bell, Daniel, 32, 146-147, 164
Benefits, see Employee benefits; Pensions
Berg, Ivar, 161
Birth rate, 3-5, 17, 40, 149, 169
  changed character of labor force, 71-73
  rise of, 170, 172
Blacks, 158
  access to jobs, 83, 95
  and unemployment, 79, 95
  and unions, 55, 71, 75
  young, and increased employment
    opportunities, 108
Blue-collar workers, 28, 55
  decline in, 74, 81, 147
  hourly wages, 95
  to white-collar jobs, 94, 106
Boulding, Kenneth, 152
Bryner, Gary, 157
Brzezinski, Zbigniew, 136
Business, 70, 97, 113
  and government, 65-67, 144
  see also Corporations

Calvin, Melvin, 175
Capital, 73, 207
  diminished productivity of, 184-186
  and nature of work, 15, 39-40
  into service industries, 189-190
  shortage of, 40-41, 73, 76
Capital-intensive projects, 45, 143, 174,
    176
Capitalism, 183-188
Careers, 15
  multiple, 25-27, 37, 149, 211
  pressures of and family, 115
Checkless, cashless society, 34
Child care, 62, 87, 99, 100, 150

and work schedules, 100-102
China, 3, 194, 196-198, 202, 209
Circuit chips, 25, 31, 183
Cities, 20, 32, 123
  population decline, 42, 153
  smaller with satellites, 28, 205
Civil Service employees, see Public
  employees
Clerical jobs, 82, 106, 189
Close, Sandy, 82
Club of Rome, 146
Coal, 26, 27, 92-93, 196
Coalition of Labor Union Women, 100
Coalition of Northeast Governors, 22
Collective bargaining, 49-52, 61, 66, 74
  and automation, 92-93
  for consumers and producers, 127
  defined, 51-52
  future trends, 52-54, 56-57, 76-79, 207
  work schedule alternatives, 117
College education, 83-85, 110, 136-137
Communal living, 154, 170
Communications revolution, 15, 23, 25-26
  and alienation, 16, 33
  see also Compunications
Communist countries, 185, 188, 194
Competition:
  and changing values, 123, 142
  elimination of, 64
  future cooperation and, 204, 206-207,
    211
  international economic, 42, 76, 91-93,
    184
  for promotions and jobs, 83, 108-109
  public versus private-sector unions, 96
Compunications, 30-38
  and crime, 36-37
  impact of, 32-37
Computer technology, 15, 36, 171
  and American economy, 183-184
  and education, 8-9
  and nonemployables, 148-149
  social effects, 9, 44, 148-149
  systems and jobs, 32-33, 147-149
  and voice communication, 25-26
  see also Compunications; Electronics
    revolution
Congress, U.S., 23, 83
  and labor laws, 50-51, 70, 85
Conservation, 22, 139, 179
Conservatives, 70, 129-130, 132

"Conspicuous conservation," 178
Consumerism, 144, 151-153
  and product problems, 126-127, 130
Consumption, 19-20, 174, 197
Corporate state, 64-68
Corporations, 40-41
  anti-union campaigns, 85, 92
  worker responsibility experiments, 165
  see also Multinational corporations
"Cowboy economy," 152-153

Decision making and worker
  participation, 66, 113, 121, 139,
    141-143, 148
  in Europe, 97, 166
  and productivity, 204
Defense and space spending, 42, 65, 88,
    115, 211
Democracy:
  participatory, 143, 205, 211
  political process, 21, 114
Democratic socialism, 61, 65
Demographic trends, 62, 71, 88-89,
    107-108
  "baby boom" generation, 137-139, 172
  table, on median age, 137
Developing countries, see Third World
Disease, 25, 89, 91, 170-181
Divorce, 149-150
Drucker, Peter, 32, 184
Dyson, Freeman, 173

Eastern Europe, 184, 209
Economic growth, see Growth rate,
  economic
Economic security, 160-163
Economy:
  and compunications impact on, 35
  conservation and efficiency, 177
  future prospects, 15-18, 39-42, 152
  income disparities, 63-65
  inflation and productivity, 73, 91, 115,
    184
  Keynesian debate, 15, 18-19
  national planning and, 88-89, 93-94
  real income and terms of trade, 19-20
  service jobs, and effects, 81-87, 125
  slowdown, 91
  structural changes, 42
  supply problems, 20-23, 40
  union-management trends, 76-79

see *also* International economy; Post-
   industrial society
Education and schooling:
   changing values, 111, 113, 123, 148, 153
   compunications impact on, 32, 37, 44, 61
   by computers, 7-9
   continuing, 5-8, 47, 210
   future challenges, 210-211, 214
   less-demanding jobs and, 83-85
   Post-industrial society, 135-137,
      139-140
   and resources for, 19, 41
   see *also* Job training
EEOC, 74
Ehrhardt, Werner, 153
Electronic funds transfer (EFT), 34
Electronics revolution, 15, 213-214
   hardware, 25
   and job creation, 47
   and productivity, 26, 82
   and products, 171
   see *also* Compunications
Employee benefits, 66, 78, 94, 110, 113-114
   equality of opportunity and, 211
   individualization of, 144
Employee rights and responsibilities, 139,
   156-167
Employers:
   authority and employees, 111-112
   and child care facilities, 62, 100
   women employees, 99-102
   see *also* Collective bargaining; Labor-
      management relations;
      Management
Energy:
   alternative sources, 27, 173-176
   conservation and self-sufficiency, 124,
      128-129, 177-178
   costs, and economic growth, 27
   and mobility, 26-28, 176
   and new technologies, 40, 196-197
   and workplace, 27-29
   international development of, 196-197,
      202
   labor problems and, 56
   lifestyle changes, 42, 153
   price deregulation, 64
   prices, 20, 174-176
   productivity slowdown, 116
   supply problem, 15, 18, 20-23
Energy Policy and Conservation Act, 177

England, 188
   economic system, 61, 155-156
   and labor unions, 74, 161, 164
ENIAC, 31, 183
Entrepreneurship, 183-188
   knowledge jobs, 189-190
   see *also* Innovation
Environment, 205
   American expectations and quality of,
      115, 123, 129, 139, 151
   compunications impact on, 35
   contamination of, and health, 28, 89, 91
   costs, and impact on jobs, 28, 56
   and economic expansion, 91, 116, 189
   energy sources and, 27, 197
   exploitation of versus economic
      security, 162-163
   and new technologies, 40-41, 44, 136
Equal opportunity, 121, 139, 149, 211
ERISA law, 66

Fair Labor Standards Act, 91
Family:
   changing character of, 149-151, 170, 205
   inherited values and reality, 153-154
   and permissiveness, 111
   predictions, 127, 169-170
   and texture, 132
   and work, 111, 115, 149
Federal Mediation and Conciliation
      Service, 77
Flexitime, 71, 78, 94, 117-118
   benefits of, 101, 147; table, 102
   older workers and, 109
   usage rate, table, 101
   women and, 100
Food, 17, 20, 24
   population growth and, 174, 196-197
Foreign aid, 198-201
Foreign investments in U.S., 188-189
Fourth World, 208
France, 73
Freeman, Richard, 106
Friedman, Milton, 19
Functional illiterates, 37
Future of the World Economy, The
   (Leontief), 195, 195n, 199

Gasohol, 175
General Agreement on Trade and Tariffs
   (GATT), 191-192, 202

General Electric Company, 36, 140, 183
General Motors Corporation, 157
Genetic engineering, 24, 170
Germany, 73, 211
  worker participation experiments, 97,
    166
Ginzberg, Eli, 81
GNP (Gross National Product), 91, 152
  and investment rate, 21-22
  Latin America and Asia, 198
  new definition of, 206
  and new values, 124
  Schumacher on, 146
  world population and, tables, 195, 199
Gompers, Samuel, 91
Government:
  changing role and structure of,
    128-130, 144
  and compunications, 32
  developing nations' projects, 208
  economic power and corporate state,
    64-65
  federal budget, 65, 87
  intervention in labor-management
    relations, 73-75, 78-79, 93-94
  as manager of economy, 28-29, 186
  national planning for jobs, 88-89
  new labor legislation, 61, 70, 74-75
  public cynicism and distrust, 92, 112
  and public employees, 53-54, 87
  regulation of business, 41, 47, 65, 190,
    205
  research and development spending,
    42
  see also Congress; Public employees
Growth rate, economic:
  and American values, 124, 152
  future predictions, 28, 146, 185, 193
  and government entrepreneurship, 186
  and service industry, 189-190
  slowdown in, 21-23, 27-28, 40-41, 91
GWP (Gross World Product), 40, 42-43,
  195

Handicapped workers, 126, 128-130, 160
Health services, 19-20, 110, 129
  environmental contamination and
    disease, 89, 101
  government role, 128, 160
  improvement of, 25, 170-171
  incentives and, 129; see also National

    health insurance
Hispanics, 55, 95
Hollirith, Herman, 31
Hours of work, 111
  flexible, staggered, 117
  four-day workweek, 78, 94, 147
  redefinition of, 100-101
  worker control over, 62, 94
  working mothers and, 99
  see also Flexitime
Hudson Institute, 43
Human potential and resources, 125,
  130
  and biological sciences, 15, 25-26
  impact of computerization, 9-11, 26,
    213-214
Human values, 124-125, 129-130, 145,
  149
Humphrey-Hawkins Full Employment
  Act, 93
Hunger Project, 152-153

IBM, 31, 36, 95, 183-184, 190
Incentives, 41-42
  American work ethic and, 163-164
  system of, 129
Income:
  American worker's dissatisfaction
    with, 113-114
  future, 42
  per capita, 195, 198
  personal, pyramid of, 63-64
  real, 19-21
Incomes policy, 93-94
Individualism, 205-206, 212
  American self-perceptions, 70-71, 143
  and education, 136
  and labor force, 61, 75-76, 79, 132
  national, 204
Industrial democracy, 114-115
Industrial nations:
  economic growth, 40, 91
  population and GNP forecasts,
    195-199
  and socialism, 129
  and trade, 19-20; see also Inter-
    national economy; Western
    European countries
Inflation, 18-19
  American thinking on, 125
  and economy, 40-42, 91

and government, 94
and labor, 57, 70, 76, 96, 129, 207
prices in 2050, 63
productivity decline, 73, 91, 115
Information technology, 15, 25-26, 30-38
Inglehart, Ronald, 151-152
Innovation, 32, 41-43, 181, 183-190
in aging society, 47
Institutions:
international economic, 191-192, 200
lack of trust in, 112, 118, 143-144
International economy:
American service industry and,
189-190
competition, 43, 76, 91-93, 184
government entrepreneurship, 183-186
new world order, 208-210
raw materials and, 73
Third World forecasts, 195-203
trade, history of, 187-188
see also Multinational corporations
International Monetary Fund (IMF),
191-192, 194
Iran, 124, 181, 187, 200
Islamic countries, 202-203, 209
Italy, 155-156, 160-161, 164

Japan, 209
economy, 19, 22, 73, 155-156
employee and quality control, 166
GNP and population, 199
technology, 88, 211
Job displacement, 45-46, 66, 92, 93
see also Unemployment
Jobs:
and flexible benefits, 94-95, 144
impact of information technology, 32,
34, 37, 66, 93
"knowledge," 189
national planning for, 88-89, 93-94
1980s and promotions, 108
in services, 81-83, 106, 148
sharing of, 94
see also Careers; Labor force
Job satisfaction, 62, 71, 148, 165
and alternative work schedules,
117-118
erosion of, 90, 110-115
Job security, 56-57, 75, 93, 161
future goals, 77-78, 160, 209
Job training, 15, 209

and automation, 25-26, 37
for working women, 102-103
Jungk, Robert, 148-149

Kahn, Herman, 21, 131
Kristol, Irving, 69

Labor force:
collective bargaining and working
conditions, 49-52, 56-57, 76-79
demographic shifts, 62, 71-73, 95,
107-109, 126
dignity and respect, 205, 210
effects of technology, 26-27, 39-40,
45-47, 77-79, 92-93
and energy, 22-23, 27, 56
future problems and trends, 15-16,
61-62, 71, 93-97, 147-149
and individualism, 61, 75-76, 79, 132
in 1970s, 106-107
in 1980s, 22, 108-118, 126
nonemployables, 148
rights and responsibilities, 156-167
structural changes, 170-172
see also Decision making and worker
participation; Productivity;
Women
Labor-intensive work, 45, 143, 161, 174
Labor-management relations, 16, 56-57,
71-79
conflicts, 28-29, 66
future challenges, 207
government involvement in, 78-79
and multinationals, 67-68, 76
Landrum-Griffin Act, 50, 55
Latin America, 18, 209
economy and growth, 193, 196-198
future prospects, 201-202
Leadership, 92
unions, 75-76, 103-104, 162
Leisure, 39, 42, 117
changing attitudes, 62, 94, 110-114,
117, 135-136, 143
Leontief, Wassily, 195, 197
Libraries, 34-35
Life expectancy, 15, 25
and family life, 149·
and retirement, 95-96, 171
Lifestyles:
"conspicuous conservation," 178
and energy problem, 27-29, 176

family arrangements and households, 149-151, 169-170, 205
need levels, 139-140
new political divisions, 129-130
new values, 115, 123-125, 127-129, 143-144, 153-154
value profiles, 1970 and 1985, chart, 141-142
"Limits to growth" concept, 28, 124, 146

McLuhan, Marshall, 148
Madden, Carl, 32
Mail services, 32-34
Management, 85, 116, 142, 171
  collective bargaining and multi-nationals, 61, 66
  irresponsibility of, 155-157, 161-172
  and job fears, 34
  new individualism and, 70-71
  techniques and skills, 210
  women in, 46, 95
  and worker responsibility, 165-166
Manufacturing industry:
  decline of, 135, 147
  and employees in, 61, 81
  trade union strength, 69, 74
Marks, Jerome, 115-116
Marriage, 150-152, 170
  and women in labor force, 99, 111
Marx, Karl, 181, 184
Maslow, Abraham, 139-140
Meany, George, 56, 75
Mexico, 176
Microelectronics, 32, 35, 38
Middle-age worker group, 108, 126
  tactics and purposes of, 138-139
Middle East, 193, 199, 209
Military spending, 65, 88, 115, 211
Minorities, 71
  access to good jobs, 83, 95, 109, 126, 128-129
  and future political coalition, 130
  unemployment rates, 99
  and unions, 55, 61-62, 75
Multinational corporations, 63-64, 188, 202, 209
  export of capital and technology, 88, 91, 93
  and labor, 61, 67-68, 70
Multiple-wage earners, 169-170
Myrdal, Gunnar, 148

National Child Care Task Force, 100
National health insurance, 65, 76, 115, 129
National Labor Relations Act, 50, 66
National Labor Relations Board (NLRB), 49-50, 74
Natural resources, 15
  of industrial nations, 195-196
  and nature of work, 39-40
  scarcity, 40-41, 73, 76
  supply problems, 17-23, 27-28
  see also Raw materials
Netherlands, The, 73
New product development, 40, 44, 178, 189, 209
Newspapers and wire services, 32, 34, 93, 213
North Korea, 194, 198
North-South partnership (American continents), 18, 209
Nuclear power, 173, 196

OECD, 43, 65, 191-192, 195
  and China, 202
  and Latin America, 198, 201
Oettinger, Anthony, 31
Offices of the future, 33, 144
  changing skills and wages, 45, 82-83
Oil, see Petroleum
Okun, Arthur, 158-159
Older workers, 107
  delayed retirement, 170-171
  in labor force, 71, 109, 126, 130-131
OPEC, 22, 175-176, 193-194, 201
OSHA, 74

Part-time jobs, 78, 81-82, 100-101, 117-118
Pensions, 66, 156, 163-164
  escalator clauses, 96, 109
  future patterns, 171
Permissiveness, 111
Petroleum:
  alternatives to, 173, 196
  discoveries, 176, 202
  gasohol jojoba plant, 175
  imports, U.S., 21-22
  and internal production, 124
  from shale, 27, 196
  tertiary recovery, 174-175, 196
Phillips Curve trade-off, 19

Plants:
-growing program, 173
and oil, 175
Pluralism, 141, 143
Politics, 64, 129
American, future coalitions, 129-130,
143
compunications impact on, 35, 37-38
and old concepts, 18, 21-23
and unions, 69-70, 73-75, 85
Pollution, 18, 28, 153
Polymer chemistry, 26
Population, world:
concentration of, 198
control of, 2-3
and GNP, 195, 199 (tables)
and median age change, 137-138
(chart)
and rising demands, 173-174
Third World growth, 195-197
Post-industrial society, 134-144, 152
aging versus maturing society, 47-48
and compunications, 32-38
transition to, 39-46
values, 138-142; chart, 141
Poverty, 64, 140, 146, 151, 209
Private-sector unions, 69-70, 96, 106-107
Production and products, 124-125
consumer complaints, 126-127
and environmental problems, 28, 40
and job creation, 88-89
labor cost of, 77-78
shifting to services, 61, 81-83, 125
see also New product development
Productivity, 20, 22, 40, 43, 85
and alternate work schedules, 99, 101,
117-118
decline, 61, 73, 78, 90-91, 185-186
causes of, 115-117, 161
gains, 45-46
"knowledge" jobs and, 189-190
multiple-careers and, 26-27
service sector and electronics, 26, 32, 44
and worker responsibility, 165, 204, 208
Professional and technical jobs, 106, 116,
147, 162, 189
Profit-sharing, 207
Proposition 13 tax revolt, 20, 65, 87, 106,
163-164
Public employees, 53-54
and budget-slashing, 87

increased, 74, 76, 106
retirement pensions, 96, 163-164
union conflicts, 69, 96
"whistle-blower" protection, 114
Pyramid of wealth and income, 63-64

Quality of life:
and changing American values,
123-125, 129-130, 142
texture in, 132-133
Quinn, Robert P., 110

Raw materials, 18, 40, 73, 76, 125
Real income, 19-21
Regionalism, 143, 208, 210
Responsibility and rights, 155-167, 207,
211
Retirement, 88-89, 95-96
increased life expectancy and, 170-171
new concepts of, 109-110, 114
Rights and entitlements, 139, 156-160
effects on economy and productivity,
161-164
retrenchment, 164-165
and worker responsibility, 165-167,
207, 211
Risk-free social environment, 160-162,
164
Russell, Bertrand, 188

Satellite towns, 28, 205
Say, J. B., 188
Scanlon Plans, 165
Schrank, Robert, 161
Schumacher, E. F., 146, 172-174
Schumpeter, Joseph, 185
Schumpeterian cycle, 43
Schurmann, Franz, 82
Seaborg, Glenn, 152
Service industries and jobs:
changing nature of, 80-83
employment in, 69, 125
growth of, 47, 61, 135, 189
national planning for, 88-89
and productivity, 44, 116-117
shift to, 32, 83-88, 147, 161
types of, 188
Shared-jobs, 94, 100-101, 117
Single-parent households, 150, 170
Single people, 145, 148, 166

Social Security, 3-5, 96, 158-159
  and retirement, 107, 109, 171
Solar energy, 27, 174, 177
Soviet bloc, 196, 199
Soviet Union, 184, 202-203, 209
"Spaceship economy," 152
Staines, Graham L., 110
Standard of living:
  and Americans, 113, 115, 124-125
  basis of, 90, 163
  decline, and government, 186-187
Stevens, J. P., Inc., 65
Strikes, 51-54, 67, 77
  Lordstown, 157, 161-162
Structural unemployment, 99, 103

Taft-Hartley Act, 50-51
Taxes, 34, 41, 64, 129
Taxpayers, 53-54, 86. See also Proposition
    13 tax revolt
Teachers' unions, 56, 76
"Technetronic Age," 136
Technology:
  assessment of (TA), 35
  bio- and information science impact,
    24-29
  challenges, 205, 209, 211
  clerical/sales jobs impact, 81-85
  corporate state and, 65
  decline of innovation, 73
  economic factors and, 17-23
  electronics revolution, 15, 23, 209
  and energy, 18, 174-177, 196, 209
  environmental impact, 40
  export of, 85
  and job displacement, 45-46, 66, 92-93
  and job security, 77-78
  questioning of, 16, 123, 136, 142-144
  small-scale, 172-174
  social impact, 39-43
  world development of, 196-197
  see also Compunications
Textured living, 131-133
Theobald, Robert, 30-31, 31n
Third World, 18, 129, 140, 146, 193-203
  agricultural production, 174
  economy, 193-197
  population, 40, 197
  population and GNP, 195, 199[tables]
  and regional blocs, 209-210
  tribal societies and commerce, 188-189

and United States, 198-199, 207-208
  war possibilities, 40, 197
Transport system, 20, 22, 29-30, 176
Trilateral Commission, 65, 67
Turnover in jobs, 82, 85, 101

Unemployment, 18-19, 21-23, 46
  benefits, 156
  of blacks, 79
  future trends, 207
  incentive system and, 129
  labor-management relations, 57, 78-79,
    207
  rates by sex, 99
  raw material shortages, 125
  structural, 99, 103
  Third World countries, 197
  underclass of nonemployables, 46-47
  see also Job displacement; Labor force
Unions:
  anti-unionism, 85-87, 93
  automation and, 93
  and corporate state, 66-68
  decline of, 46, 69-70, 74, 106-107
  in England, 161
  government and legislation, 70, 73-75
  history of, 49-51
  international, 67-68, 75-76
  leadership, 75-76, 103-104, 162
  and multinationals, 61, 67-68
  and public employees, 53-54
  tensions between, 69-70, 96
  and women, 46, 55, 61-62, 75, 103-104
  see also Collective bargaining
Uniroyal, Inc., 166
United Auto Workers, 117
United Nations, 194, 195n, 200, 209
United States:
  aging society, 3-7
  computer science and economic growth,
    41-48, 184
  corporate state and power, 65
  development of economic rights, 158
  domestic versus international economy,
    192-194
  economy and supply problems, 19-23
  labor movement, 50-51, 69-75, 90-91
  politics and values, 143
  and service industries, 189-190
  and Third World, 198-203
  and world leadership, 207-208
  see also Government

Value system (Americans):
  current thinking, 123-127
  effect on family, 149-151
  and entrepreneurship, 185
  hierarchy of needs, 139-140
  human, 124-125, 129-133, 145, 149
  Values Profile chart—1970 and 1985,
    141
Venezuela, 193-194. *See also* OPEC
Vietnam, 92, 194, 198

Wage and price controls, 64, 70, 74, 93-94
Wages and salaries:
  and employee benefits, 78, 94
  inequities, 46, 95, 111
  information and service jobs, 81-85
Wagner Act, 50, 53-54
Wagner, Robert F., 50
Watergate scandals, 93, 125
Wealth, 63-64, 91
Western European countries, 19, 22, 88,
    129
  and flexitime, 144
  GNP and population, table, 199
  investments in U.S., 188-189
  new regional bloc, 209
  worker-participation experiments, 96
White-collar workers, 28, 81, 94-95, 147
Wolfe, Tom, 132
Women, 98-105
  advancement and promotion, 95, 126
  benefits pertaining to, 78
  child care and work schedules, 62,
    99-103

continuous or intermittent employment,
    99, 127
  equalization of, 83, 126, 128-129, 149,
    159
  future political coalition, 130
  in labor force, 42, 45-46, 62, 71, 107, 109,
    126, 170, 172
  in management, 46
  and motherhood, 151
  unionization, 46, 55, 61-62, 75, 103-104
  work training, 102-103
Worker participation. *see* Decision
    making and worker participation
Work ethic, 112-113, 116-117, 149
  and changing attitudes, 90, 130,
    135-137, 143-144, 147
Working mothers, 99-100, 150
Work schedule alternatives, 78, 94,
    99-102, 110, 115, 117, 147
World Bank, 192, 194, 200

Xerox Corporation, 184

Yankelovich, Daniel, 139, 148
Youth, 5-6, 153
  and alienation, 83-85
  and authority, 111
  blacks and unemployment, 79, 95, 108
  equal access to jobs, 128-129
  in labor force, 107, 172
  and older workers, 126
  shortage in 1980s, 108
Yugoslavia, 166